A JOHN CATT PUBLICATION

T0273556

THE
PÖWER OF
CHARACTER

Lessons from the frontline

Dr Andrew Reay

"A fascinating book – thought-provoking and stimulating"
David Laws

First Published 2017

by John Catt Educational Ltd,
12 Deben Mill Business Centre, Old Maltings Approach,
Melton, Woodbridge IP12 1BL

Tel: +44 (0) 1394 389850 Fax: +44 (0) 1394 386893
Email: enquiries@johncatt.com
Website: www.johncatt.com

ISBN: 978 1 1911382270

Set and designed by John Catt Educational Limited

Praise for
The Power of Character

"*After a brutal and honest commentary on education in Britain over recent years, Dr Andrew Reay offers an alternative vision for the future with a step by step guide as to how we might achieve this. A rallying call to bring autonomy back to teachers and heads and bring an end to a 'quick fix' culture. An alternative to the obsessive focus on tests, intelligence and rankings, this book is challenging and thought provoking; exciting and inspiring in both its delivery and ideas.*"
Tim Perris, Founder and Director of 'Imagine for Schools'

"*Passionately argued, superbly researched, and filled with real stories, The Power of Character will permanently change how we see what Martin Luther King once described as the true goal of education – and how you see this within yourself – the content of our very own character and the mandate for an Education 2.0*"
Sir Iain Hall, CEO of the Great Schools Trust and co-founder of Future Leaders

"*A very readable and wide-ranging account of how a school has synthesised research evidence around motivation with historical and contemporary socio-cultural influences, in pursuit of a broad education for its students – intelligence with character. Part biography, part historical review, part survey of evidence, part polemic and part a how-to guide for ambitious schools, this book will inform, entertain, stimulate, inspire, and occasionally exasperate in equal measure.*"
Dr Barry J Hymer, Emeritus Professor of Psychology in Education, University of Cumbria

Contents

To my daughters, Iris and Betsy,

You will flourish in this life because of the power of something that runs so deep within you and with such mystery that, for now, you won't even know of its very existence. It is something that you will never be able to actually see, you may have difficulty in naming or describing it, but you and all those around you will know it is there. As you grow older, it will start to define who you are, what you do, and what you stand for in life – yet throughout your schooling no examination or qualification will ever be able to capture its true magic (nor try to I hope). My one wish is that you maintain the ability to see parts of the world through the eyes of a child; you will always believe that the impossible is possible.

This thing that I speak of is so powerful that it will even define who you become, who your life long partner may be, and what your own children and grandchildren will make of their lives, but this is all far into the future. You see this is a gift that every human on this planet possesses in abundance but few realise its power – you just need to believe in it, grab it with both hands, and run with it. Many people use the word potential, what I am talking about is something much greater; the power that is and will always be within you to reach your dreams and go way beyond what people may tell you is possible. You just need to believe in it and know that it is there.

This is the power of your character.

An extract

An extract taken from the February 1947 edition of the Morehouse College student newspaper, the *Maroon Tiger*, entitled 'The Purpose of Education':

As I engage in the so-called "bull sessions" around and about the school, I too often find that most college men have a misconception of the purpose of education. Most of the "brethren" think that education should equip them with the proper instruments of exploitation so that they can forever trample over the masses. Still others think that education should furnish them with noble ends rather than means to an end. It seems to me that education has a two-fold function to perform in the life of man and in society: the one is utility and the other is culture. Education must enable a man to become more efficient, to achieve with increasing facility the ligitmate goals of his life.

Education must also train one for quick, resolute and effective thinking. To think incisively and to think for one's self is very difficult. We are prone to let our mental life become invaded by legions of half truths, prejudices, and propaganda. At this point, I often wonder whether or not education is fulfilling its purpose. A great majority of the so-called educated people do not think logically and scientifically. Even the press, the classroom, the platform, and the pulpit in many instances do not give us objective and unbiased truths. To save man from the morass of propaganda, in my opinion, is one of the chief aims of education. Education must enable one to sift and weigh evidence, to discern the true from the false, the real from the unreal, and the facts from the fiction.

The function of education, therefore, is to teach one to think intensively and to think critically. But education which stops with efficiency may prove the greatest menace to society. The most dangerous criminal may be the man gifted with reason, but with no morals.

The late Eugene Talmadge, in my opinion, possessed one of the better minds of Georgia, or even America. Moreover, he wore the Phi Beta Kappa key. By all measuring rods, Mr. Talmadge could think critically and intensively; yet he contends that I am an inferior being. Are those the types of men we call educated?

We must remember that intelligence is not enough. Intelligence plus character – that is the goal of true education. The complete education gives one not only power of concentration, but worthy objectives upon which to concentrate. The broad education will, therefore, transmit to one not only the accumulated knowledge of the race but also the accumulated experience of social living.

If we are not careful, our colleges will produce a group of close-minded, unscientific, illogical propagandists, consumed with immoral acts. Be careful, "brethren!" Be careful, teachers!

Dr. Martin Luther King, Jr.

The Beginning

CARE more than others think is wise
RISK more than others think is safe
EXPECT more than others think is possible
ENCOURAGE where others have given up
DREAM more than others think is practical
SO THAT EVERY CHILD SUCCEEDS!

– The creed of Future Leaders

They called the programme 'Future Leaders' and, in the summer of 2009, I was one of their one hundred candidates.

We had come here, to a non-descript hotel near Birmingham, at the selection of Sir Iain Hall, a man who was to have a transformative effect on my life. Sir Iain had spent a long career as a teacher and headteacher in some of Britain's most challenging schools. If there was a part of the country's education system he had not seen first hand, it was, perhaps, not worth knowing. A calm, authoritative and visionary man, he had been knighted in 2002 for his services to education – and, though he had left the classroom behind, his life in education was far from over. In 2006 he had been on the advisory panel before co-founding the newly-established Future Leaders Trust, a charitable organisation set up in partnership between some of the UK's leading children's charities and the government, and this summer he would deliver almost all of the training on this unique programme. Its mission: to train an elite guard of future head and deputy headteachers who could then be deployed into the UK's most disadvantaged schools and, through strength of character and the leadership skills inculcated by the programme, turn them around.

I had turned to the idea of a career in education, if not later in life, then later than some, and certainly later than many of the teachers I would go on to lead. Until Future Leaders and the rigorous application procedure that brought me first to Wolverhampton – and, from there, to the National College of School Leadership, a purpose-built training centre in the heart of Nottingham – I had been riding the waves of a military career. This included a seven year commission with the RAF, first as a physical education officer, including overseas duties to the Middle East and North Africa, and then on secondment to the University of Birmingham where I researched new methods of motivation and psychology as it pertained to serving troops. The move into education had come, if not on a whim, then certainly not as part of any grand design – but my thoughts had been slowly turning this way for some time. In my final tour with the RAF as a staff officer, consulting on methods of basic training for new recruits, I had been struck by just how many young people had been failed by their education. Men and women, mainly aged between 16 and 21, had regularly arrived at our base at RAF Halton with few qualifications and little investment in their studies – but it was my experience that, after only a few weeks in the rigid, demanding structure of the military, these same recruits could become professional, principle driven airmen and airwomen who left their formal training bursting with pride.

The structure, strictness, routines and rituals of the RAF appeared to me to be transforming these young people in a way that 12 to 14 years of formal education had failed to do. Why, I had begun to wonder, couldn't this be done earlier in a student's life? How did a culture of authority and discipline steeped firmly in tradition create such loyal and principle driven people? What was it about aligning and abiding to an oath, putting the service of your country before the interests of oneself that had such a transformative effect on the purpose and mission in life of these young recruits? What was it about these authoritative role models that were transforming these young people through the power of emulation whilst equipping them with the mind-set that they can learn, breaking any cycle from their formal education that said that they couldn't? Why couldn't the principles behind the way the military helped challenging recruits be transferred into some of the toughest schools in our country? These were the thoughts that had first ushered me towards the field of urban education.

On that first summer morning, as I stood among the other 99 candidates selected by Future Leaders, I prepared to take my first step in the profession that has, ever since, defined my life. Future Leaders was designed to be both a crash course in school leadership and a brutal exposé of everything wrong in the current system. It was designed to take a group of neophytes – who had, nevertheless, shown valued character traits in getting through the long and arduous application process – and transforming them into leaders capable of restructuring, reorganising, and recalibrating the cultures of challenging urban schools across the UK. The programme would take us through a summer of workshops and lectures, a study tour to visit urban schools in the United States – where new and innovative methods were being employed to turn around the lives of children who might otherwise get trapped in the drug and gun crime so common in their neighbourhoods – and, lastly, a year long placement under a mentoring headteacher in one of the UK's urban schools situated in high challenge.

In many ways, that first week with Future Leaders threw me back to my first days in the military. Both experiences took me on an almost vertical learning curve: they were tough, unrelenting, and put huge demands on the willpower and character of their candidates. Many of my colleagues in the cohort had already been working in education, using Future Leaders as a way of advancing their careers and preparing to take the next step to school leadership; but I had come from a different background, with little knowledge of the work school leaders undertook and having rarely set foot inside a school since joining the RAF. Some of my colleagues had been educated in the independent sector, others seemed to be on the programme as a means of addressing the inequality they themselves had faced by being schooled in challenging, urban environments and, consequently, with my background in the RAF and the training of military recruits, I felt like an outsider. I did not have the 'story' many of my fellow candidates had; I was not driven to be here by a family tragedy, nor by close ties to a community whose prospects I was desperate to improve.

The sense of free fall I experienced in those first few days was only made more intense by the almost cult-like fervour with which Sir Iain and our other advisers drilled us in the programme's four guiding principles: that every child, regardless of background or birthplace, can fulfil their potential and be successful in life with the guidance of good educators; that there should never be excuses, every child must succeed and failure is not an option, only an excuse; that we should always have high expectations because children can only succeed in an environment that has the highest expectations for all who work there; and that there can be no 'islands' in education, we must learn from and work alongside the leading lights in all fields of human endeavour, because great schools cannot become great in isolation. These ideas were so central to the teachings of Future Leaders that we were being asked to adopt them with a missionary zeal; the hope was that, by the end of the programme, our alignment would be complete, and that these principles would become a self-fulfilling prophecy: if we believed them with the same fervour as our programme leaders, we would go out into the world and make them happen.

The days with Future Leaders were long and gruelling especially given my starting point in education, with each day comprising ten hours packed with lectures and workshops, and evenings spent preparing for the day ahead. Sir Iain used his incredible stories of a life lived in education to propel the days forward, speaking of how his own childhood and working life had driven him to co-found Future Leaders. Some of his stories of degradation and hope rising from the most unusual circumstances were enough to reduce my fellow candidates to tears. Much of our training was framed around a virtual school Sir Iain had conjured up, 'Future High', a model for how education might one day be if enough school leaders adopted the attitudes being passed onto us.

As we worked through these scenarios, acting out the roles of the school leaders we would one day become, simulating the day to day operations of an urban school, I soon came to appreciate the vast scale of the challenge for which Future Leaders was preparing us: the incredible gap between the most affluent and the most poor, the number of people who had access to independent as opposed to state education; the barriers of expectation, bureaucracy and structure we would all face.

Across the weeks, we were visited by the nation's top urban headteachers as well as a selection from the United States including Jay Altman, the CEO of a set of Charter Schools transforming lives in post-Hurricane Katrina New Orleans. Future Leaders was setting us up to fill a vacuum in the lives of disadvantaged children, to – in the words of education theorist David Whitman and his study of inner-city schooling, *Sweating the Small Stuff* – invest in a kind of 'paternalism', turning ourselves into surrogate parents to children who were not brought up with the values that could help them succeed.

As the summer went on, the teachings of Future Leaders began to echo more and more fiercely the lessons I had already learned in my past military career. Perhaps, I began to believe, the fact that I came to Future Leaders from an unusual perspective could even be advantageous. All of those years spent leading the RAF's fitness and health strategy, training new recruits (having already gone through the process myself), watching as directionless cadets were transformed into capable, proactive airmen and women, researching and executing strategic plans for an Air Force of 40,000 full time personnel and an equivalent number of reservists – all of this was echoed back at me as I thought about the teachings of Future Leaders and the world into which I was stepping.

If the gruelling processes of basic training could turn raw recruits into the kind of focused, driven individuals I had seen happening time and time again in the RAF and also through my wider work with the British Army and Royal Navy, what would an analogous process do for children at school – and what might that look like? Was this only about filling the parental vacuum, or did the principles of Future Leaders point to something bigger and more exacting, something we were all – from the disadvantaged child who rejects school in his challenging inner-city environment, to the boy like me who stumbled through GCSEs and A levels without any real direction or advice from my school about the next step I would have to take – missing in the way we were schooled? Could the answer, I began to think, be found in something so simple, and yet so fundamental, as character?

A nation divided

The idea that character can be taught and caught, that it is not some fundamental quality with which human beings are born, is not a new one – and, though Future Leaders emphasised its core values of 'every child', 'no excuses', 'high expectations' and 'no islands', the programme itself did not explicitly zone in on the connection between character and lifelong success. In fact the benefits are not the preserve of education alone. Across the world, businesses, governments and other organisations are waking up to the fact that the accepted sciences of motivation, work ethic and why we do the things we do are increasingly outdated – and, by harnessing the hidden power of character, are transforming the way the world is run. I had been drawn to the idea that character can be advanced through education ever since I had joined the RAF and had, myself, been transformed into a more professional, proactive and assertive individual, especially during the six months I spent in officer training. I am sure I was not the first.

Classicists like Aristotle had been proselytising that "excellence is an art won by training and habituation," that "we do not act rightly because we have virtue, but we have virtue because we have acted rightly" as far back as the third century BC. As the prodigy of Plato, then in writing the first comprehensive system on western philosophy, he believed that the 'good life' was one driven by the pursuit of excellence and governed by virtue and rationality, "We are what we repeatedly do," he declared. "Excellence is not an act but a habit." Like other classical thinkers, from both the Eastern and Western philosophical traditions, Aristotle saw character as a set of virtues that a person worked upon, acts that they refined across their lives. It was his contention that the character of a man was shaped and fashioned by the acts he performed and the ways in which he behaved across his life. Eudemonia, commonly translated from Latin as 'flourishing', describes a particular kind of happiness brought about by living a fulfilling, worthwhile and virtuous life – a life of good character. In the Eastern tradition, Confucius also emphasised tradition, study, and ritualised behaviours, as a way of instilling virtues in a man as outlined in the passage:

Sow a thought. Reap an action.
Sow an action. Reap a habit.
Sow a habit. Reap a character.
Sow a character. Reap a destiny.

Many centuries later, much of the Western school system would also be focused on developing character – this time in a religious context, where common, Church and Sunday schools focused on drilling morality into their students by daily prayer, sermonising and religious instruction. Yet, in the twentieth century, as governments became increasingly resistant to the idea of religion being at the centre of a child's education, the idea of a 'moral' or values-led education began to be seen as old-fashioned and potentially corrosive. The true purpose of school was not, it seemed, to focus on the content of our character by instilling a specific value set but to focus on academic progress and success, to drill students in certain prescribed subjects and step aside from the teaching of morality, of ethics, of anything as slippery as 'virtues' forever.

Yet, as the idea of character education waned in the United Kingdom's state schools, it continued to flourish in a sub-set of the country's education establishments. The British public school system, distinct as it is from government direction, continued to focus on teaching ritualised behaviour, on qualities that were coming to be seen as dangerously old-fashioned: on courtesy and respect, on determination and morality, on courage and good grace. Whatever the rights and wrongs of public schooling – and the debate continues, with fierce proponents on every side – it seems to be working. The United Kingdom is, after all, a nation where only 7% of children are educated in public schools – but where a full 40% of students studying at its top universities, Oxford and Cambridge, are part of that 7%. Think that statistic sounds galling? Now consider this: up to 80% of the most senior posts in the government, military and other vital areas of public service come from that 7%.

Stop for a moment, as I did upon first learning this, and think this through. One in every 15 of our nation's children are born into a family situation advantaged enough to be able to afford the high costs of a private education (the current cost of a year's education at Eton College is £36,000; a boarder at Rugby can expect to pay £33,000, and at Harrow close to £35,000; the cost at Wellington College teeters around the £34,000 mark. The cost of privately educating a child across their school career can now run in excess of £300,000 to £400,000 – a cost that prices out even most affluent middle class families). These children, with the benefits that this education provides, go on to fill almost half of the places at the country's highest ranked universities – and, more startling still, they go on to fill four out of every five top positions in public life. At the other end of the spectrum, life chances are bleak with less than 20% of students from families on the poverty line getting to any university at all. Add in cultural disadvantage on top – not being read to as a child, no trips to the theatre, museums or libraries and no overseas travel, advantages that many of us take for granted – and the bottom line is stark. If you are born into wealth and privilege, you can expect to remain in wealth and privilege throughout your life. Privilege breeds privilege. Deprivation on the other hand only serves to further starve children who are in most need of basic educational nutrients for life long flourishing. At its worst, a 2010 paper by the New Economics Foundation titled 'Punishing costs' estimated that the cost of holding a person in a Young Offender's institution topped £100,000 per year. This is close to three times the cost of sending a child to Eton whilst over 15 times the average spend per state educated pupil in English schools.

Here we had a working example of how a focus on character-led education reaped dividends for students in the long term. I was born in a working class town on the outskirts of the Lake District, schooled at a comprehensive some 25 miles from where I lived, chosen by my parents as it performed highly in inspects, and later studied at the universities of Loughborough and Durham. I had been privileged to have been brought up with a firm set of middle class values and all of the cultural and aspirational advantages that had afforded me and which I had taken for granted. Yet, it was not until I joined the RAF upon graduation that I first came into regular contact with people who had grown up in the upper echelons of our society, including those who had been educated by the very best of the public school system.

There was no doubt about the advantages that this kind of upbringing and education bestowed: these were people who knew, from an early age, where they were going in life, what they were bound to do and what specific steps they would have to achieve if they were to get there. All of this was in stark contrast to my own schooling. My goal, as a teenager, had been to study sports science at university – but the guidance from school, and on paper a good school at that, wasn't even there to tell me I would have to study the sciences at A level to do so. Instead, I had to make my own way, following detours by trial and error, never quite certain where I wanted to be until it happened. Meanwhile, my colleagues in the RAF seemed to have been schooled, from the moment they could walk, for a life in the military; they were shepherded along the paths they had chosen from a very young age, given help and advice from people who had trodden the same paths before them. Most, if not all, had been cadets while at school, some even achieving scholarships at the prestigious Wellbeck Defence College before moving onto a sponsored degree programme in a related field. Others had joined University with a concerted desire to join the military on completion of their degree and had spent three to four years in the University Officer Corp or Air Squadrons. Their attitudes and outlook, their confidence in the decisions they were making and their self-belief, were all indebted to the way they had been schooled – and, outside the school gates, the advantages it gave them were huge.

But why weren't the children in the nation's state urban schools treated the same way? Why did the plaudits always go to those who already had them? Why did the gap between the advantaged and the disadvantaged, those born to privilege and those not, continue to exist – and even widen? The United Kingdom has one of the widest achievement gaps in the developed world – but was there any reason why the advantages being conferred on public school students couldn't be conferred on those from more prosaic, under-privileged backgrounds? Was there any reason students from state school backgrounds did not go on to win as many places at the most prestigious universities, or to positions at the top of public and professional life? Was it just cronyism, the work of old boys' networks and favours-among-friends, or did it go back to something more fundamental?

Just like similar programmes designed to send high-flying young graduates straight into the classroom, including the Teach First scheme, Future Leaders meant to address this imbalance – not by sweeping government reform imposed from above, but from the ground up. The architects of the programme were determined to begin a vast, far-reaching grassroots change, to do for the general population what was being done for the precious few and we hundred candidates, just as the two hundred who had gone before us in earlier cohorts, were to be its agents. If this sounds melodramatic, if it sounds like social conditioning, then that is because it was exactly that: Future Leaders was designed to instil in us a missionary fervour, to fill us with a kind of righteous anger at the way the current system preserved the status quo; those born to privilege remaining privileged and those born in need, remaining in need. In its tone, in its content, in its execution, it was nothing more than a call to arms and, in that way, not very different from the military life I had left behind. We were to be missionaries on this new crusade, seeking to eradicate the benefits of money and birth right from the education system. For us, education would not be a career; like the military oath I swore to in the RAF, it would be a mission that would put the success of the children we served before anything else. Every one of us would embark on our new lives rich in the belief that the work we would do would not only change lives, but change societies for the better.

Failure is not an option

In August of 2009, as our summer-long crash course with Future Leaders was coming to an end, we were looking forward to our first deployments into disadvantaged schools. We were despatched to the United States to experience first hand the way innovative school leaders on the eastern seaboard were redesigning the classroom experience. They were moving dramatically away from a model that not only tested both its students and its staff by the results they achieved, but more toward models that instead emphasised building – and in some cases learning from scratch – a specific set of character traits that would give the best chances of success in the grown-up worlds of work and study. Some of my Future Leaders colleagues were sent to New York, others to Chicago and Washington and Philadelphia, all places Sir Iain and the other founders of Future Leaders had visited as they sought to pull together our own programme. My own journey would take me to Boston, where I would see direct evidence of the way inspirational school leaders can challenge and subvert the expected norms and seemingly work wonders for their students.

The Charter School movement began in earnest in the late 1980s and, much later, would directly inspire the academies and Free School programmes of the United Kingdom. Their mission was simple: to create a succession of schools with a more flexible approach to education, founded by teachers, parents or other activists and subject to less central control than other educational establishments.

As no single Charter School is identical to another, nor are all necessarily successful, it is difficult to generalise – but at Boston Prep, Roxbury Prep and Amistad Academy, three of the highly successful schools I visited, the shared characteristics were stark. An extended school day was the basic principle, giving 'more time on task'. The teachers and leadership teams of these schools were often head-hunted and provided with huge levels of training and on-going support. Their pedagogical planning, delivery and reflection was as much a science as it was an art, with instruction consistent across each classroom and age group. They all had incredibly high expectations of their students; they embraced structure, routine, and ritual relentlessly. They valued aspirations above all else, with the goal that every child should be accepted at college, and frequent testing, remediation and personalisation of lessons happening day in day out to achieve this goal – failure was not an option.

Each year group was designated the 'Class of 2016', the 'Class of 2017', 'the Class of 2018' and so forth, focusing the students' minds on the year they would graduate and begin their college career. Each corridor was covered with motivational quotes and posters; every student recited mottoes and mantras daily, as there was an explicit and deliberate strategy to mould the values of their students. College was not just a vague idea but also a tangible goal for even the most under-privileged student, who might be the first person in their family to even consider, let alone achieve, a college career. Every child had been asked to define his or her ambition from an early age and, along with their teachers and guidance counsellors, they built a tangible pathway toward achieving it, an aspirational journey published and promoted on the corridor and classroom walls. They called it the 'Dream it, Do it!' pledge.

Though many of these students came from financially restricted, challenging backgrounds, the teachers here showed a level of paternalism far beyond anything I had seen in a school back home; these teachers were actively trying to fill the void left by their student's upbringing, striving to prove that there was a way out of the poverty trap, that their students' aspirations did not have to be limited to doing the same as their parents had done; and that, in the most extreme cases, there really were options beyond the gang and criminal lives in which these students might naturally have been expected to become immersed.

In the same year, the inspirational story of Geoffrey Canada, CEO of the Harlem Children's Zone, was published by journalist and author Paul Tough. The schools some of my colleagues visited in New York were not only typical of the Charter School experience I had seen first-hand in Boston but also of all of the teachers and senior leaders written about by Tough's immersion in the war on poverty in Harlem. They approached their jobs with the same missionary zeal as Future Leaders aimed to inspire in us. They were narrowing the gap between the achievers and the under-achievers not just by strong-arming their students in academic principles but also by paying attention, first and foremost, to aspects of character and culture. They emphasised ambition and aspiration by creating an environment in which every single child, no matter what the circumstances of their backgrounds, were expected to succeed, where no excuses of upbringing and lack of privilege were made for poor behaviour.

The word that Canada used when talking about his cultural paradigm shift on introducing a 'Cradle to College' educational pipeline was the process of 'positive contamination'. He wanted all families of Harlem to adopt the middle class virtues espoused by those in more affluent suburbs of New York, whilst still keeping the value set specific to Harlem. Focusing on aspects of character and culture was key to the formula's success – but it did go against the grain of state education, which had moved away in many schools from the traditionally didactic, heavily teacher-led and learning-by-rote approach to more progressive approaches. For those of us who had come to observe, it was a startling change (if not return to the old days) of tone. Students were being drilled on discipline through simple social norms and routines, the ability to track the person they were speaking to with their eyes, the basic courtesies of politeness and how to greet somebody with a firm handshake, how to sit up straight and pay attention to everything that was being said, how to respond in full sentences; put simply, how to engage. This was made consistent by a social blue print for every school within the same charter chain, including various acronyms encapsulating the specific modes of behaviour to which students were expected to adhere. Prominent among these was SLANT, in which students were expected to Sit up, Listen, Ask questions, Nod and Track with their eyes whoever was speaking in the class, whether that was a teacher or a student. Furthermore, all positive actions were reinforced and reflected on publically so as to make the expected behaviour explicit for all to see.

This simple self-improving cycle – to firstly bring to light every unconscious positive habit, reflect on it, move it into their student's consciousness, repeat it, refine it and as a result improve their character was unleashing incredible powers of self-belief and self-worth from within which had previously laid dormant. The successes of these high-performing Charter Schools – and the statistics are remarkable, with the achievement gap between black and white, poor and privileged dramatically smaller in these schools than in the United States' high-performing public schools – were down to something as fundamental as a culture shift, and the attitudinal adjustment of their school leaders. This was not about resources and capital investment – most of these schools were housed in disused business offices or warehouses – but about the investment of time, energy, and a new, independent spirit.

Some of the schools my Future Leaders colleagues and I had visited belong to a much larger cohort of independent organisations across the US that are placing character strengths high on the agenda alongside traditional academic subjects, schools like KIPP – the Knowledge is Power Programme – Uncommon Schools, Amistad, Harlem Children's Zone and First Line, that, in recent years, have become the poster-child for the Charter School movement. In recent years there has been a groundswell of debate amongst educators, academics, social policy experts and journalists, all seeking to unearth the true merits of this approach.

The research into character is only just beginning but it is already wide and varied. As books, journals and newspaper articles have repeatedly pointed out, there is now empirical evidence to suggest that teaching children moral, intellectual, performance and civic virtues and encouraging awareness of their emotional and psychological character traits will significantly impact their chances of achieving positive results, both at school and far into their adult lives. These Charter Schools, with their innovative and character-led approaches, were living proof of the fact that the old systems were tired and unresponsive, that a daring and innovative teacher (or set of teachers) could revolutionise a school and get children who would otherwise have no investment in their education actively thinking about their future. It was to be our task to bring this thinking back home.

Looking to the future

That summer with Future Leaders was the first step on the road to what would eventually lead to the creation of a brand new school in 2012 that would become focused on character. King's Leadership Academy Warrington was founded by Sir Iain Hall with Shane Ierston as principal, who was one of my Future Leaders colleagues, myself as vice principal and three other colleagues. The school was set up through the company Great Schools for All Children which would later become the Great School's Trust as it would take on additional free schools and help to turn around the fortunes of existing urban schools in difficulty (more on this later). At the time of writing, the doors of King's Leadership Academy, Warrington, situated mid-way between Liverpool and Manchester has been open for four years. Its stated goal: to bring the benefits of character education to the masses, to do for the free school system what has already been done in Britain's public schools and grammar schools for untold generations, and to closely emulate the ambitions and spirit of the American Charter School movement.

After four years, our statistics show the academy to be well ahead of the national average: daily attendance is over 98%, we have a 99.9% measurement for punctuality and positive attitudes to lessons; with predictions of the government's premier performance measure, the English Baccalaureate or EBACC, being three times the national average. In 2015, the school became formally recognised as the first National School of Character, as an institution putting character education at the very heart of what it does. We have been lauded on the national stage as the model for how this revolution of education might best be implemented, and the now trust has been tasked with assuming control of other schools in the local area and leading their rejuvenation. Above all else, we have shown clearly, in the results our students are achieving, the benefits of putting character at the heart of what a school does. We are showing, day in and day out, the way that the old, out-dated model of education was betraying our children and how the benefits of educators focusing on building character can belong to all, no matter the wealth into which they are born.

This book is the story, not only of King's Leadership Academy Warrington, the Great School's Trust and the school culture we strive to create, but of a sea-change in the way we, as a society, are looking at education; a quantum leap forward in the way we are equipping young people to harness their real potential and succeed in the world beyond the school gates. For too long, we have been working inside the confines of an out-dated model, one not fit for the purposes of the 21st century. Now, and thanks in part to the free school system, a new breed of educators are challenging the accepted norms, daring to imagine that there might be alternatives, that our children can be better served than by strategies that have been endured, tweaked but never transformed, since Victorian times.

By investigating the sciences of motivation, the ways we form and maintain habits, ambition, and how character is formed, we are beginning to build a new model, an Education 2.0. It exposes the frailties on which our education system has traditionally been built and levels the playing field so that the opportunity for success is being offered to all our children, no matter how privileged their backgrounds.

The Power of Character has three parts. Part one will look at the systemic problems in our education establishments, the way specific government initiatives have turned our schools into cost-centred and target-driven organisations, with teachers and headteachers incentivised to 'game' the system in order to retain their jobs, at the long-term cost to their students. Part two will peel back the layers further and investigate the scientists, theorists, and statisticians whose research into the nuances of character and how we function as human beings is offering educators the tools by which they can buck the trends of the old system, introducing new ideas to the classroom and new structures to the schooling system that are revolutionising the way we teach: the mandate for our Education 2.0. Finally, part three will be your very own field manual and turn the structure of *The Power of Character* on its head with direct challenges to the reader to look at their own lives, their family and work situations, and challenge their accepted norms with lessons from the book.

This book is naturally centred on the story behind the setting up of King's and the benefits of the development of character in our youth but its lessons and the potential for growth its ideas offer can be translated to many other fields of life. In this part, we will also look briefly at how the science and theories on which the new model of character education is being built can have direct relevance to family life, business life and beyond.

This book, then, is the story of the first steps we, as a society, are taking down a long road to reinventing the way we approach who we are – and a challenge to every reader to bring these principles into their own lives, for the betterment of themselves and everyone around them.

The Proof of the Problem

On curiosity

Children are learners by nature. I had known that by instinct, but perhaps it was not until my daughter was born that I knew it as fact. Watching as she grew from being a baby to a toddler was an education in the very building blocks of character and how we learn. Without having to be guided or persuaded, she was inquisitive and curious, daring and bold. She would play for hours without any external driver, nor any incentive to continue, playing simply for the inherent joy and pleasure it would bring. Unperturbed by thoughts of either success or failure – because the very ideas were inscrutable to her – she seemed, to me, living proof of the joy children can find in learning, in making mistakes and discovering new things for themselves and not for the promise of any reward but for the simple pleasure of the process.

The idea of children as young as two enjoying the process of trying something new, mastering it, and gaining autonomy was a powerful one that I would keep coming back to across my career in school leadership.

The first day of that career took me to an industrial town in the northwestern part of England, on the northern bank of the River Mersey. The school here was to form the final part of my Future Leaders experience, a year-long residency in which I would be exposed to everything, good and bad, which the school system had to offer. I had barely set foot through the door, nor gained my bearings in this sprawling school, when I had my first taste of what the year would be like.

Future Leaders had drilled into us the idea that high expectations led to high results, that we needed to ensure our first contact with students set the appropriate tone of expectation and mutual respect. So, on that very first morning, I took up my post at the school gate, intent on greeting every student with a handshake. Apparently, no other member of staff had ever done the same and soon the students coming through the gates were looking at me as if I had two heads. Still, perhaps grudgingly, my hand was shaken, before each student tramped on into the building – until the moment when, upon seeing a new group of boys shambling through the gate, I asked one of them to tuck his shirt in. This time, the response was more than grudging. He looked at me once, the disdain on his features plain to see, and promptly told me to 'fuck off'. From that moment on, the day just got worse.

This was my first experience of urban education; a month earlier I had been a military officer in an organisation that valued respect, routine and rank, and here a 14-year-old boy with his shirt hanging out was swearing at me. This would not only be my first urban school but an abject lesson in how drastically things can go wrong in an environment where there are few social norms, where the relationship between teachers and pupils has no practical boundaries and where ritual and respect are entirely missing from the day.

I was reminded of that boy as I watched my daughter take her first tentative steps, as she built her earliest towers out of the building blocks from her toy box, as she fitted the pieces of her jigsaw puzzles indecorously together, or worked out – by trial and repeated error – the way she could open up her safety gates and scurry into new, undiscovered parts of our house. What happened, I wondered, between one and the other? The Charter Schools of America had the belief, as did I, that it was possible for every single child to succeed at school, and in life, no matter what their circumstances and background. The boy who had spat and swore at me that day – one day, in the not too distant past, he had been a toddler and the same age as my daughter. Once, he would have had a curious and inquisitive mind, eager to discover new things, caring neither for failure or success, but only the pleasure of learning. Somewhere along the way that had changed; now, like so many others in this school, he was detached from the learning experience, seeing his days here as things to be survived, endured, and done battle with or rebelled against.

The fact that his was not an uncommon story, in this school and countless others, was soon to become self-evident. Yet, there had to be a reason. What were we doing to our children to kill off that love of learning with which they are born? What turned those naturally inquisitive minds inward? What turned off the love of discovering new things?

King's Leadership Academy Warrington opened its doors in the September of 2012, three full years after the day I first set foot inside this school. Its ambition was to synthesise all we had observed in our careers and to build something innovative and new, a school with a sense of social justice at its heart. In thinking about how King's Leadership Academy might work, it was first necessary to ask exacting questions about the organisations we had all worked in, about what succeeded and what failed. Every remedy needs its diagnosis and if we were to arrive at our model for a new school, our Education 2.0, then we first needed to pick apart the lessons of the past.

Education 1.0

The long hot summer of 2011, London was ablaze. In stark images across the fronts of every newspaper, flickering on the television screen on the nine o' clock news, buildings were being ravaged by fire. In the London boroughs of Tottenham, Croydon, Peckham and Dalston, double-decker buses sat gutted by the sides of the roads. In a video uploaded to *YouTube*, later to become infamous, a young man named Ashraf Rossi was attacked for his rucksack by a group of men before then being, seemingly, rescued by a second group only for that group to then take his rucksack while he was looking the other way.

Warehouses, cycle shops, restaurants and pubs all became the victims of sudden, sporadic attacks, sometimes by opportunists, sometimes orchestrated over social media. Later, estimates would put the number of businesses who had fallen victim to these attacks at around 48,000.

The London riots, five days of widespread destruction in the August of 2011, were precipitated by a stand-off between police and Mark Duggan, a resident of Tottenham in North London who was shot dead on the fourth of August. The protest that followed descended into pitched battle between the police and protestors.

Perhaps the most troubling thing about those days of sporadic violence and random aggression was that when the moment had passed and lawyers, the judiciary, and journalists began to take stock, they could see that the people involved in the rioting were not, in general terms, intimately related to Duggan's death. What had begun as a protest had quickly been seized upon and used by people from across the social spectrum. By the middle of August that year, 3,100 people had been arrested for offences that included arson, looting, causing severe criminal damage, as well as more violent offences including murders and rape. A number of those arrested had prior criminal records but many did not. They came from a cross-section of society and included those ordinarily thought of as middle class and affluent.

The riots were not contained to just London. Violent scenes were witnessed across other cities in the mainland UK too, including Birmingham, Manchester, Bristol and Salford. These riots were later branded 'copycat riots' with the presiding feeling being that the lack of immediate boundaries in London had encouraged people across the nation to take part in the violence.

Later, debate would rage as to the causes of the riots. Were they the results of the policies of austerity instituted by the government after the economic collapse of 2008? Were they a reaction to high levels of unemployment and uncertainty about the workplace? Were they the product of gang culture, of poor race relations in the city's multicultural areas, of a failure in the penal system or the natural outcome of the disenfranchisement felt by the city's young? Or was it, as some academics would later suggest, simply for fun? Was there a sense of carnival in the marching and looting, the wanton destruction? If that was the case, what, then, did that say about the nation's character and the sense of moral and civic virtues being imparted to our young?

There are terrifying statistics to suggest that we are failing our young people on a moral level. A Home Office research paper of 2010 showed that young people commit a vastly disproportionate number of crimes compared to the rest of the population, with those under the age of 18 committing almost a quarter of all reported offences but only comprising 10% of the population. Frighteningly, more than half of all robberies, a third of all vehicle crimes, and a fifth of all sexual offences are perpetrated by our young people. Pertinently for the future King's Leadership Academy, we need look no further than our own school gates for the worst example of this kind.

In 2007, only 500 yards from where our Academy would one day stand, Gary Newlove – a middle-aged Englishman and father of three – confronted a group of youths who he believed had vandalised his wife's car. Moments later, he was on the ground, being kicked to death. It would later transpire that the group that murdered him had previously subjected other innocent passersby to acts of unimaginable violence. They were formed of a nucleus of key members but were part of a much more disparate group of young men and women whose lifestyles was unfixed and revolved around deliberate acts of terror. The trend for young people to fill the vacuums in their lives with criminality could never be clearer.

In 2011, Civitas – an independent think tank – postulated that a number of factors contributed to this trend: the lack of strong moral guidance within families; the sense that anti-social behaviour was an accepted norm inside certain urban micro-cultures; the pressure of peers already entrenched in anti-social and anti-authoritarian behaviours and, perhaps most strikingly of all, a fundamental lack of aspiration among our young. In 2011, a Prince's Trust report found that a full quarter of young people from our socio-economic poor believed that none of their dreams of a career were realistic, simply on the basis that 'people like them don't succeed in life'.

For more than a third of these young people, school was seen as an irrelevance in their home lives; more than a third had nowhere to do schoolwork at home, almost half did not have a desk, and a quarter no access to a computer. This lack of aspiration, some commentators noted, had direct bearing on the causes of the 2011 riots themselves, with young people propelled into joining the riots simply on the basis that if others were getting away with it, so could they. Why not, after all, if their aspirations were so low?

It was not long after the dust of those riots had settled and the examinations began that the question of how to remedy this failure in our national character turned to the idea of education. Moral education had long been thought of as deeply unfashionable, a throwback to an earlier time when the church and school system were irrevocably entwined but, soon after the riots, a cross-party enquiry was established to investigate its causes and make recommendations to ensure it did not happen again. There, amongst its recommendations, was a call to champion character building in schools and for each school to publish its specific policy regarding the building of character. "In asking what it was that made young people make the right choice in the heat of the moment, the panel heard about the importance of character," the enquiry declared. Character education was back on the national agenda.

Welcome aboard Air 53

Schools can be like societies in microcosm, and in a lot of ways my year long residency experience reflected the debates that would rage after the London riots. A glance at the whole school photograph is often a quick and easy way to reveal the expectations, culture and ethos of a school. And so it did here, where boys and girls wore uniforms with ties and hairstyles that would not look out of place in a 1980s American high school movie. A picture literally paints a thousand words!

My residency school was, in my opinion, a school in crisis. Contextually, its performance was deemed successful as later that year on my departure it would even be rated as Outstanding by the national inspectorate. In reality, it was failing almost half of its students to attain the basic requirements needed to move into education after the age of 16. That sense of crisis, after all, was why we had been brought in to train here, both to expose us to some of the worst that the school system had to offer and for us to do what we could to effect real change among its staff, students, and school culture.

Let's look at this failure rate in a different way. Would you board a plane in full knowledge that your pilot had successfully arrived at his pre-planned destination on only 53% of his previous flights? If, as you boarded the plane, slapped across the aircraft there were congratulatory messages of 'Well done Air 53, our best year yet!'? What about booking your child in for an operation with a surgeon who boasted of having a success rate of 53%, one of the highest performing surgeons in the area? The two scenarios are absurd, yet firstly this figure of 53% is exactly the number of students who achieved the government's national benchmark of five good GCSEs (at grade C and above) including English and mathematics in 2015. Secondly, it highlights the scale of self-delusion that school leaders often fall victim to in order to justify their existence on, around, or just above these mediocre standards. Let us look at it from the opposite angle.

At present rates, almost one in every two of our state school students are not gaining the basic qualifications needed to proceed into further education with any level of academic buoyancy. Those who fail to meet this standard might proceed into post-16 education or training (indeed, they now have to) but their levels of educational currency put them at a disproportionately higher risk of failure, disengagement or dropout. It's important to note, too, that these figures are just an 'average' with schools in urban and more deprived areas often faring much worse than their more affluent counterparts. In some areas of the United Kingdom, our urban schools record as low as a 10% pass rate.

What if you wanted to board that plane and travel first class? The government's first class equivalent in educational terms is the English Baccalaureate, a collection of good GCSEs in the subjects of English, mathematics, sciences, modern foreign languages and the humanities. In 2015, only one in four state-schooled students achieved this arbitrary measure or, in other words, three out of every four state-educated students failed to achieve a standard highly regarded by top colleges and universities. You might be wondering what the point is in these analogies? When you board a plane or book in for a surgeon, you ultimately have a choice. Yet in schooling it is rarely so simple.

Only the most privileged of parents have a choice over which school they can send their child to – selection by house price in order to be within catchment of a high performing school; selection by income in order to pay for private tutorage to help your child pass the 11 plus – unless, of course, they have the means to pay for a private education.

Schools, like the one to which I had been posted to, are often described as 'deprived' but the word has a connotation that is not strictly true. In reality, these schools are funded just the same as any other. If anything, they accrue more funding due to the challenges of their locations and benefit from further funds through schemes such as the Pupil Premium/ Free School Meals budgets. No, what my first weeks were to prove to me was that deprivation is not purely a matter of budgetary constraints; schools can be deprived in other, less easy to measure ways and this was a crash course in what manner of things could go wrong.

During Future Leaders, we had been taught to visualise the Four Horsemen of the Urban School Apocalypse – aspirational deprivation, cultural deprivation, basic skills deprivation, and the deprivation of basic social and professional norms. These horsemen cantered through the corridors of my own residency school with wild abandon. Nor was this an unusual set of circumstances. Soon, many of the other Future Leaders in my cohort would report back that the urban schools to which they had been sent displayed exactly the same problems. These were not issues being faced in isolation; they were widespread and deep-rooted in our education system. The most pernicious thing of all was that, for almost all of these children, there was no other choice.

Having come from a military culture, where order and routine was king and strict discipline key to the smooth running of the organisation, my first foray into education left me wondering whether the move had been a sensible one. Here was a school where order was absent, where the students were effectively left in charge while the teachers strove to survive their days. Sanctions against unruly children were loosely enforced, students walked the corridors whenever they felt like not being in lessons, basic respect between teachers and students had eroded to the point where expletives and abusive language abounded and where violence was not uncommon. To me, steeped in military culture, this all boiled down to a lack of aspiration and basic social norms.

During my first days as a military officer, I had been provided with a career 'flight path'. This informed me of exactly what options I had open to me over the course of my career, with the promotional opportunities mapped out as a timeline in front of me: whether that was in research and strategy, military parachuting, adventurous training, or survival and evasion instruction, the options were numerous and motivational. Yet, in stark contrast, the children here had little ambition to do anything with their lives and had, for the most part, never been drilled in the basic social codes of courtesy, respect and gratitude.

At the same time as I was taking my first tentative steps in residency, a secondary school teacher turned author, Charlie Carroll, had published his account of life as a supply teacher in the UK's inner city schools, travelling from one to another in his iconic VW camper van. Carroll's account was filled with the same kind of order and ill-discipline I saw in my first weeks, but more shocking still were the accounts of a pupil stabbing in Nottingham, a girl passing vodka around in her history lessons in Birmingham, another pupil using his IT lessons to deal drugs in Sheffield, and a 13-year-old boy so confident and aggressive that he could bully his teacher out of a school in Yorkshire. That these kinds of incidents demand reporting are not the point; the point, rather, was the laissez-faire way with which they were articulated.

Incidents that must seem outrageous to outsiders, as I then was, were banal to somebody inside the system. Whilst I had left the likelihood of operating on the battlefield long behind, the battle in the urban classroom appeared to be one of daily survival on the part of every teacher, with one report even citing that as many as one in ten practitioners had suffered physical violence in their previous 12 months of teaching, a majority having reported regular verbal abuse. Only the strong willed teachers were surviving, the rest either moved on or changed career. This was the norm.

My residency experience was typical of other state schools too in that there existed a culture of excuses, among both its students and its staff, with the children's postcode and upbringing constantly being pinpointed as the reason for their poor behaviour and lack of academic ambition. Among the children, hard work was not fashionable; it was cooler to be a class clown than it was to be conscientious and well mannered. Although this might be said to be a character trait inescapable in children, the way that it was encouraged and fed back by the staff seemed, to me, particularly problematic. The expectation was that learning had to be 'active' and, indeed, the focus of staff training that year was 'Kagan', a co-operative learning system founded in 1968 and designed to make the classroom experience enjoyable.

In principle, this might seem a good thing – co-operative learning has been shown to be effective at teaching both values and academics, at conveying basic life skills such as listening, communication, solving conflicts and working together, and at the same time building a sense of community inside a classroom. It's also been shown to foster greater acceptance of classmates from different ethnic or racial backgrounds. Indeed, the Kagan organisation argues that student-engagement and results overall can be greatly improved by the adoption of their methods. Here, in my residency school at least, it seemed to comprise of students constantly working in groups, always away from their desks with little classroom control and even less direct teaching of the subject by teachers, what I had assumed to be the essential foundation of knowledge in order for further building blocks of learning, such as application, analysis and critical thinking, to develop.

On the face of it, students were active but, in reality, because the teachers had failed to teach the knowledge underpinning a particular topic first, the students were being expected to analyze new concepts through play without being firmly grounded in them. As the saying goes, 'if you don't know what you don't know, then how are you supposed to know what to do?'. The reality was that students were being expected to run before they could walk and, as would be expected, the co-operative learning methods became reduced to a succession of party games with little deep learning. What we would later come to term 'funky' teaching, it was designed to appease the 'type' of problem children the school perceived that it had. Teachers even became armed with a range of soft balls and squidgy objects that they could throw to the students who had difficulty paying attention.

When I had been in the military, if a basic recruit could not stand still or pay attention (and believe me there were many with pre-diagnosed attention problems and special educational needs), they had to return that night and early the following morning in full formal dress for inspection by a senior officer. As a result of these high expectations and structures, few if any did so. As I watched this form of delivery in the classroom unfold often into chaos, mixed in with regular bursts of 'visible progress checks' such as thumbs up, smiley faces and a range of acronyms to tell the students what they were learning or about to learn, I could not help wonder what had gone on (and wrong) in educational research between my school days and now.

The time of teachers as authority figures stood at the front as the expert, the font of all knowledge, actually teaching the class a difficult and challenging concept, still with an air of respect and admiration, where had these role models gone?

Paradoxically, the discovery-based phenomenon had made the art of teaching tougher on the teachers and easier on the children. Amalgamating classes together and teaching them in large open 'learning plaza' spaces quickly became the next craze in brand new purpose-built urban schools; buildings and teaching spaces often designed solely by architects with beautiful designs and awards in mind rather than in consultation with teachers who could have given their views on what worked best.

When social norms are well established and respect and professionalism in classrooms are in abundance, the children can thrive and the teachers can teach, however what I was seeing was the polar opposite of this approach: what was lacking were clear structures, rules and regulations and, instead, students were setting the agenda. Like so many other schools, my residency school was trapped in a vicious cycle with the clear lack of boundaries incentivising the students to push further and further and inculcating in them an aversion to authority, while the teachers responded by finding new ways to appease. In doing so, they steered them further and further from the heartlands of education.

Freeing pupils from the overbearing authority of teachers, allowing them to follow their own interests, and making learning fun as opposed to coercive all appear sensible in theory but, like in so many other urban schools, it had gone too far and, with the exception of a small number of strong willed teachers, it was having a devastating effect in and around the classroom. The staff training and pedagogical focus was also a 'one size fits all' approach.

Every teacher, from the strongest to the weakest and the most experienced to the most recent graduate, all had the same diet of training, as did the students have the same diet of learning; there lacked any form of diagnostics to make delivery personalised. What was it that led schools like this to become organisations in which the relationship between students and teachers was so problematic, in which progress was curtailed by a culture of blame and excuses, and in which basic social norms were not observed? The cornerstone to Aristotle's definition of human flourishing or 'phronesis' (translated to practical wisdom) is knowledge. Often seen as the master virtue, knowledge is literally the font of good character, yet what I was witnessing in the classroom was a deliberate attempt to brush over this stage altogether.

The key to understanding why this was happening, I would later discover, was rooted in understanding how the role of the school leader had changed over the preceding twenty years, and how a specific set of circumstances, ranging from inside forces such as the attitudes and policies of central government to outside forces such as economic collapse, had reimagined the very nature of a school.

Lies, damned lies & statistics

Since the economic collapse of 2008, and the waves of austerity that followed, there was undoubtedly a sense of anxiety in workplaces across the United Kingdom. With unemployment figures rising, news stories recounting lay-offs and businesses closing, having a job – and holding onto it – became more valuable than ever.

These pressures were felt keenly inside the schooling system; schools do not exist in a vacuum and my residency school was no different; it could not exist outside of the austerity, fears of unemployment and financial chaos that were colouring those years. The reality is that schools have been subject to similar pressures for much longer than this brief period. In fact, over the past several decades, schools in England have been radically transformed by the pressures being applied on them and, in particular, the way a succession of different governments have transformed the roles of school leaders.

As early as the 1980s, when schools were given responsibility for their own financial resources, headteachers found themselves not only as the leaders of cohorts of teaching staff and students, but financial managers as well.

Cost-centred leadership encouraged headteachers to manage their schools like businesses where every student was a financial commodity, not only when they stepped through the door each morning but when they achieved good grades. Budgeting spreadsheets became the bugbears by which schools were governed and the freedom to use money to find creative ways of teaching became secondary to the need to make the budgets balance.

Meanwhile, a system of targets and league tables were being set up to measure, rank – and, in theory, drive up school performance. In 1992, as a result of then Prime Minister John Major's 'Citizen's Charter' – an attempt to improve public services and make them more accountable to the UK taxpayer – the old, loose system of school inspections, largely being the preserve of local government, was replaced by Ofsted (Office for Standards in Education, Children's Services and Skills) who report to the central government and are responsible for every state run educational establishment nationwide.

Soon afterwards, the first school league tables were published. The hope was that they would give the parents of school children – or 'customers' as they could now loosely be called – an instant snapshot of the quality of the schools to which their children might go and the chance to make an informed choice about their children's education. In principle, the free market approach to education was a good thing but, in practise, it also began to take autonomy away from individual schools.

If a school measured badly in the league tables, or was seen to be stagnating or not improving, policy makers could now target that school. The data harvested by inspections could directly be used to steer the school system, with new directives being imposed from above. As a result, the autonomy of headteachers was slowly being diminished. The responsibility for steering the specifics of a curriculum were being adopted by the government and the role of headteacher was transforming into somebody who implemented, rather than set, the agenda.

Across the 1990s and 2000s, as the league table system was refined – and, in large part, in response to resistance by schools themselves – factors other than results began to be built into the ways in which schools were measured. By 1997, schools were being rated according to an 'improvement index' that aimed to rank them in terms of how much better the school had become since its last inspection. Soon after that, the first attempts were made to metricate how much progress an 'average' student made in each school, each year. Students no longer became known as a person with a name, a story and hope and dreams like any human would expect to be treated, but as a statistic. Not only did this sudden obsession with student targets and expected progress start to dampen expectations for many students, it also began to exert unnecessary pressures, with rates of anxiety and depression amongst the young seeing a steady increase.

The national strategy on 'Gifted and Talented' in schools even went as far as specifying that there should be a particular quota of students within each year group who were better than the rest. What this did indirectly was assume that a pre-set limit existed in students' capabilities and for those who did not make the arbitrary cut off point, provide them with a convenient opportunity to believe in a series of self-fulfilling excuses based on how their deficiencies were grounded firmly in their inherited DNA. How often do we con ourselves into thinking that we were not lucky enough to be born with the 'maths gene' or the 'music gene', for example?

As far back as 1869, Sir Francis Galton argued in the publication *Hereditary Genius* that maximal performance was determined by heritable genetic traits. It has only been more recently that a number of researchers, the most prolific of whom is Professor Anders Ericsson, have studied the myth of innate talent and so called 'prodigies' and the findings could not be clearer. There is no evidence to suggest that anyone is born without the innate 'gift' or 'talent' to do mathematics, play music, compete in sport, draw beautifully or myriad other things to a high performing level. It just requires unwavering belief, hard work, repeated practice, personal endeavour all mixed together with lots of timely feedback. I had navigated my way through school having had exactly this mind-set – that I was born to be good at sport but did not have the gene or 'talent' for music, art, drama or technology-related subjects.

As a result, I dropped these subjects as soon as I could at the age of 14 but what I failed to realise was that I was only good at sport not because I was 'gifted and talented' but because I practiced it more than anything else. Yet, why was the education system actively encouraging me to make these decisions? In stark contrast, the military training system I had left behind as an adult had taken me onto its officer programme having had no prior military experience at school or at university, nor any family ties to the service whatsoever.

By the end of the programme, I had to meet exactly the same level of output standard as a fellow cadet who had grown up in the service; a fellow cadet who had been a part of the cadets whilst at school and had gained military sponsorship whilst at university. In the end, it just meant my learning curve was longer and far steeper, yet with belief, hard work, repeated practice and feedback (mixed with good old-fashioned military wit) it was achievable. Yet, the education system appeared to be doing the exact opposite – it was breeding a culture of mediocrity, the nod of approval to say that when you arrived at your pre-set, pre-determined level predicated on what you had achieved by age 11 or 14, it was okay to stop learning and improving as there was nothing higher to achieve, unless of course you were classed as gifted and talented.

Worse still, if you did not make the grade straight away it was okay to try something different, something easier such as the myriad vocational qualification 'equivalents', after all not all of us can be good at maths or do the sciences, right?

As the years went by, the system of rankings became so complex that it became distracting – and, what was worse, teachers and head-teachers were themselves being ranked and examined according to the findings of this system; a poor performance might mean a black mark one year but it could easily mean a lost job the next. By the mid 2000s, the algorithms by which schools were rated were being revised to draw in data from other fields.

This system, which went by the name of CVA (Contextual Value Added) aimed to rank schools more fairly by allowing for other factors affecting achievement. These factors included ethnicity, gender, the poverty of the specific area in which the school was to be found, and any other special needs provision the school caters for.

In principle, this was an improvement on the old system, which valued only the raw hard facts of exam results, in allowing other factors to be accounted for. Schools in areas with greater levels of poverty, or schools whose children faced greater challenges and traumas outside the school gates, would not be compared on a like-for-like basis with schools in more affluent or progressive parts of the country. Yet, in real world terms, the extra nuance CVA added to the system was a distraction; schools might have now measured students differently based on their life circumstances but employers could never be asked to do the same.

A trainee scheme at a bank, or application process at a university, would never employ or admit an applicant with poorer qualifications than a competitor, purely on the basis of what post code they came from. Can you imagine Oxford University saying to a student applying from a leafy middle class suburb that they can have a place as long as they achieve three As at A level, while simultaneously saying to a student from an urban school that they could be admitted on three Cs? Or a graduate trainee scheme saying the same? The idea is comical and, yet, that is exactly what schools have been doing across the last twenty years; turning qualifications from hard, objective scores to softer, subjective ones riddled with excuses based on circumstance.

In reality, CVA did nothing to remedy the overriding flaw in the system: though they might have started with best of intentions, league tables effectively moved schools away from being student-focused to being target-focused organisations. Now, headteachers, who were already grappling with their new roles as financial overseers, were being handed down targets and measured against them in the same way that salesmen and commission agents are incentivised and, more recently, general practitioners and medical practices. The effect was a slow eroding of the head's traditional role; no longer were they concerned solely with bettering their students, now the focus had shifted and they were instead being incentivised to get good Ofsted reports. At first sight, the two things might seem the same but there are actually subtle, and very specific, differences. Principally, there is more than one way of getting a good Ofsted report and getting a good Ofsted report does not necessarily mean having the best interests of your students at heart.

While I was working at my residency school, beginning to understand the ways in which a school without aspirations and basic social norms might work, one of my fellow Future Leaders experiences situated in a different part of the country had made it clear the manifold ways a school could navigate their way through the Ofsted system without putting the long term needs of their students first. The goal was for every student to achieve five passes at GCSE, including in mathematics and English. This school intended to succeed in this, no matter what the cost.

Here, children were entered for GCSEs in mathematics and English twice a year, every year, from the ages of 12 to the age of 16 until they passed, regardless of grade. If this didn't happen, other options had to be taken and, though GCSEs were the standard qualification, there were alternatives at that time that could also count in how a school was rated. If a student failed their GCSE after eight attempts, they would be sent away on a study weekend to a local hotel, and upon their return they would have been awarded a BTEC in mathematics, the GCSE alternative. That's right; eight failed GCSEs mattered not at all because a BTEC could be achieved in just one residential study weekend.

Students were also entered three times each year for the Adult Literacy and Numeracy, or ALAN, test that, at the time, could also count towards the government's performance measure where each student at a school was rated. The problem was that the ALAN test was multiple choice; students sat it alongside a teacher and, if they didn't pass it by their fifth attempt, they would be designated as having special educational needs, given an in-school support plan and be allotted a reader who would help them sail through the test on their next attempt. The result was that nobody ever failed; the definition of special needs was extended to such a point that even students reasonably outside that designation could be given special help and their grade effectively assured.

Other times the school deliberately picked and ushered children into qualifications demonstrably easier to achieve than standard GCSEs. Under-performing children were sent away on a residential weekend to gain a BTEC in Fish Husbandry, which the headteacher argued was a useful qualification to hold in a challenging port town; others were sent on a weekend course to a local hotel to earn a diploma worth two GCSEs in hospitality.

Some stories were even more difficult to believe and, instead of showing how a school played the system, showed a school in flagrant opposition to it; an external investigation in 2013 found the school guilty of copying coursework from another establishment. All of this done, not to the betterment of the students but to the betterment of the league tables and to preserve the roles of school leader and staff. It is no surprise that, in those days of CVA taking into account postcode as a part of how children's success was measured, this school had one of the highest CVA scores in the country.

Considered together, it is hard not to get the impression that, in the first decade of the 21st century, the UK's schools were not designed to be serving their students, but simply to carry on existing against an avalanche of statistics and government red tape. This was the age of lack of authority, teaching methods designed to appease rather than teach, low value qualifications focusing on the performance tables rather than the students. Across this period, the artificial inflation of students' grades – caused by easier exam content, lower exam grade boundaries and an unprecedented scale of perverse incentives – led to fewer students studying a foreign language, with schools opting for 'easier' subjects such as ICT and media and film. BTECs in obscure, and sometimes unpragmatic, subjects were valued above the harder core subjects at GCSE, students were being drilled in their subjects through countless re-sit examinations, and sometimes even being fraudulently pushed over the line by teachers focused on raw data rather than real world results.

By the time I arrived for my residency experience in 2009, schools had been labouring under these conditions for almost three decades; and the erosion of what we might think of as 'traditional' school values – the investment in children as our future, the respect and responsibilities between pupils and staff – seemed, at least here, to be complete. Teachers and school leaders were obsessed by their students' target level and 'getting them over the Grade C line' was their raison d'etre. When I was at school I had no idea what my academic targets were nor did I care, we were just made to always try hard and, if I didn't, my teachers would inform my parents.

The point is, because I had no concept of my attainment targets for my age, my teachers never created any glass ceilings for what I could achieve, nor did I feel pressured to hit a predetermined target that cannot for one minute account for the 'true' potential within us all. I was encouraged to do my best, whatever that might be – as it turns out, my grade Cs in English and Maths at GCSE did not dampen my spirit and prevent me from gaining a PhD from a top university nor did it tell me that I was not good enough to aspire to become a military officer. I often wonder to this day whether I would have had that confidence had I been told that I had reached my true potential the day I was awarded my GCSEs, "Well done Andrew on your Grade Cs, you must be very proud on reaching your full potential!"

But what lessons can we draw from this when we begin to devise a formulation for our Education 2.0? If the practicalities of the system are not going to change – if schools must go on being inspected to uphold and (quite rightly) continually improve standards, if teachers must go on being held accountable for the results their students achieve – is there any way of recasting school life, recalibrating school culture, to avoid the need for teachers and head-teachers to trick the system? Might there be a way of returning to the core values that once underpinned teaching, and yet still survive in a modern world of Ofsted, league tables and trial-by-exam-results?

The quick fix

If there is one thing that the transformation of headteachers into manipulative statisticians – the type who might 'game' the system to protect their jobs – shows, it is that we live in a 'quick fix' culture.

In 1895, Joseph Malins – a temperance activist who emigrated from Worcester in England's West Midlands to the United States, where he worked on the railways – wrote a poem that perfectly captures the idea of the quick fix culture. In *A Fence or an Ambulance*, the walk to a beautiful sightseeing spot is made perilous by a sheer cliff face, down which many good men have plummeted. When asked what should be done about the danger, the citizens who live in the area have two different schools of thought: the first suggest a fence should be built around the edge of the cliff; the second shrug their shoulders and say "put an ambulance down in the valley."

In his scathing verse, Malins was perfectly caricaturing the types of decisions with which we are so often faced with. Do we opt for the course of action that provides the greatest long-term benefit, but demands the most effort or do we opt for the path of least resistance, something to patch over the problem without stretching ourselves? Do we build fences to prevent accidents, or do we simply wait for the accidents to happen and clean up afterwards?

The idea that we live in a quick fix culture is not a new one and, indeed, Malins was parodying the idea as far back as the 19th century. Undoubtedly, its roots go even further. There was a time in mankind's history when quick fixes were needed. Imagine prehistoric man running from predators on the ancient African savannah. Could he stop and debate the cost/benefit ratio of erecting a fence to keep those predators at bay – or did he just need to keep on running? Back then, reaching for the quick fix provided a bona fide evolutionary advantage and perhaps, as a result, our brains are hard-wired to reach for the easiest, most immediately effective solution to a problem instead of automatically considering the long term. After all, biologically speaking, we are still that same prehistoric man, fleeing predators across the Savannah. Yet, as societies formed and civilisations rose, the benefits of the quick fix were rapidly eroded.

In a world where millions of us must co-exist, where the actions of one individual invariably effect the lives of countless others, the quick fix culture presents a catastrophic lack of foresight and a willingness for us to bury our heads in the sand and delay disaster. Nowhere was this more evident than in the financial collapse that began in 2008.

The financial crisis of 2008 is considered by many economists to be the worst since the Wall Street crash of 1929 and the Great Depression that followed. The collapse of large financial institutions, the government bailouts that stopped the avalanche from proceeding, the plummeting of stock values and the rapid decline in consumer wealth – all of this has been well documented in the years since the crisis. What has been less well documented is its simple root cause. Though debate has raged between academics and economists as to the true origins of the collapse – was it the bursting of the American housing bubble in 2004? The easy credit conditions that led to predatory lending by banks across the world? The limitations of the financial modelling systems used to regulate the global economy?

In a lot of ways, the debate does not matter because there is one factor common to every argument and counter-argument the theorists invoke and that's the quick fix culture itself – the way the system incentivised banks and brokers to take bigger and bigger risks to make immediate gains, without thinking about their long term implications.

President Barack Obama hit the nail on the head in a speech of June 2009. A "culture of irresponsibility" in the banking sector, he declared, was at the heart of what had gone wrong. Financial institutions across the world were "rewarding recklessness rather than responsibility". In other words, in the pursuit of fast profits and big bonuses, corporate bankers worked without scruples. In seeking to maximise their gains over the short term and win bonuses big enough to set them up for rich, indulgent lives, investment bankers were ignoring the long-term stability of the financial world.

President Obama's ire did not end there. The bankers were at fault, he explained, but so too were the world's governments, who were happy for the financial sector to take these risks and refused to regulate them too closely. So too, he said, were the American citizenry, decent family men and women who bought homes "without accepting the responsibilities" of the debt they accrued. The message was vivid and would last long in the international imagination; the quick fix culture extended to every corner of modern life, from the very big to the very small.

The financial crisis is only the biggest and most striking example of how rapidly a quick fix culture can become unstuck. Look around you and you can see the quick fix culture proliferating in the many and varied corners of life. Think this is just in the financial sector? Well, think again. The university students paying an online service to write essays for them so that they can avoid the long hours of study and writing the essay might take? That's the quick fix culture at work. The other students turning to online encyclopaedias instead of investigating primary sources or reading further afield? The overweight man from down the road who, rather than putting in long hours at the gym, turns to gastric bands and other weight loss surgery instead? The patients who would rather take cholesterol-controlling drugs than make the necessary adjustments to their diets?

These are all examples of the way society, and we as individuals, reach for the easiest option available. We are living in a world in which we are constantly incentivised to go for the immediate solution, rather than one that takes more effort but, in that effort, might enrich our lives. Ask any geneticist and they will tell you that, on a basic level, we are still the same animals we were five million years ago – we are stone-age humans living in a tablet-aged, information rich world, and, as is our nature, we take every 'energy saving' opportunity we can. This is what our species has learnt to do across millions of years of scarcity, to preserve energy by taking the shortest route.

There's a danger in harking back to older, better times; the idea that there was once a Golden Age in which everything was perfect, which we must work hard to return to is a powerful one. It grounds us and gives our modern lives context but it is not true. Golden Age thinking would have us believe that a time before modern medicine, before the civil rights movements of the 20th century, before the welfare state, was an age worthy of recreating.

There's growing evidence that the rapid technological advancements made since the industrial revolution of the 19th century, and particularly since the information revolution of the late 20th, have had a seismic effect on the way we not only interact with each other and the world in which we all live, but in the fundamentals of how we think. If we want to understand the fullness of the quick fix culture, the science can shed some interesting light.

At the dawn of the 20th century, penicillin was a thing of the distant future; manned aviation had not yet begun in earnest; horse-drawn carriages were still more prevalent than motorised ones, and would be for years to come. Yet, by the dawn of the 21st century, mankind had set foot on the moon, developed atomic weapons capable of destroying the planet, decoded the blueprint for the human genetic code, cloned animals and ushered in an age of instant, mass communication. The technological advancements of those hundred years outweighed, by a great degree, the technological advancements of all of human history. This was a century in which a person could begin their life with the threat of an early death from an infected graze but end it having survived any number of diseases that would have killed his forebears, having taken in man's first visit to space and the birth of the computer age along the way.

The speed of this technological change, and the changes it has necessarily made to our cultures, would be dizzying to anyone who lived before it. Though it could be argued that we live in a world vastly more connected, safe and secure than in ages past, in recent years scientists have committed great resources to defining exactly how our minds and mental capabilities have started to change as a result of this rapid progress. The results aren't encouraging.

A 2015 study, by the National Centre for Biotechnology Information in Maryland in the United States, sought to uncover the effects the deluge of information we are subjected to, by the internet, our social networks and other media, has had on our attention spans since the social media boom of the early 2000s. Their thesis – that our attention span has diminished in the face of so many external stimuli – was borne out by the data.

The study found that the average attention span in 2015 was eight and a quarter seconds, down from 12 at the turn of the century. It also found that the average internet user reads less than a third of the words on each page they visit, with almost a fifth of all pages being visited for less than four seconds at a time; and that the average office worker checks their email inbox every one and a half minutes, down from every five at the start of the century. A similar study by computer giant Microsoft had corresponding results. By using electroencephalograms (or EEGs) to monitor brain activity, they discovered that those with heavily digital lifestyles – defined as consuming more entertainment, engaging actively with social media, and adopting new technologies at an earlier point – had difficulty focusing in environments where long term attention was needed.

The world has sped up. Communication is instant, we absorb more but consume less – and it would be foolish to suggest that none of this has had an effect on the way we use our brains. A 2009 UCLA study has suggested that just five hours of internet browsing is enough to show, in the patterns of our brain activity, how our brains function differently. A group of students asked to give up their mobile phones for 24 hours were observed showing signs of restlessness and anxiety disorder, perceiving phantom phone vibrations in their pockets and constantly reaching for phones that were not there.

The statistics are stark enough, but we have all seen it – teachers, perhaps, more so than any – the lack of focus in conversations, the temptation to constantly be checking phones for messages and updates on social media feeds, the changing nature of online news as newspapers and other sites work to lure readers into their pages and keep them there with a succession of short, snappy articles, designed for maximum impact over the shortest number of words. As we spend more time engaging with others online, the nature of those conversations is changing our expectations, and therefore our abilities: we are less focused and less engaged than we were fifteen years ago on a cultural level.

It's easy to blame this on the age of the internet and the life-defining culture of social media but it would be wrong to think of this in isolation. The fact is, in a number of tangible ways, culture has been shifting inward for half a century or more. Most of man's history has been defined by the things we do not have – the constant hunt for food and security of our hunter-gatherer ancestors, the need for fuel to burn and keep us warm, the need to accumulate wealth and, in that way, protect ourselves across much of our civilised history. If there was once a time in which all our waking hours were spent accumulating the things we needed to simply keep ourselves alive, that is not the case today. Thanks to the technological, scientific and cultural advancements we have made, the presiding feature of our modern lives is not one of scarcity but of abundance. The things we once strove for – food, fuel and shelter – are things we now take for granted. We are deluged with entertainment and information. In most cases, whatever we want – be it a cold drink, something fine to eat, a new movie or book in which to lose ourselves, or a new experience on which to venture out with friends – is right there, at the tips of our fingers. There are choices everywhere that we look.

It would be easy to say that the standard of living we have achieved, in the Western world, is unimaginable to our forebears. Our grandparents' generation would, perhaps, think ours a golden age for this very reason. Yet the ease with which we can access and achieve the things that we want has not necessarily made life more straightforward or happier. A world of abundance is a world packed with choice – dizzying, electrifying choice, and the demands that makes on our attention. For every action there is an equal and opposite reaction and what we might think of as the traditional values of hard work and endurance have transformed, in an age of abundance, to a kind of 'I want one now' culture. Prosperity has given us much that's good but what it has also given us is a need, a demand, for more prosperity. It has been like a sugar rush, its chief result being a need to consume more. Children raised in an age of abundance, naturally, have no context for that abundance; for them, abundance is the norm.

As a species, we seem to be programmed to want more than we have. That's a survival tactic inherited from our earliest ancestors. The delineation between the things that we need and the things that we want has been eroded. Yet, my daughters will now have to navigate their way through a world defined by the instant transmission of information and consumerism and they, like all of their generation and those following, will need to be able to differentiate between what is reality and what is not. At what cost will this have to their character? How many times in the past year have you seen something you want to buy and, unable to come up with the funds immediately, reached for a credit card to make up the difference? The transformation of our economy from one predicated on funds in hand to the concept of credit has generated untold growth, but – quite apart from the cycles of boom and bust that easy credit has precipitated – its repercussions can be felt in our character and how, as a culture, we are increasingly unwilling to delay our gratification, how we reach for easy, quick answers to life's problems more often, regardless of what challenges this might pose further down the line.

According to a 2013 study by Gabriel Fineberg of the University of Pennsylvania, the number of families spending money on credit cards – choosing to buy now, pay later, or to put it more clearly, purchasing goods they cannot yet afford – rose from 16% in 1960 to 64% in 1995. When the fast food giant *McDonald's* first allowed credit card purchases in the United States, the average diner spent $2.50 more by card than they would have done in cash. The availability of credit changed the way we thought about cash and, in turn, about commodities. It transformed us from a culture of saving and spending within our means, to a culture growing up needing instant results.

People want things – money, a new car, a bigger and better house – and they want them now. No longer do we routinely put things off until we can afford to pay for them. Our 'buy now pay later' sense of entitlement means that we feel we shouldn't wait; we see it as our right to be gratified straight away. This culture of instant gratification is inextricably linked to the quick fix culture itself; it's everywhere we look. You can see it in the homogenisation and concurrent lack of diversity in the entertainment industries, the rise of short-form sports such as Twenty-20 cricket in preference to long-form sports like Test Cricket, to the nose-diving popularity of books that demand engagement and long-term investment and the soaring successes of the first *YouTube* megastars, dispensing bite-size nuggets of advice to their millions of subscribers daily.

In the US Presidential race of 2016, commentators contrasted Republican nominee Donald Trump's sound bite style with the denser, more involved style of Democratic candidate Hilary Clinton. They found that Clinton's style, though much richer with substance, was less palatable to the public. The way we look at the world itself is changing. Instant gratification is king. Schools and their leaders have not been immune from this drive toward swift or instant results. We have already seen the tactics some head-teachers would revert to in an attempt to jump the hurdles of the Ofsted system. My first experiences of teaching outside the Future Leaders programme was to provide a striking example of how the cultures of instant gratification and the quick fix were further impacting our schools.

The iceberg effect

After the year I spent teaching at my residency school, I gained a senior leadership post at a large urban comprehensive on the Wirral, a metropolitan borough of northwest England with strong connections to Liverpool. The Wirral is an interesting place, in that it is one of the few remaining regions of the country with a significant number of grammar schools, mirroring the affluent coastal towns of Hoylake, Caldy and West Kirby that exist nearby. Only a short drive away, the town of Birkenhead is plagued with high levels of unemployment and underperforming schools, as the non-grammar school comprehensives face similar challenges to the old secondary modern schools of the 1960s and 70s.

The college to which I joined was only a short drive from Birkenhead and had a greater affinity with the urban, inner-city areas of Liverpool than with the leafy middle class coastal towns. The college was, by all official measurements, an exceptional school. Just as I joined its staff, it had just won a national award after its most recent outstanding Ofsted inspection. My first days there were a stark contrast to my first days in residency.

Over the preceding five years, the college had achieved the status of National Support School, with the headteacher also working as a National Leader of Education (or NLE) to provide support to under performing schools in the local area. The journey to reach this position had not been easy. Five years prior to my arrival, the college had been in crisis, defined by a culture that was negative and forbidding and in constant competition with the local grammar schools. Like in so many other parts of the country, disaffection – coupled with a non-working and dependency-based family unit – meant that students had little respect for their education.

This had been a place where the four horsemen of the urban school apocalypse ran wild: there were low aspirations, low social capital, low cultural capital and very few basic skills being imparted. Low aspirations naturally lead to complacency and inertia, with a bare minimum of teaching and learning being undertaken, and at the Wirral school this cycle had become ingrained and particularly stubborn to break. A lack of self-belief was leading to low expectations, and when the schooling culture is one that actively advocates making excuses – these children can't do well because they don't do well – standards quickly unravel.

At Future Leaders, we had been taught that turning a failing school around involves taking five steps, each one supported and underpinned with massively high expectations: get them attending, get them behaving, get them learning, get them achieving and get them believing. You cannot have students believing they can achieve if they are not firstly in school or, if in school, if classrooms are disruptive and unruly. The initial steps therefore have to be an intense focus on punctuality and professional standards, and that was exactly how the headteacher here had turned things around on his arrival, with a relentless focus on discipline and systems. Whether through the immediate exclusion (or in severe cases the expulsion) of students who had disregard for authority, or through constantly reasserting the very highest expectations he had for his students and staff, the head had steered the school into such a position that it was finally flourishing.

This was now a school that espoused many of the traits of the American Charter Schools we had visited with Future Leaders: poor behaviour was dealt with effectively, no excuses were made for students not attending school or engaging in good practice, students were given firm boundaries in both their academic and extra-curricular lives and were routinely excluded if they failed to meet expectations. A system of repeated and sustained practice permeated the school and, at first glance, it seemed one of the most well-oiled operations I was likely to see.

I learned a great deal from an inspirational headteacher here: the importance of strong discipline; clear and consistent teaching routines and working practices; strong branding and outwards communication; forensic scrutiny of performance data; the benefits of recruiting huge numbers of English and maths teachers to get class sizes consistently below 15, and, of course, the way the school was constantly striving to give urban working class students the same level of social and cultural capital that students at private schools and the local grammar schools routinely enjoy. Yet, in spite of the incredible successes the school had had, it was here that I began to think about the bigger picture nationally and the long-term effects of effective urban school leadership happening in turnaround schools. When change was imposed upon an organisation – albeit necessarily and for the best intentioned of reasons – where did that leave the organisation when the leadership changed or moved on? In schools where the leaders have improved poor situations through strict discipline and rigour, regulating staff almost as closely as students, are the staff fully engaged with their work – or do they feel micro-managed and unmotivated as a result? And, if staff and students are not empowered, how can change last positively for any real length of time?

It was on the Wirral that I first began to think of school leadership in terms of icebergs. Think that sounds nonsensical? Well, think again. Icebergs are curious things; we think of them as big chunks of ice floating on the water but, in fact, they're much vaster than that. What we see are only the tips of giant mountains of ice hewn from the Arctic and Antarctic ice sheets, with most of their bodies, over 90% of it, being entirely submerged. In other words, only 10% of what goes on is 'outward facing' or in plain sight for all to see; the rest is 'inwards facing'. When we talk about scratching the surface of the problem, sometimes we talk about seeing only 'the tip of an iceberg'. Dentists have a similar expression and express it with their own mordant sense of humour: they talk about getting to the 'root of the problem.'

The way schools are examined and held to account, and ranked against each other, does not encourage teachers and school leaders to do the same. What was occurring in Britain's failing schools, even under the stewardship of strong-willed and driven school leaders, pointed to this very fact.

To turn an unsatisfactory school around takes great willpower and ferocious strength from its leadership. Too often, however, these transformations were driven by tip-of-the-iceberg thinking because of the way the inspection system works; change has to be fast and only change that is imposed by brute force can be rapidly effected. To outside observers like Ofsted, the transformation strong school leaders could affect must have looked revelatory, but to what extent were the long-term implications of these blitzkriegs being taken into account? What happens to an institution, to a culture, when its head is cut off or removed, literally? If change has been imposed, rather than cultivated from below, what happens when that imposition is taken away? Can change be lasting if it is forced, or does it just wither away? Does a school or any other organisation for that matter start to nosedive when their leader is removed or moves on to bigger and better things? If it does, this points to an overt focus on 'tip of the iceberg' thinking; in other words, the organisation has succumbed to the 'iceberg effect'.

What was happening in successful turnarounds up and down the country was remarkable and inspiring in so many ways, but I wondered if they also risked being subjected to the quick fix culture – a legitimate reaction to the demands of the system, perhaps, but still an example of how momentary improvements could be made at the expense of long term thinking. As Confucius once said, 'you reap what you sow'. Was education now a system that actively encouraged heads to become 'seasonal gardeners', sowing new seeds each and every year yet only tending to a select group of their flowers at the most important times of the school year – and defining that importance in terms of them and their positions rather than the long term benefits of their students.

The idea of a head becoming a 'constant gardener', somebody who plants and nourishes every seed, attends to each and every flower equally, regardless of species or time away from the annual village show, with the same rigour and commitment every day of their working lives wasn't actively encouraged by the system into which our school leaders were bound. We might laugh at the colourful comparison between leaders of education and those of horticulture, but look a little closer and think about what we, as teachers, do in comparison to gardeners. We plant the seeds in September, we ignore them for four years, expecting all our flowers to grow in a linear fashion then, when the summer show is fast approaching, we cram in all the quick fix techniques and miracle grow cures we can, keeping our fingers crossed for a perfect summer bloom. Just as Aristotle has taught us that habits are the cornerstone of every behaviour, positive or negative, if we fail to prepare the minds of our students effectively over the course of their childhood, is it any wonder why so many adults fail to develop into life-long learners? Rather, our students become more adept at cramming and see education as something to be endured, all at the expense of developing mastery and a lifelong passion for learning. Education, just like horticulture, is based on an ecosystem requiring constant seeding, nurture and cultivation to achieve its true potential. So why do we take short cuts year after year in our schools? Why, in spite of our results consistently showing almost half of all students not proceeding into further education with a basic level of educational currency, do we succumb to the iceberg effect? Why was education trapped in its very own Groundhog Day, the process repeating itself year after year with no discernible change?

If there was a valid Education 2.0 out there, it would have to be one that somehow went against the grain of modern living, one that put value in the solid and long term instead of the fleeting and momentary; and one that, in eschewing the rush for instant gratification and putting the desires of the present ahead of the needs of the future, laid long-lasting foundations. Was there a way of taking the kind of change the school leader at the Wirral effected and ensuring it lasted? If nothing else, Education 2.0 would be focused on 'below the iceberg' principles, hewing close to the character virtues and values that set students up to be successful in the long term, not just to appear successful in the short.

The 'constant gardener' knows that a truly flourishing life starts at the root. Although it is impossible to make a flower grow in a linear fashion, we can create a culture that fosters the right conditions to maximise growth for the long term. As the old adage goes: give a man a fish and you will feed him for a night; give him a fishing rod and he can feed himself for a lifetime. That, I now knew, would be Education 2.0's principal goal, to help us better help ourselves. The word paradigm comes from the Greek. It is more commonly used today as a change in theory, perception or framework. In other words, it is a different way of seeing the world. My experiences in the next school to which I was posted would only bolster my belief that there was no quick fix to the problems of the quick fix culture: at its heart, the system needed fundamental change – a new paradigm.

The surgeon

We have already seen how the Ofsted system and the gaming of the school league tables transformed school leaders, and their teachers, from being student-focused to being results-at-any-cost focused. This then encouraged school leaders to become 'seasonal gardeners', or dentists focused only on the surface of the tooth rather than its dark, broken root. The cost of the transformation was a shift from long term to short term thinking and a slow eroding of what might be seen as the traditional values of our schooling system. The more tangible cost has been the generations of children ejected from school into the working world with qualifications that might, on the face of it, seem encouraging but which, in reality, hide the stark truth of their under-preparedness from view. There is another striking cost to the way the school system has been transformed across the past decades, one whose impact lasts through generations of different children and that is the way the system has challenged and transformed the role of schoolteacher itself; how staff, like students, are persistently being let down.

In 1994, when Sir Christopher Woodhead – a teacher and lecturer who had also held several posts in local government educational development – was appointed the new director of Ofsted, then only two years old, he made a bold declaration that would echo in the education system long after. Woodhead had a style many found abrasive, and his opening declaration that 15,000 teachers were unfit for purpose bought him many enemies in the profession. Even at that early point in Ofsted's life it was felt that Woodhead was using data out of context to attack the schooling system. Indeed, 15,000 teachers only represented 3% of the teaching profession, implying that the vast majority of teachers were exactly the right people to be driving the nation's schools forward.

All the same, Woodhead had thrown down the gauntlet and, in the midst of all the opprobrium and resent that would follow, had made at least one salient point. The school system's most prized assets were its teachers, those missionaries on the ground whose task it was, day in and day out, to engage and challenge their students, to get the very best out of them even when they didn't believe they could get the best out of themselves. Woodhead may have been berating the very people he was meant to defend, but he had one thing right: a school was only as good as the teachers who walked its corridors. That was a truth self-evident; they had to be the best.

After my year on the Wirral, my next posting took me to suburban Manchester, and a school that was to give me first-hand experience of the cyclical trap into which schools can fall victim to the iceberg effect, rather than being fundamentally addressed for the long term. Myself – along with another two colleagues - were despatched to Manchester for eight months in the hope that we could help effect real change in a school that Ofsted inspectors feared would soon slip into its 'special measures' category. Manchester was also my first role as a deputy head, and as such the first that truly allowed me to see the inner-workings of a school from every angle.

Turnaround school leaders are trained, as we were with Future Leaders, to enter problematic schools and rapidly effect change. Like everyone else, they are measured not only by the results they procure – but also by the speed with which they procure them. They are trouble-shooters by nature, tested and ranked by the swiftness with which they turn failing institutions around, and it was in this capacity that we entered the Manchester posting with the purpose of effecting real change.

My colleagues and I arrived with a non-apologetic approach. What had worked in other successful turnaround schools nationally would work here in Manchester, and we soon resolved that our focus would first be on the behaviour of the school's students, instituting order so that a productive teacher/student relationship could be developed. On arrival, it had seemed as if the students were in charge of the school and we readdressed the balance by enforcing a new behavioural code and excluding those who refused to follow our rules. We had a 'no excuses' policy on uniform, and the school's senior staff began standing at the school gates every morning to send those not dressed correctly home. We turned the same exacting eye on the staff and soon discovered that the school showed a specific trend that could be observed in many coasting schools across the country, with the classes of the top performing students being taken by the teachers who had worked in the school the longest, and the most troublesome sets being given to the newest, youngest and least skilled staff.

Effectively, the senior teachers were coasting, leaving their less experienced colleagues to confront the school's most problematic students alone. This was a culture we worked hard to change. Word quickly spread around the community that we were adopting a new approach and, with the support of parents and the local population, we soon began to see real change. In a little over eight months we had improved the school's headline statistics by 20 percentage points compared to the previous year making it the highest performing state school in the area.

In spite of the pride we took in pulling the school back to respectability, there was no doubt that many of the tactics we used to effect that change were typical of the quick-fix culture of which we were measured against. In a results-oriented culture, school leaders brought up, trained, measured and ranked inside the same culture are as limited and trapped by it as the students themselves. I have worked with many wonderful individuals, all of whom were set upon improving the lives and life chances of others, yet in our sincere attempts to achieve significantly better results in Manchester, I added my own name to the roster of people who did so using a variety of short term approaches. Just like in the school my colleague had seen during his Future Leaders residency, in Manchester we entered all of our students into English and maths GCSEs up to three times during our eight month intervention period and, in the event that they failed to get a C, we simply dismissed the results and re-entered them to be examined by a different board.

We focused exclusively on those students at risk of not accomplishing this C grade, neglecting the rest; in this way, we were 'seasonal gardeners' in the truest sense of the words, leaving the rest of our garden to grow wild while we committed ourselves to a select few. Perhaps more problematic still, we identified those at risk of not achieving five good GCSEs and entered them all onto a week long residential course which styled itself as a 'certificate in personal effectiveness' and which counted for two GCSEs at grade B – a sure-fire way of getting them across the five GCSEs worth A*-C line. It worked, but it was the quick fix culture at its worst, real tip-of-the-iceberg thinking. This was a qualification that did in one week what would ordinarily take two years of teaching at around six hours of study each week. Corners were cut, yet results rapidly improved, and all in the name of gaming the statistics that would dictate whether this school was 'saved' or remained unsatisfactory. A few months following the published results, the school was inspected and rated good in all areas. On the face of things the support had been a great success, or had it?

After leaving, I had been left wondering how a school transformed by dynamic leadership alone could last without that leadership in place – and, here in Manchester, I got my answer. For, after the support team had moved on from the school, the situation quickly reverted; three years down the line, results were falling, poor and disruptive behaviour was prevalent again and the old dysfunctions between students and staff had returned to such an extent that, at its next Ofsted inspection, the school would plummet into special measures, with serious concerns in every category. The school would later be taken over, some staff would lose their jobs and the school would be re-branded under a new academy chain. At last, in case I ever needed it, I had experienced the peaks and troughs of the quick fix culture at its worst. Here was solid proof of the way a school can be quickly dragged up to statistical respectability, only for its successes to disappear just as dramatically.

Schools were not just at risk of becoming tangled in a football league table like culture, headteachers became no different to football managers and were being recognised, rewarded, and even honoured, by the speed of movement up the league table. Those who produced the quickest results got the biggest bonuses; those who failed were sacked instantly. This experience would later mirror the findings from a 2016 review of 160 schools in England, published in the *Harvard Business Review*. If ever there was to be a study to show the negative impact of the quick fix culture through short-termist 'surgeon' headteachers, as opposed to the benefits brought by the 'architect' headteachers who took the longer-term approach by re-building a school from the bottom up, it was this.

If Education 2.0 was ever to become a reality, there had to be a way of making changes that endured, and Chris Woodhead had at least got one thing right: above school buildings, above school equipment, above computers and other progressive technologies, teachers were a school's most prized assets. However education changes, it cannot change without the commitment and investment of its soldiers on the ground. "Great vision without great people is irrelevant", as Jim Collins would write in his classic book, *Good to Great*. Nothing matters more than the decisions that leaders make about how to hire, whom to hire, how to train, and who to fire or, as Collins says, it is about getting "the right people on the bus and sat in the right seat."

Staffing crisis

It has long been known that there is a staffing crisis in our schools, but determining the reasons behind that crisis has proven to be a slippery, problematic affair for successive governments. This is a world in which the variables are many, in which the numbers of children in each school year can vary greatly, in which problems of population, social deprivation and the international economy all play their parts. Amidst all of this, one thing is clear: the staffing crisis might not be new, but its severity is startling.

In 2015, it was reported that more than 50,000 of the UK's teachers walked out on the profession for pastures new, the worst year since records began being kept in 1997. Over one in ten new teachers quit after a year on the job; a staggering one third of all new teachers who started in 2010 had left the sector five years later. Over 100,000 teachers are estimated to have completed their teacher training but never taught since. The deficit threatens to become even worse in the years to come, and many of the attempts governments have made to address the situation, most recently with a review of teacher work-life balance, have been met with limited success.

Perhaps the problem easiest to identify is the pay gap between what school teachers can expect to earn, both at the outset and across their later careers and the expectations of their peers in other industries. In 2016, a freshly graduated teacher in the United Kingdom could expect to earn around £22,000 outside London, while a first year solicitor might expect to earn £34,000 per year, a graduate accountant £30,000, and a graduate moving into the financial services sector can expect to earn anywhere between £30,000 and £40,000 per year. More problematically still, the salaries for teachers have a necessarily lower glass ceiling than they do in most other industries; commensurate as they are with other roles in public service, a school teacher should not expect to earn much beyond £30,000 a year unless they also move into school management. Therefore, it follows that the cost of training to be a teacher is a greater burden than for various other careers: at 2016 rates, a student training to be a teacher in England can expect to pay £9,000 in course fees. As a percentage of guaranteed future earnings, this is greater than in almost any other profession.

Recruiting enough teachers to meet the demand of our schools will always be a challenge, especially when potential teachers are also being met with forceful advertising by the slick graduate schemes offered by corporate banks, private business and other fields. More troublesome, still, is recruiting teachers to schools in the country's most challenging areas, where the lifestyle needs of young teachers and their families are much more difficult to meet. These schools are often the schools beset by problems of academic performance, lack of aspiration and lack of engagement. Yet, without being able to attract the best candidates, the way out of the morass is not clear. It is at this point that school cultures stagnate, and children are failed; lack of aspiration is a learned behaviour, just like ambition itself and without the school leadership and teachers to teach aspiration and engagement, whole generations of children can be lost to simply perpetuating the system.

In 2016, Sir Michael Wilshaw – then the chief inspector of schools – reported on the alarming rate of 'brain drain' from the profession, that more than 100,000 teachers who had been trained in the United Kingdom now worked overseas, a figure that had increased by 25% over the course of a single year. In the preceding twelve months, 18,000 teachers left England for schools abroad, while only 17,000 graduated into the profession – a deficit that, though it might seem small, remains unsustainable in the medium or long term. Teacher vacancies were nine times as high in 2016 as they were in 2011, and across 2015 the number of classes being taught by roving supply teachers more than tripled, the cost of which exceeded £800 million for state run primary and secondary schools.

Staff shortages can be crippling to a school. They lead to inflated classroom sizes, lack of attention being paid to individual students and, inevitably, the poor results that follow. Here's where things get sticky because it is exactly these situations, where underpaid teachers in under-staffed schools are struggling to make their organisations work, that lead to a reliance on the quick fix culture, on getting children through their exams in whatever ways possible, in gaming the system so that its systemic failures do not reflect negatively on the teachers striving, in imperfect circumstances, to help their schools survive.

The prevailing policy response to the staffing crisis is, quite naturally, to inflate the number of supply teachers available to plug the gap and yet this, too, is a symptom of our quick fix culture, papering over the cracks instead of interrogating the problem's root cause. What becomes clear, by interrogating all of the data, is that the staffing crisis is not actually a result of a fundamental shortage in the number of people training to be teachers and then not entering the profession at all. This might provide momentary blips, as the system finds itself in want or in surplus according to the diktats of any particular year – but more pressing is the way schools invest in and retain their staff. More than enough teachers enter the profession to carry our schools forward but the increasing number of teachers leaving the profession for reasons other than retirement leave us with a deficit difficult to manage.

Compensation is certainly a part of this, but it is also true that teaching was never a profession that people entered because of its pay. Like nursing, teaching was traditionally a vocation, a role entered because it is one in which people can make a genuine difference in others' lives. And, once you start approaching the problem with this in mind, it suddenly becomes clear that, though the staffing crisis is propagated by all of the many things we have investigated, though poor pay and poor prospects certainly play their part, one factor overrules all else – and that is the way the role of schoolteacher itself has been transformed.

While it's already clear what cost the quick fix culture can have for students, how short-termism leaves them under-prepared for life beyond the school gates, there is another cost to the way the education system is rigged, one that's less immediately obvious but equally important to the system's long term health and that's the effect it is having on its staff.

We have already seen how the policy changes of the 1980s and 1990s changed the role of school leader, transforming them from being student-focused to being focused on cost and efficiency. This was the age of school leader as business CEO, with all of the sacrifices that transformation entailed. Yet, just as autonomy was being taken away from headteachers, making them answerable to central government in a way they had not been before, autonomy was being taken away from individual teachers as well. Imagine a food chain in which central government policy makers are at the top, school leaders in the middle, and teachers – education's ground troops – are sitting at the bottom of the ladder. Now imagine the way autonomy was being drawn upwards, away from the school leaders to the policy makers and institutions like Ofsted, with the impact it had on the way schools could be run.

Well, the food chain works only one way and, as headteachers toiled under the pressures of the system, constantly battling to keep their schools afloat and ranked at a good level by Ofsted inspectors, they did it through techniques like the ones I'd helped implement in Manchester. They did so by imposing rules from above, by dictating the terms by which a school should be run, by prescribing policies for behaviour, school culture, how rules should be enforced and problematic situations resolved, and then sticking to those policies with a rigidity that borders on fearless. I had seen for myself, especially in Manchester, with what swiftness a failing school could be turned around under these conditions but I had also seen how quickly that could fall apart when the rigid conditions were taken away and, just as importantly, what effect these conditions can have on a school's staff.

The primary goal of any good school should be to retain 100% of its teaching staff, assuming they are on 'the right bus and sat in the right seat'. Under these coercive conditions, however, it is not unusual for schools to have retention rates as low as 50% and find they have to replace 40-50 teachers annually – not because all the teachers didn't make the grade but because many chose to leave.

For staff in schools like this, there has been a fundamental shift in the nature of their job. For them, teaching has crossed the line from being a vocation to just being a job. Under the strict controls of a coercive school leader, pushed into being that way by the demands of central policy, teachers find themselves stripped of their autonomy. Unable to make decisions for themselves, hemmed in by the diktats of the school structure, they find themselves not teachers in the oldest sense of the word, but rather reduced to being cogs in a machine of somebody else's design.

Mission command

Without the freedom to choose the way they teach, to develop and follow their instincts in how to approach and tackle challenging subjects and students, they become depersonalized. In these conditions, teaching begins to happen by rote, it has become a service industry rather than vocation and, consequently, staff engagement and morale are incredibly low. That was what had happened in Manchester, that was what was happening across the United Kingdom's most challenging schools.

For me, this knowledge came as a shock. Having entered educational leadership straight from the military, I was used to certain principles being taken for granted and the idea that different levels of autonomy should be given to different ranks has been enshrined in military cultures for generations, for some very specific reasons. For the military, the 19th and 20th centuries were transformative times, not only technologically but culturally too. Historically, soldiers were nothing but the tools of their commanders, condemned to do or die at the behest of one of their superiors. Nowhere was this more evident than on the bleak battlefields of the First World War.

This idea largely persisted through the Second World War, but catastrophic episodes thereafter gave rise to a new school of thought, one that suggested decentralising command was actually key to making successful and more rapid movements in war. Speed has always been important to the military but for most of history it has been limited to what a human or human on horseback could see and do.

Whilst technology in the 20th century increased the speed of communication to and from the battlefield, this same technology also created many new problems with the amount of people who could have and wanted to have 'control' of the same information. Perhaps the most striking example of this is in the Normandy Landings, the pivotal moment of the Second World War in which allied soldiers landed on the beaches at Normandy in their attempt to liberate France and start driving Nazi Germany back across the continent. Faced with vast, unexpected resistance from the shore, the casualties incurred on the beaches of Normandy were staggering and yet the soldiers who made the landings had little alternative as they were ordered to land and take the beaches.

By the time they could call back to the command post to relay the latest intelligence and the command post could place a call higher up the chain of command, request new orders, and relay them back down the line, the moment would have passed. On the Normandy beaches, many thousands of men perished because of the glacial pace with which decisions could be made.

The problems with rigid, centralised command will never be clearer than this: in times of war, men have often died waiting for commands from their superior officers. Nowadays, the modern military has moved away from over-dependence on centralised command. Vivid catastrophes such as the Battle of the Somme, the Normandy Landings and more showed the frailty in a system when only those at the very top could make decisions. To overcome the impossibility of a commander being able to communicate with and direct the actions of all of his soldiers at all times, the time element of acting in less time than their opponent had to be to empower decision making down to the lowest practical level of competency.

Clearly the military is extremely hierarchical and, with rank and orders, will always continue to be. Paradoxically however, independent thought and rapid innovation are strongly encouraged amongst troops, even training its young officers to think in a formulaic way, especially in chaotic and fast-changing conditions that prevail on the front line. Whilst command and control from up high and far away is of no use to troops serving on the ground who need to make split second decisions all of the time on the battlefield, neither are traditional ethical frameworks based on rules or consequences. Somehow there had to be a way of troops making moral and ethically correct decisions in a fast changing life or death situation. So how do you create strong moral agents, experienced in perception, who are able to make decisions from a stable mind and a virtuous disposition? Decision making can be as much an art form as a science and military strategist Colonel John Boyd developed an iterative decision making cycle he called the OODA Loop. Following the success of American F-86 pilots against their MiG-85 opponents during the Korean War, despite flying a technically inferior aircraft, Boyd realised that successful pilots were those who decision-making cycle was more effective.

They Observed, Orientated, Decided and Acted in the most timely and decisive manner. Having firstly seen what was happening around them and filtered it through a common value system (observe); secondly assessed, analysed and synthesised all necessary information (orientate); thirdly formed the right choices aligned to the stated mission (decide); and finally acted upon those intentions (act), those who continued to repeat and adapt to the OODA cycle successfully, assuming that every action creates an equal and unpredictable reaction, became the most agile, able to make life saving decisions before their opponents did. This art of practical reasoning, making decisions by thinking forwards into actions and consequences, became the cornerstone of mission command.

Mission command dictates that soldiers in the field be given 'earned' autonomy and trusted with making key decisions without needing to constantly refer to their superiors. Brigadier John Thompson OBE, a governor of King's, is also former deputy commander of the Territorial Army Land Forces. Graduating from Sandhurst Army College in the 1973, it was not until 1991 that military officers in this country began to be trained on the principles of what he describes as the "decentralised control, the empowering of the level below and actively encouraging all troops to join 'our' battle not 'my' battle. It became my release to be creative rather than simply be the purveyor of orders." In other words, by pushing decision making down the chain of command, the autonomy to act is given to those closest to the information, those with 'eyes on the ground' who are able to make rapid assessments of constantly changing variables.

According to the principles of this doctrine, the goal (why) of any particular mission is described along with the enabling tasks (what) to a unit of soldiers but without the path (how) to its achievement being fully proscribed. Understanding their commander's intentions, the soldiers in the field are then given the freedom to act how they see fit in order to accomplish that mission, so long as they remain within the operating boundaries of the commander's intent.

The system has certain key advantages. Even in this age of near instant communication, timing is vital and, following the principles of mission command, allows soldiers in open conflict to make decisions more quickly, at their most informed. More than this, it elevates soldiers above being simple tools. It recognises them as human beings rather than instruments, it trusts them with the intelligence to make important decisions at critical moments, it hands them the responsibility for their own survival and that of the soldiers around them. It makes them feel valued, trusted, and as if they truly have something to offer. In his book *Principle Centred Leadership*, Stephen Covey highlights the power of this form of delegation by creating a purpose to one's work greater than any one thing or individual. "The scientific paradigm says *pay me well*," Covey writes. "The human relations paradigm says *treat me well*, the human resource paradigm says *use me well* but the character based leadership paradigm says *involve me in the vision and mission of the organisation and its goals. I want to make a meaningful contribution.*"

People, it seems, have a natural desire for self-direction and want to be a part of a mission that transcends their individual day-to-day tasks. In other words: we are all in the pursuit of autonomy, self-efficacy and purpose and transferring responsibility to other like-minded, skilled and trained people means growth, both for individuals and for organisations. It was this same sense of autonomy, of being trusted enough to drive lessons forward and tackle problems head on, that was missing in the schooling system. Teachers reduced to being cogs in a machine quickly fall out of love with a job that takes real love and commitment to survive. Without those teachers working at the best of their abilities, what hope is there for the children in their care? How could Education 2.0 return some level of autonomy to staff? How could it remove the sense of them being only cogs in a vast educational machine, and in doing so return a sense of vocation to the profession? Was there a way that the lessons of military mission command could be translated to a classroom situation – and, in an age of constant metrication and micro-management, could there ever be a way of empowering staff members once again?

Management guru Peter Drucker coined the phrase, 'Efficiency is doing things right; effectiveness is doing the right thing'. Like many schools caught in this cycle, they may be doing things right with the greatest of intentions – but were too inflexible to be able to do the right thing. If there were to be a rounded Education 2.0 out there, waiting to be formalised, it would have to be one that answered these fundamental questions: how could the right staff be located and, more importantly, retained? How could those staff be encouraged to invest wholeheartedly in the profession and consider it a lifestyle for the long term, instead of a phase through which they passed on a different, multi-faceted career? Could it, like so many of the other problems facing modern education, be a simple question of culture and character? Culture and character are, after all, the foundations of effective mission command.

Clearly, there will be mistakes made along the way: a soldier might misunderstand a commander's intent; he or she might not truly buy into the vision in the first place; or, they might have been empowered prematurely, before they were fully competent. Creating this bridge between leaders and the people they lead, having a 'safety net' to empower action in subordinates in full acknowledgement that there will at times be failure and encouraging an environment of 'constructive dissent' where we can speak freely and challenge orders without fear of consequences, requires the nurturing of the highest form of human relationship: absolute trust. And it is this trust, between people high up in an organisation and those on the ground that transforms organisations. In his book *Leaders Eat Last*, Simon Sinek calls trust an organisation's "circle of safety", a circlet that can lead to instant, safe, and effective communication.

Brigadier Thompson reiterates this point succinctly in that "by empowering a subordinate, I am showing that I trust them. Cultures founded on suspicions and fear of mistakes are dampened and instead become founded on openness. Mission command literally is the be all and end all." Could it be that this was what was lacking in our schooling system?

My experiences in both the Wirral and Manchester had made one thing abundantly clear: permanent change, I was discovering, could not be imposed from above. Changes dictated to a school and forced upon it by a dynamic leader might improve things in the short term, they are often essential in a turnaround situation, but over a longer period, it was not enough. Trust and control share an inverse relationship, as one goes up then the other goes down and all too often in low trust-high control organisations team dynamics become based more and more on competition rather than collaboration. In turn, this leads to greater levels of cynicism, tension, staff walking on egg shells and protecting their own backs – in other words a blame culture ensues which can quickly become intoxicating.

If Education 2.0 was to become a reality, true change would have to come from somewhere more fundamental – leadership was important, but more important still was culture. My experience was proving what Future Leaders had been promoting all along: if there was a new model for education out there, it could not be the vision of just one headteacher; the changes would have to come at a grass roots level, and permeate every corner of a school. The quick fix culture was not working, nor was the single-minded revolutions of a strong-willed school leader; whatever came next would have to be a holistic approach.

Testing times

The system of league tables and school rankings changed the nature of schools themselves, often to their detriment. But, what of the ways schools test and examine their students? Could it be that we are letting our children down through the very nature of the way they are examined?

The debate around how children should learn, what they should learn, and who they should learn it from is one that provokes heated discussion. Whether that be among the policymakers of Westminster, Washington and other seats of government around the world, or around the school gates where parents congregate to share their opinions of the schools that their children attend. Some still fiercely propose that children should be seen and not heard, lined up in front of a figure of authority and drilled in the rudiments like the Victorians of old. Others propose adopting techniques they label 'progressive' and which, like the Kagan system I had observed during my residency year, put their emphasis on lessons built around cooperative, collaborative, group based activities, designed as much to elicit pleasure as to inform. Should education be a simple, individual experience? At its best, is it a group activity, designed to let students discover things as if for themselves, rather than being dictated to by others? Are our students better off being crammed full of facts and figures and purely academic concepts that might encourage a higher level of thinking but be forgotten soon after their schooling finishes, or is a curriculum based on real-life skills and future vocations the best route to take? Perhaps most crucially of all, who should be doing the teaching? By what definitions are we choosing the next generation of our nation's teachers, and are we getting it right?

The statistics are not encouraging. The New Labour government that came into power in 1997 got there, in part; because of the emphasis they placed on education in their manifesto pledges. Indeed, when they came to power, they invested much in fulfilling those promises. Across the next governments, total expenditure on education rose by 78%, with £50 billion being spent in 1997 and £89 billion being spent by the time the Conservatives were restored to power in 2010. Yet, by the time 2015 came around, a report commissioned by the Organisation for

Economic Co-operation and Development (OECD) found that one in five British students left school without competency in basic language and mathematic skills and ranked the United Kingdom only twentieth on their list of highest-ranking nations, lagging far behind the Asian nations that dominate the list.

England, the report outlined, was the only developed country in the world whose school leavers had lower mathematics and literacy skills than their grandparents' generation. For all of the extra resources pumped into the education system across those two decades – a rush of new initiatives, new school buildings, fresh recruitment drives and research into the best methods of educating our young – statistically, our children were no better off than they had been before. So the question remained: what was the flaw in our system that meant so many children slipped through the cracks, regardless of the enormous amounts of public money being poured into our schools? Nor was this a problem to be viewed in isolation. As the OECD education director Andreas Schleicher said, in introducing the report of 2015, "the quality of schooling in a country is a powerful predictor of the wealth that that country will produce in the long run." The inference is stark: quality schooling leads to wealthier, more fulfilled populations. If it wasn't a question of material deprivation, then what was it?

We have already seen how central policy pushed schools into a situation in which they were gaming the league tables in order to stay afloat. The long term impact was grade inflation – students being awarded grades they had not empirically earned, just to satisfy inspection criteria – and the ushering in of replacement easy subjects. All of this had undoubtedly contributed to what Mike Harris, of the Institute of Directors – the UK's longest running organisation that brings together company leaders – has called the "credibility gap" between "exam pass rates and employers' real-world experience of interviewing and employing people." In simple terms: the CVs of the United Kingdom's students might have shown them as academic and adept, with multiple exam passes at various grades, but in the more exacting world of work, their skills did not match up.

In his book *The Road to Character*, author David Brooks suggests that, for most of us, there is an imbalance between what he calls our 'resume virtues', the skills we bring to the job market which contribute to our external 'tip of the iceberg' successes, and our 'eulogy virtues', the deeper, core virtues, hidden from plain sight yet are those that get talked about at our funerals and are our *rasion d'etre*. We all know what these 'eulogy' virtues are – respect and integrity, to name a few – as they are not limited to a particular nation, they know no boundaries, they transcend all cultures, religions and nations, and they also meet the rule of reversibility: the idea that we would want someone else to treat us with exactly the same virtue. As the British astronaut Tim Peake said in a tweet delivered from the International Space Station to a Character Symposium in 2016: "Your CV will get you the interview, but only your character will get you the job." However, most of us, Brooks suggests, have a stronger idea of how to achieve success in our careers than we do of how to go about developing a profound character.

Harris's observation – that we are not equipping our children with the long-term skills they need to succeed beyond the school gates – is much more illuminating than it first seems. Yes, it calls into question the soft subjects, the weekend residential courses and multiple-choice exams that students were being ushered into so that school leaders could successfully meet grade quotas and avoid slipping down the league tables, but look a little further and it actually calls into question the fundamental nature of what we're doing in our schools. No matter what your preconceptions, it is not immediately obvious what children should learn. We think of traditional subjects only because they are that: traditional. We hark back to what we learnt as children and assume this is fundamental, in large part because this was the way our brains were first wired. Scratch beneath the surface and interesting questions start to present themselves. Perhaps the most interesting in the entire field of education is not the debate around how we learn; it's the debate around why we should.

What we think of as a standard curriculum, one built upon the fundamentals of mathematics, the English language and the sciences, has its roots in the 19th century and how the early state school system grappled with the challenge of equipping a generation for employment in the new industrial workplace. While students from more privileged backgrounds were funnelled towards an education with the classical world at its heart, most enjoyed an education of basic language, mathematics and practical skills designed to deliver them as ready for work on the factory floor. At a basic level, this is the way our curriculums have stayed ever since. Trends have come and gone, an era of grammar schools and secondary moderns, new subjects have been added and then stripped away, but fundamentally we think of education in the same way we did under the reign of Queen Victoria.

Across that period, mankind has fought two world wars, developed flying vehicles, travelled into the vacuums of space, decoded the human genome and begun to develop therapies that can rewrite the very essence of what we are. Yet, though the world and its workplaces have changed beyond all recognition, our classrooms have remained the same. Harris's 'credibility gap', then, reaches much further than to the preponderance of soft subjects students are being examined in to game the league tables. Rather, it flags up the fact that our schools might not be fit for purpose in a deeper way and that we are educating 21st century children with a 19th century approach.

In recent years, and following the digitisation of the workplace, schools have turned their attention to bridging this divide and bringing computers and the latest tablet devices into the classroom, with certain innovative school leaders pioneering the teaching of computer coding from an early age. These efforts push us in the right direction, refocusing on modern skills for the modern workplace, but the truth is that the challenge of defining what constitutes a 21st century skill is not easy, in large part, because it is a constantly shifting thing.

Most of us would agree that needlework is, perhaps, a subject best left to the 19th century classrooms in which it was taught, while learning to code in a basic computer language is a skill vital for the world in which we now live. Should we now be thinking in terms of coding being an essential core 'language' for learning just like English? Yet the scale of technological progress witnessed over the 20th and early 21st centuries, and the seemingly exponential rate at which that progress is still being made, suggests that any new subject added to a curriculum will itself be marginalised or superseded very quickly. It suggests that, if we accept education as part of a pathway preparing us for adult employment, our schools are destined to lag behind in the race to ensure the next generation is best equipped. Such is the rate of 21st century change, as old professions are wiped out and new ones rise up in their place.

Guaranteeing to a class of 11 year olds that the computer languages they learn, the specific applications they are instructed in how to use, will still be relevant by the time they enter their first employment is much more precarious than it was in an earlier century, where simple mathematics and language skills were at the core of what schools did and what employers needed, and could be expected to stay that way. In the study of physics, the 'Theory of Everything' is a hypothetical theory that could encompass and explain every rule of the physical universe, the theory behind all other theories. Perhaps, the key to answering our own debate is in looking beyond the classroom, in interrogating what we are not teaching as much as what we are, in searching for our own unifying theory.

One thing is certain: tackling the question of what children should learn will not be resolved by shuffling the deck, introducing new subjects or removing others. If it is apparent that education will always lag behind the demands of a rapidly changing workforce, then what we must be preparing children for is not a life of education followed by employment but a life in which education is a constant thing, one in which new skills and attributes must be being developed all the time.

As the saying goes, we should be preparing our children for the test of life, not simply a life of tests. Long gone is the age when a person could enter a job straight out of school and expect to remain in it until their retirement 50 or 60 years later. In an age when a worker might be expected to go through four or five different phases of a career, potentially in vastly different fields, we must equip children for the experience of learning itself – not as a means to an end, but as an end in itself. Children, it might be said, must 'learn how to learn' but something as intangible as this cannot be easily proscribed. What we are talking about is interdisciplinary, a lesson that cannot be compartmentalised and that must underpin everything we do in our schools. What it boils down to is our focus: whether we are teaching subjects at school, or whether we are teaching children.

The answer to this can only lie in the ethos of the schools in which we're teaching. The origin of the modern English word ethics actually derives from the Greek word ethos and its etymology means habit or the way customs are adhered to; in other words 'how things are done around here'!

Culture is king

I had twin visions of the differing ethos in schools during the year I spent with Future Leaders. In residency, where I first taught, the school motto was emblazoned across the front doors which promised ambition, hard-work and sense of community spirit but never was it referred to, looked upon, or even noticed by the students who filed underneath it each day. The vision was literally framed rather than followed. Yet, in the Charter Schools I had visited in Boston in the United States, school ethos – the beliefs, values, codes and culture – was central to how the schools operated from not only a set of written rules and routines but also, more remarkably, it was the level of fluency and connectedness with which unwritten scriptures were recited and turned into everyday action by everyone involved.

It does not require the intellect of a rocket scientist to know a good school the moment you enter it. There is purpose to all inside, classrooms and corridors are calm, and the relationships between students and staff, students and other students, and staff members with other staff, is underpinned with respect and professionalism. There is also a palpable sense of collaboration amongst staff; teachers share ideas with one another, seasoned staff coach more junior colleagues to improve instructional practice and, as a consequence, staff collegiality flourishes. In my residency school, as in many other schools in the United Kingdom, the set of school values might have existed in the copy on the school website, or inscribed upon a wall few ever looked upon, but they were never spoken about and nor were they at the heart of how decisions were made in the school.

In schools like this, the school's 'vision statement' is a parlour trick, all smoke and mirrors, designed for outward appearances but, ultimately, empty. The Charter Schools of America were the opposite of this in every way. Their fundamental principles – considering that every child could succeed, no matter what their circumstances and background; that a culture of high expectation led to high aspiration and high success –

were the defining factors in how the schools were run. They were the foundations upon which everything else was built.

For the Charter Schools, grades were important. Grades were, after all, the key to their students getting access to the college courses and future opportunities those courses represented, and access to college was one of the fundamental ways in which they measured their worth. Intellectual achievement was not seen as the first, nor necessarily even the most important, step. Rather, their principal aim was to develop the emotional wellbeing of their students, a form of paternalism that sought to replicate in the classroom what their under-privileged students were lacking in the home environment – to help students first and foremost with what has been termed their 'emotional intelligence' rather than their academic intelligence. By first addressing the values, ambition and emotional security of their students, these schools sought to instil an ethos that would allow academic success to follow. The success of these schools was plain to see in the statistics, in the lives turned around and students sent off to colleges when, otherwise, they might have found themselves trapped in cycles of low aspirations and crime. But was this down to intellectual rigour, or was it down to inculcating a specific set of beliefs and character habits, in teaching students how to manage their own emotions and, in doing so, make the best decisions?

The term 'emotional intelligence' was first coined by psychologists John Mayer and Peter Salovey in an academic journal in 1989, and subsequently popularised by the science writer Daniel Goleman in his book of 1995, *Emotional Intelligence*. The concept is striking, at its heart it is an attack on the way students and people more generally had always been ranked and compared – for the theory posits that intellectual intelligence, or our traditional IQ, is not the best way of measuring or predicting success but that an emotional quotient, or EQ, can better foretell how an individual might succeed in life.

Goleman defined EQ as the ability to monitor the emotions of both yourself and others, and to use the insight gleaned from this to guide the making of significant decisions. His definition takes in the ability to empathise with others, the ability to manage relationships and successfully steer them in the right direction, the ability to make decisions based on gut feelings or reactions, and – crucially – the ability to regulate the emotions in times of high anxiety. Goleman's research prompted the development of certain tools to algorithmically measure a person's emotional intelligence, and this in turn opened up an entire field of study, with future researchers going on to both develop and critique Goleman's work as they attempted to further refine the concept. The Charter Schools we had visited as part of our Future Leaders experience had put these concepts at the heart of how they taught: academic prosperity, they knew, could only come if the mind-set was correct, before academic success came emotional security and emotional success.

In the United Kingdom, we want students to be able to persevere and be resilient when faced with failure but our quick fix culture often prevents us to consider the deep roots of those skills, the steps that every child must take, developmentally, to get there. A 2016 paper by the New York think tank Turnaround for Children describes these early capacities as "building blocks for learning", a theoretical framework that charts a path towards academic behaviours. According to the author of the Turnaround paper, Brooke Stafford-Brizard, schools must first develop a foundation of executive functions, a capacity for self-awareness, and relationship skills before other character habits can be developed. Equally, the greater and steeper the development phase, the wider the foundational EQ base required.

In so many of our coasting schools, mission statements, sets of proscribed values and the like, are pretty pictures on the school walls or website. Like at my residency school, they are never spoken about, never discussed and, as such, never become part of the school's fabric. Lessons happen by rote, students are drilled to sit their exams but the school has become a factory floor designed to process students into exam results, serving its continued existence without reference back to the often-lofty aims of the way the schools are branded. Schools might style themselves as being driven by values and investing fully in the lives of their students but often they disconnect with how the school outwardly presents itself and how it engages its students beyond the syllabus.

In an environment in which schools are being measured by exam results, with careers on the line, it is perhaps natural that school leaders relentlessly zone in on how they can inflate those statistics and we have already seen the lengths to which our school leaders will go in the service of this quest. Yet, might it be that there is a way of improving our schools' performances by resisting the slippery slopes of the quick fix culture? What if adjusting our focus to the values underpinning our schools, committing to emotional intelligence alongside academic rigour could give our students the foundations to flourish? I had already had grounding in the strength of a value-led organisation during my time in the RAF. On enlisting, the very first thing given to new RAF recruits is the Core Values booklet, outlining the precepts of the RISE code – Respect, Integrity, Service (before self) and Excellence – on which the service is built. These were qualities on whose details we were tested mere days into our officer training.

By the end of the first day and similar to professions such as medicine, we swore allegiance to Queen and country and had to recite an oath as a mark of our integrity, commitment and responsibility of character that our future career would behold. Throughout the course we were immersed into the culture of the RAF, a culture founded on a set of prescribed qualities that is expected of everyone who wears the uniform. It was this sharp focus that helped transform raw recruits into efficient members of the service as each of us modelled our new behaviours and patterns of thinking by emulating those who led our training. High expectations, strict discipline, and the pressure of peers also helped but none of that could have existed without being underpinned by a clearly defined set of values in which all recruits had to invest. These virtues were imparted to us through the use of a common language and typology of virtue throughout training via stories, case studies and role models. Although only formed in 1918, everywhere you walked in RAF Cranwell was steeped in history, buildings and rooms named after past leaders who embodied the key virtues of the service. To put it simply, alignment to the *rasion d'etre* was in constant sight.

If one thing is certain it is that, though committing to the factory floor of education might boost schools up the league tables by brute force, its effects are never lasting, nor will it ever achieve a '100%' success rate. If we continue down this road, the 'credibility' gap with PISA will only get wider, nor is there a guarantee that testing our children's academic success so relentlessly will generate the best academic results. Whilst a selection of Far East nations have dominated academic performance for several years, a direct comparison may be of limited benefit due to vastly different cultures and associated expectations. Things however, can still be radically different in other parts of the world who are more culturally aligned to ourselves.

The constant gardener

Finland is one of the highest performing non-Asian countries, which was ranked sixth out of all world countries in the 2015 OECD survey, and has been top in previous years. Finnish students have scored top in the skills of science and problem-solving, have ranked either first or second in reading and mathematics, and have one of the smallest gaps in achievement between the most and least academic. What is most noteworthy though is that more than 99% of all Finnish schools are state-funded. That is right, almost every school in this high performing nation has a totally comprehensive intake, even spending approximately 30% less per student than we do here in the United Kingdom!

This comes despite the fact that, during school reforms, many teachers were faced with classrooms of children of differing abilities for the first time. Regardless of that, all students were expected to reach the same high academic standards. Although we must be mindful about why and how the transition took place (not least over a significant period of time dating as far back as 1947 when the debate first started through to full curriculum implementation by 1985), this represented a major paradigm shift from their previous two-tiered approach that had streamed children from the age of ten into either an academic or vocational pathway. At the peak of reforms during the 1970s, Finland was plagued by an educational model that was based on high control, low autonomy, and low trust. Teachers not only had to keep diaries recording what they taught each day, national school inspectors made regular visits to ensure that all schools were following guidelines outlined in a 700 page centralised curriculum.

Today, however, autonomy amongst school leaders and teachers is highly valued and they are free to experiment and write their own curricular to ultimately design a more creative and self-directed system than any level of centralised control could ever do. There is no such thing as Ofsted: schools are simply not inspected in the same way as they are in the United Kingdom. League tables do not exist and students are not separated into sets defined by their academic achievements. In fact, 'streaming or setting' by ability and test scores was actually made illegal and for the first six years of their education, children are not tested academically at all. The government conducts only standardised testing of targeted samples to ensure schools are performing as required. There is only one mandatory standardized test taken in the Finnish school system at the age of 16.

The Finnish philosophy is that children's mental health and wellbeing are closely related and therefore just as important as their academic achievements. As such, Finnish children do not begin formal schooling until the age of seven, some two to three years later than children do in the United Kingdom. They are assessed during kindergarten for school readiness with some starting a year later, if required. This later start was intentionally made in order to encourage greater physical, cognitive, social, and emotional development in Finnish kindergarten's through a focus on 'play'. By developing children's social, emotional, and decision-making skills, their belief is that children will have the attitudes and character to better apply the skills required for reading and writing. Once they are in full time education, those requiring extra time and tuition to catch up with their peers are provided with it immediately. Every school has full and immediate access to school psychologists, counsellors, social and health workers.

In Finland, teaching is also seen as a prized career, in the same way as being a doctor or a lawyer. Gaining entry into teacher training school in Finland is as prestigious as gaining entry into medical or law school. This means that only the top graduates with a real sense of purpose and mission gain entry into the profession, even having to pass an interview focused on moral commitment while the weakest are weeded out from the very start rather than years down the line. Consistency across teacher training providers is also a core feature of their education system that, in turn, has led to a traditional yet consistent approach to classroom practice and relative uniformity of delivery both between and within different classrooms and schools. High quality textbooks, using the latest research and guided through teacher input are common for each subject across most, if not all, schools. This may also be a reason for little variation in performance when comparing different schools from different regions of the country.

Now compare this to the UK: how many of our own teachers join the profession because it is truly their vocation in life and how many do so because they see it as their only viable option? Is it right that we have a saying that alludes to exactly this thing: 'Those who can, do; those who can't, teach'? In 2010, an extraordinary 6,600 potential teachers applied to take only 660 places for trainee primary teachers in Finland – an oversubscription of 900%. Could, then, what at first appears to be counter-intuitive prove to be true? Could stepping back, easing the pressure on our students and refocusing on the long term reap the lasting results we are looking for, closing the credibility gap forever? If we have passed through the age of school leader as financial leader, school leader as manipulative statistician, school leader as dictator keeping their schools alive at any cost, is there a way we can enter the age of school leader as social worker, seeing their role as part of a wider commitment to children's services? This could introduce a holistic model that would see a student's emotional stability and integrity as the first step toward lifelong success.

Clearly, a lesson to be learnt from Finland is that teacher recruitment and training, based on a set of pre-determined beliefs, values, and intentions, is critical. Going back to our Air 53 analogy, are our state school GCSE results languishing because we have, in effect, recruited flight instructors of a calibre capable of landing the plane safely only 53% of the time? What is it about the recruitment strategy within the Finnish education system that is attracting 'top gun' pilots – those with a strong moral purpose and unwavering desire to continuously improve? If our proposition for Education 2.0 could not change the fundamental way children are examined and schools are inspected in the United Kingdom, perhaps there is still a way that we could approach those examinations and inspections differently thus putting our children and teachers in a better position to not only survive their days, but to prosper from them.

The last decades have exposed the fundamental disconnect between the grade a student achieved and the real-world value of the skills they had acquired. It has also exposed the problems hidden within the inspection of our schools – is there a lack of trust and autonomy in the system because we have actually failed to recruit and train teachers with the right beliefs in the right way?

Interestingly, whilst Finland's PISA performance has slipped since 2013, education leaders did not back away from their latest cutting-edge approach known as phenomenon-based teaching. This is an interdisciplinary student-led approach related to important life skills that is supported by on-going, in-class research. Finnish educator Pasi Sahlberg stated in *The Conversation*: "You may wonder why... The answer is that educators in Finland think, quite correctly, that schools should teach what young people need in their lives rather than try to bring national test scores back to where they were". How refreshing – mission command in its truest sense!

However Education 2.0 looked, it would also have to build a bridge across this chasm, reconnect the level of a qualification with its fundamental worth and, in doing so, implicitly understand the relationship between academic and emotional intelligence and how one can influence the other. If IQ and other standardized tests could not adequately measure the growth of our non-cognitive skills – our personality traits, our resilience, the fundamentals of our character – how could Education 2.0 help a generation of children develop these qualities and use the science of emotional intelligence to prosper? Outwardly, Education 2.0 might look the same but inside, where it mattered, what a student took from their qualifications would have to feel radically different.

*

So looked the landscape of education in the first decade of the 21st century: schools transformed by central policy into being cost-centred, target-driven organisations; a system that corralled school leaders into adopting short-sighted, if pragmatic, strategies to drive their schools forward; NLE 'surgeon' headteachers parachuted into schools deemed to be failing and tasked with rapidly turning them around – even if that meant employing tactics designed to serve not the students of those schools but the league tables designed to measure them, despite the very best of intentions. These patterns had become entrenched and were self-serving: the very design of the system encouraged short-termism and insular thinking.

Yet, across the world, there were glimmers of the way things could be. The Charter Schools of America, where character and long term success was prioritised above the immediacy of results; the dynamic school leaders abroad and at home, whose schools – like in the Wirral – had been transformed by force of will and, if handled correctly, might stand the test of time. Future Leaders, through the vision of Sir Iain, had been the thing that exposed me, among the others in my cohort, to the way the future might be but, until now, we had taken only a few tentative steps to making that happen.

Along the way, I had even indulged in the very short termism that I had come to regret. If anything was to change, if the lessons we had learnt from modern education were ever to be put into effect, it had to start somewhere and it could only start by utilising education's most important resource: its teachers. There was no value in diagnosing the ills of the system unless we could prescribe a solution as well. It was time to make Education 2.0 happen.

Education 2.0

"Be careful of your thoughts, for your thoughts become your words.
Be careful of your words, for your words become your deeds.
Be careful of your deeds, for your deeds become your habits.
Be careful of your habits, for your habits become your character.
Be careful of your character, for your character becomes your destiny".

– Chinese Proverb

The true goal of education

By the summer of 2011, the idea of an Education 2.0 was finally beginning to crystallise. Through experiences prior to 2009, then with Future Leaders and latterly in the schools we had worked in following our residency, we had been exposed to everything that was wrong in the education system: the way policy makers had transformed the roles of school leaders, the way the autonomy of staff was being diminished and had created a culture of mediocrity in the staff room, the way schools were being treated as factory floors in service of the league tables rather than in the service of their students. For every bad thing we had seen, we had also seen the good: in the shining examples of the Charter Schools of America, imaginative school leaders were transforming the classroom experience, setting children from deprived backgrounds on course for genuine achievements in life and in work. In the United Kingdom, dedicated staff could turn a school around through sheer willpower, even if keeping it that way was a more difficult endeavour.

The last three decades of policy in the United Kingdom had turned schools into financial and target-driven institutions, fronted by headteachers who had to transform themselves into creative statisticians just so that they could navigate their schools through the inadequacies of the system. Education 2.0 had to change this. If there was a way of resisting the quick fix culture, of returning school life to the core business of educating young people, it would mean school leaders taking a different tack – becoming not financial leaders, nor target-driven leaders, but, in some ways, social services leaders, visualising their roles as part of a broader service to the community, rather than just factories designed to churn out false outcomes for the sake of a school inspector.

Time and again, in examining the flaws of the system we had all entered, Sir Iain had kept returning to the idea of character. "Intelligence plus character," Martin Luther King had said. "That is the true purpose of education." We had seen the way the Charter Schools of America had championed character-building as a central part of their ethos; we had always known the way Britain's public schools put character at the forefront of what they do and how that propelled their students on to statistically greater successes than almost any other school in the state arena. I, myself, had watched the way a rigorous process that focused on aspects of character could transform a raw military recruit into a productive and well-rounded member of the military community. When these things were possible and being proven possible, what reason was there for limiting their scope? Why should up to 50% of all places at Oxford and Cambridge Universities go to students from the 7% of our country who were privately educated? Why should 80% of the country's highest positions be drawn from the same pool? Why could these lessons not be brought to the wider student population, those opportunities not be afforded to children from our most economically and culturally deprived areas? Wasn't there a way of returning autonomy to staff like what had happened in Finland and in developing a school culture that didn't take short-cuts, that resisted the threat of rankings and took the road less travelled? Wasn't there a way that we could put character first and, by helping shape our students' outlooks and attitudes, guarantee their future success long after their school days were over?

It was time for us to put our instincts into practice. Education 2.0 would be all these things and more: an attempt to resist the temptations of the quick fix system; a model of education that sought to have lasting, long term effects by addressing issues of character and development alongside academic achievement; a culture that looked after the long-term prospects of both its students and its most prized asset, its staff.

It was with these principles in mind that, in 2012, King's Leadership Academy was born.

Aspiration high!

The summer of 2011, a full year before the doors of King's Leadership Academy Warrington would open for the first time, and the task placed before us was proving more problematic than we had hoped. Sir Iain Hall, Shane Ierston, the founding governors and I had gathered as the Board planning to establish a new school, to put together the particulars of Sir Iain's 200 page bid. Though there was much to discuss – the way a new school structure might work, the standards that would make the bid stand out from all of the others, the way we would train and recruit staff outside the standard industry norms – at the top of the agenda was how to define the school's ambition.

The genesis of King's Leadership Academy and the Great Schools Trust had been a trip Sir Iain made to Chicago as part of a Future Leaders programme that was taking place after our own. Across the past year, Sir Iain had been coaching Shane and I in our second school, having progressed from the Future Leaders programme, and in recent conversations we had begun to draw the line between the ambitions of Future Leaders and the advances being made in the study of character by certain valued psychologists and theorists.

The idea of how a school might put character education at the very heart of what it did was never far from our minds, and Sir Iain – still exposed by Future Leaders to the continuing successes of the Charter Schools of America – perhaps most of all. Returning from that trip, with fresh evidence from Chicago's schools already percolating in his mind, one in particular whose motto and sole purpose was 'Character and Academics', Sir Iain became separated from the group he was travelling with and, alone at the back of the aircraft, spent the journey dreaming about how such a school might look in the United Kingdom.

By the end of the flight and on touch down in Manchester, his notes amassed to over 30 pages. He approached Shane and I with a challenge, days after his return, when the seed that had been planted was now in full bloom. Shane was to investigate how the teaching and learning in a 'school of character' might take shape in the context of the United Kingdom; and me, with my background in motivational study and the military, to investigate how character and leadership might itself be brought into the classroom, for the betterment of our students. What if, Sir Iain had wondered, a new school could be built on these principles? What might it look like?

Defining the ambition of a potential new school in broad terms was the first, and least challenging step. Breaking that ambition down into its constituent parts so that we knew how to deliver the education and culture we envisaged on a day-to-day basis, not at some far remove, was by far the most problematic. How to define 'good character'? How to inculcate those traits in our children in a way that made use of the most up-to-date thinking on motivation, drive, ambition and education itself? Though articulating our ambition, 'to develop the academic skills, intellectual habits, qualities of character and leadership traits necessary for every child to succeed at all levels and become successful citizens in tomorrow's world', was a first step, we also knew that this needed to become the DNA of the organisation, permeating everything that we did.

The implications of this were far ranging, but what they boiled down to was the specific belief that pursuit of exam performance and pursuit of a student's personal development were not in conflict. Rather, we believed that they directly fed into one another and that, if a student's mind-set was correct and commendable, then diligence, application and the thirst to succeed naturally followed. How do you locate and develop the right mind-set? How do you make this ambition a reality without paying lip service to the idea? How do you become a school that does more than put the obligatory school motto above the door but never brings it into its students' lives? How do you take the long-term view in a world and culture that actively encourages a short-termism and, on some level, specious, magical thinking?

King's Leadership Academy would become the first state school in the country to focus completely on attributes of character and leadership but what that would mean, and how it would be enacted, was still very much up for debate. For the moment, all we could do was roll our sleeves up and get to work in defining the essence of what our school would be. The one thing we knew for certain was that, if we were going to do this, we were going to do it properly. No child would be left behind, no excuses made, and we would have the same high expectations for all. It was in that spirit that Sir Iain titled the initial bid: Aspiration High!

Ghosts of the past

Making character the keystone in what we had planned was not an idea specific to us, nor was it unique to the Charter Schools of the United States. Programmes intended to make schools invest in developing the character of their students had been trialled in the United Kingdom before, even as recently as the Labour administrations of the early 2000s. SEAL – or Social and Emotional Aspects of Learning – had been an initiative specifically targeting the development of motivation, empathy and social skills in primary-school aged children. It was piloted by a small set of local authorities in 2004 and then rolled out across the following years, first to more primary schools and then to students of secondary age.

The Labour government's version of character education sought to help children manage their emotions and grow effectively by imposing an explicit taught curriculum that focused on ideas of togetherness, understanding others and self-discovery, alongside more tangible activities outside of the classroom. Ideas included the setting up of anti-bullying initiatives, peer-to-peer mediation services, school councils and 'worry boxes' in which students could privately post messages concerning things that troubled them at school. SEAL was built closely upon Daniel Goleman's writing on Emotional Intelligence and its influence, even above academic skill-sets, on an individual's long-term success. In principle, it was a valiant attempt at addressing issues of character – and, at the very least, it was an acknowledgement that our schools could, and should, be doing much better in helping our children develop good character. But, on being scrutinised, SEAL was found to have had, at best, mixed results. Data collected from later inspections suggested that, while the application of SEAL structures and lesson plans had had a marked effect on children of primary age, its influence in secondary schools was negligible. Reports showed that SEAL was only truly effective in schools which already had a clearly articulated ethos, ones in which there was already a clear and manageable relationship between students and staff and in which the precursor to SEAL – what we used to know as Personal and Social Education, the part of the National Curriculum which included moral, social and sex education – was already strongly emphasised.

The truth was that, in spite of the millions of pounds poured into its researching, composition and implementation, SEAL had become an overwhelming failure for the Labour government and was quickly jettisoned when the Conservative/Liberal Democrat coalition moved into Downing Street in 2010. SEAL had meant well but it had sought to turn the education of character into a strict, bureaucratic process where 'good character' was defined so assiduously as to leave no room for nuance, in which every way a person could be considered of 'good' character was rigidly prescribed. The initiative was handled by central government and imposed, by them, on local authorities. Just as in the schools where I had taught, those at the forefront of the initiative – the teachers themselves – were not given the true autonomy that would have allowed them to connect with and guide their students onward. They were provided with a specific set of learning materials – the same for every school across the country, regardless of its context – and expected to teach these in a strictly laid out way.

The absurdity is stark: here were teachers expected to deliver lessons that promoted emotional wellbeing, empathy and autonomy of thought but without being permitted their own autonomy, and their own sense of engagement and wellbeing. In effect, SEAL was a quick fix approach: it had diagnosed the problem correctly, seen in Daniel Goleman's wildly successful work a solution, but then failed to implement it in a lasting way. SEAL might have sought to subvert it, but in truth it was just another example of the quick fix culture, short-term solutions valued over lasting change.

SEAL had died its death in the early years of the Coalition government and yet it was only a year later that, prompted by the widespread rioting of August 2011, the focus of think tanks and policymakers returned to the best ways of developing character in our young. By the time I started teaching on the Wirral, SEAL was all but finished but its effects still echoed through the schools in which my Future Leaders colleagues and I taught. Its rhetoric sounded good, the way it sought to re-fashion schools as part of a wider community rather than isolated institutions, the values it sought to instil in its students and the depth of research which backed it all up – but the reasons for its apparent failure felt clear: in seeking to provide a one-size-fits-all method of character education, it had foisted its assumptions and processes onto schools from the top down.

Though its content chimed with much that we ourselves were thinking, what SEAL had initiated was actually dictatorial in nature; in failing to begin from the bottom up, it had not been able to effect the changes in culture and mind-set that character education needed if it was to properly flourish. Its version of character education had been flow-chart and rote process and, just like in those schools where strong leaders had forced change through strict discipline and micro-managing staff, it had drawn autonomy away from the very teachers it meant to empower.

However we formulated Education 2.0, we knew it had to eschew this approach. Aspiration High might have drawn on some of the same research as the progenitors of SEAL, but our goal was for change to be lasting – and this meant interrogating aspects of school culture not addressed by schemes of the past. The traditional purpose of moral and character education – giving children the practical wisdom to make good decisions for their own benefit and the benefit of others – has never been more relevant in today's society. At Aspiration High, this would not only mean thinking and acting in ways that are beneficial to yourself and others but doing the right thing both when nobody else is watching and when peer pressure to do the wrong thing is strong. Influencing behaviour in positive ways, we now knew, would be at the root of what we did; coercing positive behaviour would not. Coercion was quick fix, and the quick fix culture was something we meant, at all costs, to belie. As fortune would have it, there is a rich body of research into behavioural change and the psychology behind it – and it was to this that we would turn as we began to lay the framework for how Education 2.0 might work.

The character code

The decisions we make often have their genesis from the perceived value of taking an intended action or route. We have already seen how the OODA Loop was used as a strategic decision making tool by the military and one which I, myself, was assessed on during my officer training. It demonstrates how our actions are often pre-determined by an information phase (observe) and the means to what we can do about it (orientate). Yet, what if the utility sought at the 'decision' phase could be altered for the better? What would happen if you could intentionally shape the information a person receives and the methods he or she applies when orienting upon it prior to their 'action' phase? Icek Azjen, a professor of psychology at the University of Massachusetts, undertook possibly one of the most powerful pieces of cognitive research, in the late 1980s to the early 1990s, to define how people's actions can be changed for the better.

Ajzen's *Theory of Planned Behaviour* was to become a landmark text in the field of social cognition and would directly inform the way we structured our vision for character education. Ajzen's thesis is alarmingly simple and yet its ramifications are almost too vast to properly take in. His thesis was based on an earlier piece of research titled the *Theory of Reasoned Action* that Ajzen developed with fellow psychologist, Martin Fishbein, in 1975. It suggests that three things shape the architecture of our choices and decisions, which then leads to intentional behaviour. Firstly, our attitude toward the behaviour we are about to perpetrate; secondly, the social pressures we feel to either engage or not engage with certain behaviour; and, lastly, our sense of how much we are in control of whatever our behaviour will be.

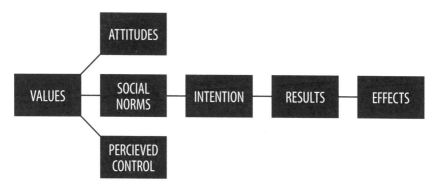

According to Ajzen, focusing upon these three 'awareness' factors, through their underlying belief and value set, provides a framework to act upon our intention (Ajzen also uses the term Implementation Intentions), the junction of our choices and decisions, which then directly dictates the actions we undertake, for the better or equally, for the worse. At its simplest, the theory provided a framework to change people's habits, to move people's automatic and engrained habits into their consciousness and as a result, enable them to make more rational based decisions which in turn and through training, could lead to more positive behaviours and outcomes.

Ajzen's research would go on to be utilised in many varying fields, with its central conceit being especially influential in healthcare where it was tailored as a form of cognitive behavioural therapy to better engage patients in dieting, exercise and quitting smoking through a deliberate form of habit programming or re-programming. Some later theorists, taking advantage of more modern techniques in neuroscience, would go on to critique Ajzen's thesis by contending that human beings are not entirely rational creatures and that, because Ajzen's thesis suggests we make decisions rationally based on what data our minds have acquired, it is not sufficient to properly explain human behaviour. Yet, what if we could bring our irrational actions into our consciousness? What if, just like highly successful forms of cognitive behavioural therapy, we could train ourselves to become more self-aware of our underlying, automatic habits and were able to consciously shape, refine and, where required, change our behaviours for the better?

The simplicity of the model (and taking into account its limitations) would become the foundations for what we planned to do at King's, providing us a framework in which to nestle our version of what character education could be – one founded upon education and abstract reflection, repetitive practice, positive habit formation and the unleashing of personal leadership.

On a fundamental level, character education is about mind-sets and facilitating behavioural change. A student may begin apathetic or lazy and, through a process, become more engaged and hard-working; they might begin with debilitating self-confidence and gradually become a poised and self-assured public speaker, capable of standing on their own two feet in the world outside the school gates. Let's take an example common in every classroom – the failure of a student to hand in homework of a good standard. How many of us immediately rush to the conclusion that the student in question is simply disorganised or lazy?

By focusing on the tenets of the TPB, it allows us to first question the student's beliefs about how they perceive the importance of homework and producing quality work. This is the critical first and most important stage. If they do not believe in (or equally cannot see through their personal lens) the importance of the task then you will not change their habits and behaviours. Was their attitude to this particular task positive and if not, why not? Did their friendship circle act in the same way and how supportive and involved are their parents in this? Were they actually confident in the first place of completing the task to a good standard? Accepting the way the brain works on impulse alongside its capacity for rational thought, this approach enables us to burrow down to the roots of behaviour, the building blocks of why we do the things we do.

How do we persuade people to make the right choices? How do we define what those choices are? How can we provide children with the capacity to do this for themselves without prescribing every possible life scenario in precise detail, or defining meticulously what a 'good' decision was as the progenitors of SEAL had tried to do? How, in a nutshell, can we usher children through a process of education to a level of autonomy where they have all the skills and personality traits to make a success of their adult lives?

Changing poor behaviour patterns has always been an aspect of what schools do. The schools we had all worked in tried to change patterns of poor student behaviour by brute force. They imposed strict disciplinarian regimes, punishing slight infractions – a wrongly knotted tie, a contravention of dress code, tardiness or distraction in lessons – by punishments that might reasonably be said to have outweighed the offence, great punitive gestures designed to stamp out problematic patterns of behaviour in an instant. According to Ajzen's reasoning, this kind of punitive reaction ended up creating the right behaviour for the wrong reasons. It changed the outcome – or the behaviour of the students – without changing the intention behind the behaviour, nor the attitudes, beliefs and other antecedents that had propagated it in the first place.

What about instilling patterns of good behaviour in our students, rather than simply punishing or working to eradicate the disruptive, the malcontent, the bad? We knew, from the start, that behavioural change at King's would not be focused on correcting the misbehaviour of our students. Schools that work solely this way can never be anything other than reactive, waiting for infractions before bringing character-forming efforts to bear. At King's, we wanted to be proactive from the start, actively helping shape our students' futures and to do this we knew that sanctions would only stop the rot, yet changing beliefs could change behaviour. Our work would therefore be concerned with instilling the correct attitudes in our classrooms, in shaping mind-sets so that students actively wanted to flourish, in developing the best intentions and beliefs so that our students were in the best possible place to flourish in their lives ahead. Accepting of the debate around the brain's chemistry and the seeming battle between impulse and rational behaviour in all human lives, what we drew from Ajzen's work would go on to initally become our 3 Element or E's approach.

First, to **EDUCATE** our students in the fundamental values that underpinned our version of good character thus serving as a mechanism for them to examine their unconscious beliefs and values; then to **EQUIP** them with an understanding, through habit formation, of the beliefs, basic social norms and rituals that will aid them to prosper in future life. Finally, to **EMPOWER** them with the ability to make good decisions for themselves, together instilling in our students the character traits that, we hoped, would give them the long-term ability to succeed. As we put this philosophy into practise, it became clear that the 3 Es, vital as they were to how King's would be structured, needed to be introduced and buffered so that our students would get the most out of them.

To this end, we introduced a further three elements, **ENABLE**, effectively an induction programme that would expose students and parents to the beliefs and expectations of King's and introduce students to the journey on which we intended to take them. Having introduced our principles clearly, we sought to cap them off, with our **ENTRUST** and **ENGRAVE** steps. First entrusting that the habit and consistent ways of behaving and making decisions we had equipped our students with would go on to be used outside of the school building and, finally, a farewell step that ritually declared that the values of King's Leadership Academy had been engraved upon our students and as such they would be able to live a more flourishing life.

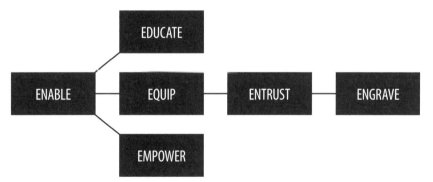

All of this is a roundabout way of saying that the lessons we hoped to pass on to our students would become fundamental parts of them. We would enable them to understand the precepts of our plan; we educate, equip and empower them with the knowledge and self-belief to go out into the world and act upon the values which they'd been exposed to across their education. We would entrust them to carry these lessons on with them across their lives. The word character itself, we would teach them, takes its root from the Greek word *kharakter* – a chisel, or marking instrument, designed to be used on metal or stone. Character is something that endures, that stands the test of time, and so would it be for each one of the students who passed through our doors. Our hope was to engrave a mark of good character on their lives so deep that it left an enduring imprint.

ENABLE
"Be careful of your thoughts, for your thoughts become your words"

Transient times

It was clear from a very early point that the first days of King's Leadership Academy would be some of its most important. These were the days in which we would set the tone of the school, unfurling the path on which both students and staff would travel. As I can remember only too well, the first day of secondary school can be a traumatic one. First impressions count – for schools and students – and there cannot be a teacher in the country who hasn't been fascinated by the emotional tussles that are played out, year in and year out, as one school year finishes and another begins.

There is a widely held belief that the most stressful moments in our lives include getting married, moving house, starting a family and changing jobs. For me – having lived it and observed it for many years – the single most stressful time in our lives is probably the one we have tried to forget or put to the very back of our minds: the transition from primary to secondary school. In fact, there's growing evidence that a child's experiences as they transition from primary school into secondary school can mould lasting connections in the circuitry of the brain. As I stood at the school gates in September 2012, waiting for the very first day of King's Leadership Academy to begin, seeing those nervous faces staring up at me as they passed and shook my hand for the first time, I was starkly reminded of this very fact. At the age of 11, the chances were that these students had been settled in a school that had formed a major part of their lives for the past seven years, perhaps even more if they went to pre-school or nursery in the same place. These students passing me now had gone from being the oldest and most respected students in their primary schools to being the youngest, least respected in their new one.

Chances are that, when you were 11, you were confident of the school in which you operated. You were veterans. You knew your teachers, you knew your classmates, and you knew every nook and cranny of the school that had been a second home for as long as you could remember.

For many of us, our primary schools were small, almost family affairs: small school, small classes, a small set of teachers and assistant teachers who you all knew by name. Secondary school changes everything. To an 11 year old, secondary school is like tilting the world on its axis. Everything that was once so familiar is now so strange.

My own experience was not dissimilar to this. I went from belonging to a school of 90 students to a school of over 2000; spread over two sites a whole mile apart. My friendship group at primary school, who had been a critical part of my life from the age of four, had all splintered off to many different secondary schools. From having lessons in the same class each day, delivered mostly by the same teacher, we now moved lessons every hour. From being top of the tree, I was suddenly right at the very bottom and trying to avoid daily scuffles with others and being terrorised by the older children became my number one priority. This may just have been my first year in secondary school but I am sure I speak for many and, not surprisingly, many students have difficulty managing these new demands.

Students graduating from primary to secondary education are, in fact, experiencing an earthquake in the relative calm of their lives. The academic, social, and emotional demands are different. Students are expected to be increasingly independent at the exact moment when, to effect a smooth transition, they need support the most. It is little wonder that this key moment provokes wild and varied reactions. Paying attention to this transition and investing the most time for our newest and most vulnerable year group, ENABLING our students to have as smooth a transition as possible and inculcating them early in the beliefs, values, social norms and opportunities of King's Leadership Academy. This was a vital first step in how we perceived the school operating.

A brief look at the science of child development is all it takes to properly understand that this is one of the most significant steps we as educators can help our students take. Most researchers agree that the first three or four years of a toddler's life are those in which their brains are 'wired' on a fundamental level. In this period, the brain grows to being about two thirds full size, developing at a rate that will never be seen again. Though the foundations of our social and emotional selves are laid here, our brains do not stop developing. Just as science has shown that severe stress experienced by a toddler – whether that's because of lack of attention, encouragement, support, or more criminal neglect – can impact how the brain is formed, so has it been shown that children experiencing adolescence, a period in their lives where the brain is again in flux, developing and changing at a rate not seen since those earliest years, can be impacted in the long term.

Bullying, neglect and stresses of all other kinds have a lasting impact on the human brain; this is seen most forcefully at times of flux. So what difference might the positive or negative experience of transitioning from one school to the next have on our students? On leaving primary school, how many of our children go from being confident and optimistic to becoming closed, cautious, fearful of failure or of looking silly in front of their new peer group?

The wonder years

Most educators assume that high rates of regression from primary school through to the start of GCSE study – a major Ofsted paper called *The Wasted Years* chronicled this exact phenomenon – are due to students having a lack of basic skills or sufficient academic challenge in their early years of secondary education. What if we could get this transition process right and focus equally on a child's social and emotional development? What if we brought into their consciousness the power of personal leadership – the knowledge and awareness that one's beliefs are the only thing we can truly control ourselves and the only way to effectively take control over one's destiny is to accept personal responsibility for each and every action we take? Stephen Covey, in his book *The 7 Habits of Highly Effective People*, has a wonderful way of describing this phenomenon as being 'response-able'. Would we then be on our way to empowering our pupils to flourish and compete on equal terms with their peers from wealthier backgrounds, often schooled from ages 4 to 18 at the same institution, for long term success? Enabling our new students would only be half of the battle. Parents are not only their children's primary character role model and teacher, they are their most constant and enduring influence.

In other words, the beliefs, words, actions and habits of parents are contagious to those closest to them and will likely cascade down onto their children. In the book *The Power of Habit*, author Charles Duhigg calls our most important habits 'keystone habits'. These are particular routines that have a multiplier effect on a range of other behaviours. For example, Duhigg documents findings from studies with parents who set the routine of having dinner every evening as a family can also lead to their children having "better homework skills, greater emotional control and more confidence".

Children who make their own bed every morning starts, what Duhigg calls, a 'chain reaction' of other positive behaviours. As such, when students attend school from a wealthier background they are more likely to come from a more stable and intellectually stimulating home where they are well cared for and where they are encouraged to do their best. Under these circumstances, student achievement undoubtedly benefits several fold onto what a school can add on its own.

In less affluent areas, we must be also be mindful of a decline in such things and an increased chance of children being brought up by a single parent with limited disposable income and leisure time for their child's educational development. In these cases, it is not unusual to see respect for authority, good social skills and a willingness to work hard and diligently erode to such a level where students arrive for school tired, hungry and less ready to learn. Bad habits must therefore be replaced with good ones. Therefore, at each stage of our induction process, ENABLING each and every parent to understand, align, internalise and act upon the same expectations as ours would be critical for the lessons of King's to be continued beyond the school gates each and every day. This included the reinforcement of our beliefs and values in the home but it also went much wider to include some important determinants of success such as attendance, punctuality, behaviour, dress and deportment and methods of developing social and cultural capital. This would create a shared consciousness between the school and the home to enable a student's whole environment to support their growth.

King's Leadership Academy opened its doors for the very first time in September 2012 and our first intake of 38 students, all 11 years old, filed past me through the gates. I did not yet know if this was the start of something vast, or an experiment that might end in noble failure. What

I did know was that what looked like any other day actually represented these students going through their toughest schooling challenge yet. Get this right, and there was a chance that the rest would follow.

In the main hall, the *Triumphal March* by Aida roared out through the sound system. Staff wearing gowns stood at the gates to welcome our new intake, each student gently tapped the heads of the academy's two lifesize stone lions 'Archimedes' and 'Aristotle' as they entered and wished for good luck, a ritual to be performed by every successive year group to come.

This was only their fifth day as Year 7 students. The previous four, along with a five stage transition programme whilst they were still in their primary school, had been dedicated to our ENABLE stage – becoming immersed in daily rituals, in class and out of class routines and our values based ASPIRE code (Aspiration, Achievement, Self-awareness, Professionalism, Integrity, Respect and Endeavour). This was our set of values that we hoped would permeate every aspect of the school and run through our students like the words on a stick of Blackpool rock.

For each of the values, a series of historical role models had also been studied to enable students to get closer to what the value truly meant to them by learning of the heroic actions of people such as Edmund Hilary, Rosa Parks and Mahatma Ghandi. We hoped students would learn to one day emulate these people implicitly. Emulation was also developed explicitly, from learning how to walk and line up in straight, serious and silent lines, to shaking hands and speaking in public confidently. Students would practice our classroom rules, it too following the ASPIRE acronym – always be ready to Ask questions, Sit up straight, Pay attention, show Interest to the subject, Respond to questions professionally and with good manners and always maintain Eye contact. A day would also be dedicated to researching and planning their flight paths – a personalised crusade for each student to envisage where they one day hoped to be and define the steps that would take them there.

The stage was now set for our students to formally pledge allegiance to the values of our school, and the ASPIRE code itself. This, we had decided, would be an annual rite of passage, a transition from one state to another, the moment a student stepped out of their primary school lives and into their secondary school career. Through this pledge they would dedicate themselves to becoming young leaders in our new type of school, an academy with the ethos and culture of a public school but one that was open, inclusive and free for all.

As I watched the children assemble, an elderly lady appeared on the gate. "Excuse me," she said, "I'm here to meet my daughter but I'm a little late. My grandson has started secondary school this week. I don't know the name of the school, but my daughter said it was the new Harry Potter school. Is this the one?" It was with that remark that I knew we had taken our first step toward success and hit our first target set by Sir Iain: to create 100 years of tradition in less than 100 days. Our journey had begun.

Flash forward four years, and the stage was set exactly as it had been on that opening day. Inside the main hall, our fifth intake of students – this time 120 strong and taken from over 400 applicants, each determined by proximity to the school – sat in their groups at the front. Aged only 11, four new students lined up on stage. This would be their first experience of a public speech that they had written themselves. At their sides sat four older students. Each of them wore a maroon jacket – the blazer we called our ASPIRE jacket. Over the preceding four years of King's Leadership Academy, staff and students had voted for these students as the students of the year. These were students who epitomized our values day in and day out. The ASPIRE jacket was highly sought after among the student body and had been their reward. Just as a professional golfer hungers after the green jacket, at King's acquiring the maroon jacket had become the pinnacle of a student's journey.

Finally, the ceremony began. There was no principal to lead it, nor any other school leader. Instead, the four new students took their places on the cusp of the stage and began. Speaking eloquently for several minutes to an audience of 300, they introduced the principal to the stage and, at that moment, the formalities began.

In turn, each of the students beginning their King's journey that year approached a table. Here they were introduced to the school by their leadership tutor, and signed an oath to the ASPIRE Code, a personal contract, that they and their parents promised to always follow the academy's values – not just in school but at home and in the community as well. Once their names were inscribed in the school ledger, they marched on to our principal, Shane Ierston, who formally asked each student: 'Do you agree to follow the ASPIRE code? Will you always endeavour in your studies?' Once each student had agreed, the principal placed a King's tie over their heads and finished their rite of passage with a firm handshake. It was at this moment that each student received the King's ASPIRE pamphlet.

This is a constant reminder of the seven habits we expected them to develop and nurture, and by which a King's student could always be known, the seven habits of character that would, from now on, define their lives. At the back of the booklet, the poem *The Road Not Taken* by Robert Frost stands as a constant reminder of the journey these student were about to undertake, a different but tougher path, one which will get more difficult and more demanding each and every day. Rather than taking the common, easier route, the King's journey would turn them into a better person – a person who understands that the good life, a life of good character, comes from not just performing the difficult tasks of life repeatedly well but doing so in the face of failure and constant set-backs.

This is the story of how King's promotes those habits of character and the sciences behind them – how the key to unlocking the hidden strengths of character is open to us all, whether we be a primary school student just embarking on an educational career, or an adult who has long ago left the school gates behind.

EDUCATE

"Be careful of your words, for your words become your deeds".

Defining character

The history of character education is long and varied but before embarking on our own iteration, we would have to confront the same challenge that our forebears had and find answers to the arena's single most fundamental question: what is good character, and how can that be succinctly and effectively defined? In seeking to answer this question, the theorists of the past had formulated all sorts of different designs. Education 2.0 would have to have its own.

The challenge we had handed ourselves, in the year before King's Leadership Academy opened, was a challenge the architects of America's Charter Schools and many others, had approached with different methodologies and wildly varying results. To most of us, the idea of 'good' and 'bad' are as black and white, and that's a way of thinking that has been drilled into us since we were children. "Be a good boy," we were told, "be a good girl" – without any real interrogation of what that might mean. Scratch beneath the surface, though, and the question is as complex as it is short.

The problem is that, though our instinct might be to think of 'good' character as a binary thing, a little interrogation quickly reveals it to be a subjective and slippery question. More often than not, it depends on context. Consider, for instance, the prison inmate who obediently shuffles from his cell to the exercise yard each morning, returns to his cell in an orderly fashion until he is called for a meal, eats serenely in the prison canteen and then, at the tolling of another bell, returns calmly to his cell where he waits until the next morning so that the whole ritual can be gone through again. To a prison overseer, this is exemplary behaviour and yet, if you were to supplant the same man into a performance-based business environment, being passive, quiet and obedient is quickly seen as problematic. In one context, passivity is championed; in another, it's positively decried. Consider how ideas of what an 'admirable' quality is might change across different landscapes and times.

In his book exploring the Charter Schools of America, *How Children Succeed*, Paul Tough makes a good case: in Victorian Britain, Tough suggests, chastity, piety and social graces were the qualities that might generally be considered to rank a person as 'good' or 'bad'; on the American frontier of the same century, there would have been little to commend in these very same traits. In that place and time, the values that a 'good' man might need had much more to do with 'courage, self-sufficiency, ingenuity, industriousness and grit.' Jump into different times and places and the question only becomes more complex.

Should attention-to-detail be valued over the ability to empathise with others? Should willpower be rated more highly than flexibility? The ability to work well with others and be tolerant of others attitudes and behaviours might be invaluable in a dense urban environment, but might that very same trait hinder somebody on a frontier who needs to make rapid decisions, regardless of their effect on others? What good are social niceties to someone attending a council of war, or sitting across a table hammering out the details of an important business deal?

Take a step back and it becomes clear that asking what constitutes 'good character', and therefore what character traits we should be developing in our children, is an organisational nightmare. In 2004, one pair of researchers published a book that attempted to do exactly this and, by looking past the specifics of history and geography, to articulate a definitive set of characteristics valued by all societies across the globe. That book, *Character Strengths and Virtues* was intended to become a volume analogous to the *Diagnostic and Statistical Manual of Mental Disorders,* which is commonly used to assess issues of mental health. The idea being that *Character Strengths and Virtues* would become the founding stone for further researches into how our characters are developed and how they inform the things we do. Its authors, professors of psychology Christopher Peterson and Martin Seligman, took in a wide survey of contemporary and historical thought – canvassing opinion not only from classical thinkers like Aristotle, religious and spiritual texts like the Torah, but also popular children's cartoons, fairytale and fiction – and eventually settled on 24 specific 'character strengths' that they divided into six classes of 'virtue', and with which, they claimed, they could actively measure character.

Peterson and Seligman's 'core virtues' were only the latest in a long list of attempts to classify and denote what makes a character 'good'. Our earliest written texts give a hint at how our forebears tried to answer the same question. The 'Cardinal Virtues' of antiquity – derived from the Latin 'cardo' as the meaning that all other virtues 'hinged' upon them – were first derived by Plato and went on to be expanded by later thinkers like Cicero, Thomas Aquinas and Saint Ambrose.

This quartet of virtues (Wisdom, Temperance, Justice and Courage, with nuanced definitions of each) would go on to inform the Christian tradition that brought religion into the debate by defining its own set of virtues in the context of our relationship with God: faith, hope and charity. Christendom's divergent branches and their thinkers continued to debate what living a 'virtuous' life actually meant – across the next centuries, humility, hospitality, reliability and many others all vied for their inclusion in the canon – but what Peterson and Seligman were trying to do went beyond this. By losing the specificity of the many and varied codices they looked at, they aimed to achieve something universal, outside of landscape, culture and time.

Across the three years, during which they worked on their study, Seligman and Peterson broke down their virtues into six distinct classes: virtues that contributed to wisdom and knowledge; virtues that concerned strength; virtues that concerned humanity, justice, temperance and transcendence – with this latter, intangible as it initially feels, being to do with our ability to appreciate beauty, to hope, to gain pleasure from the optimism of others and, at the very last, to have a coherent belief about the meaning of our existence on Earth. The idea of a set of virtues common to all societies and sub-cultures of Earth is tantalising stuff. There's a chance it even points to something fundamental about our human nature. Why do codes of chivalry of striking similarity appear in creation myths across the world? Why do the knights errant of European mythology behave in exactly the same honourable fashion as the samurai of Japanese history and legend, and within the same bounds of chivalry as the semi-mythical cowboys of America's own founding myth? Seligman and Peterson seem to suggest, through their work, that reduced to a base level, our ideas of what constitutes good and bad behaviour are hard-coded into our genes, that we grow up with the same moral barometers irrespective of ancestry and culture.

Perhaps the most revolutionary aspect of *Character Strengths and Virtues* is the idea that these 24 specific characteristics are not actually ways to define what we already are; rather, they're ways to define what we can be, what we could be if only we behaved in certain ways and developed certain patterns of behaviour. The relationship between what we are and what we do is complex but, where the theorists of the past had thought of character in terms of absolutes, with life a process of discovering a basic, inherent self, the notion that Peterson and Seligman were tabling was radically different. What if, they suggested, character was a constantly changing force, if every day we woke up one person and went to bed another, constantly evolving – for better, or perhaps worse – across our lives? What, then, might that mean for the ways we think about ourselves and each other?

Think you've heard this somewhere before? Well, you have. We have already seen how Aristotle himself was grappling with the same idea almost 2500 years ago through his unique form of virtue ethics. Contrary to other philosophers at the time who believed character, like personality, was true to its etymology – an engraved and permanent mark on the soul – Aristotle believed that character could be moulded through the shaping of one's environment and learning from, and on reflection of, one's acts. His book *Nicomachean Ethics* (written for his son Nichomachus) promoted the idea that for a man to have a character of excellence required habitually doing the right thing, at the right time, in the right way.

Concentrating more on the actions one takes to become virtuous required the moral agent (me and you in other words) not just to have the will (moral knowledge and beliefs) which his mentor Plato had long preached, but also the skill (practical experience) and the drill (the will to act morally yet decisively well) to be of good character. Consider the analogy of learning to swim by reading the bestselling book 'a beginners guide to swimming' (I made this book up by the way!). Can you imagine reading the manual from front to back, then proceed to jump into the deep end?

Knowledge on its own is of no use unless we have the opportunity to practice and improve – we must put virtue into practice. There also has to be an explicit and intentional connection between what virtue is and how this translates into our everyday behaviours; our very habits as Aristotle would say. This profoundly optimistic view of character lifted people beyond the fixed traits of good or bad and adapted the meaning to something more akin to leaving the very best imprint on the world. "Excellence," he believed, "is an art won by training and habituation… We do not act rightly because we have virtue, but we have virtue because we have acted rightly… We are what we repeatedly do". This to Aristotle was the cornerstone of 'phronesis' (translated to practical wisdom and good sense), itself seen as the master virtue, directing the application of all other virtues. It also represented the first stage of the 'Golden Mean', the intellectual capacity to make well-balanced and well-judged decisions, thus avoiding too much or too little of a good thing.

Courage, for example, is the golden mean between cowardice at one extreme end and foolhardiness at the other and the only way to know the difference between the two excesses and hit the right balance is found through purposeful practice and refinement until it becomes a habit. As well as aiming to provide a universal definition of good character, in *Character Strengths and Virtues*, Peterson and Seligman had belied centuries of thinking that bound character up with religion and the permanence of the soul and returned to a classical principle: that human beings are not absolutes. Character is a sliding scale and, by habituation, a person of what could be termed 'poor' character could develop and transform. For educators this is seismic; it provides a scientific reasoning to back up those dedicated and forward-thinking teachers who will not give up on students from under-privileged backgrounds, or students with behavioural problems and low aspirations. It provides a solid footing for those who believe that low aspirations are not permanent, that children can succeed in life no matter what their backgrounds – and that, importantly, schools must make no excuses for poor performance based purely on a student's postcode or familial circumstance. For the rest of us, it might be the most forgiving of life's mantras: a mind-set trained to think this way could let go of the past, unburden itself of fears of what it has been, what it is now, and concentrate solely on the things to come.

This was a notion the Charter Schools of America had taken to their heart and around which they specifically structured their teaching and educational 'cradle to college' pipelines like those seen in the Harlem Children's Zone. If Seligman and Peterson were proposing that the character traits in their study were ones that could be developed, practised, and refined in the same way as ball skills, arithmetic, and almost any other discipline, then it followed that they were also skills that could be taught. That was exactly what schools such as KIPP, Uncommon, Amistad and First Line had been doing: a direct attempt to teach character.

Lessons from across the pond

The time I had spent in Boston with Future Leaders had always stayed with me as a direct example of how educators concentrating on developing character could better position students for success at school and, later, at college. Paul Tough's exploration of the wider strategies employed by the Charter School programme provides further elucidation. The schools in the KIPP programme, among the others with whom Tough spent time and whose methods he set out to chronicle, were often directly inspired by Peterson and Seligman's definition of virtues. They defined their school ethos specifically in terms of the types of character they wanted to develop so that, while the goal of a particular institution might be for 75% of its graduates to go on and complete a four-year degree from a college, the way of attaining this was through strict adherence to the particulars of character laid out in its ethos.

Variously, qualities like 'grit', 'determination', and 'zest' were prized highly, with each school's ethos a refined and truncated version of the broad vision Peterson and Seligman had described. Tough's investigation threw up yet more nuances and a close look at them gives more credence to the idea that defining what 'good character' means is a slippery business. Some of the schools Tough investigated prized what we might call 'performance-related' virtues most highly. These were the virtues of hard-work, dedication, determination and desire identified as markers for how well a student might succeed academically and, by extrapolation, in a later business career. Other schools prized more emotional virtues most highly, reining close to those characteristics that better fostered a sense of community: openness and honesty, kindness, gratitude, and the ability to successfully manage relationships with others. Still more emphasised what we can think of as civic-minded virtues: citizenship, fairness, and integrity.

These observations were made more widely when author and academic Scott Seider composed his book, *The Character Compass*, mapping the academic achievements of three Boston Charter Schools. Seider's investigation followed schools that each focused on a different sub-set of values – performance, moral or civic – and how academic outcomes varied according to each.

Seligman and Peterson had incorporated all of these different traits into their study and, as we put our bid together to open King's Leadership Academy, we knew that we wanted our own school ethos to be anchored in each port. Tough talks at length about the imbalances that can be developed by focusing on singular characteristics too heavily. Peterson and Seligman had contended, for instance, that there was "no true disadvantage of having too much self-control". Other psychologists, including University of California's psychology researcher Jack Block, expound the opposite view: too much self-control leads to students denying themselves pleasure, effectively punishing themselves through virtue, or what we might think of as a borderline sadomasochistic response.

Similarly, researchers have argued that too much willpower can be to the detriment of a person's flexibility; that too much grit or determination can have a negative impact on a person's ability to empathise with others, or their tolerance for those whose abilities to do not match their own. Balance, we decided, was key. As the age old adage goes: too much of a good thing will kill you.

The ASPIRE code

If our version of Education 2.0 was to be underpinned by the strong ethos we had seen in those Charter Schools, which we knew from experience was the foundation of a school that might succeed in the long term, we would need to identify our own set of values specific to our school and code them into the school's DNA from the outset. As early as the writing of the first bid, that was exactly what we did. Beginning with Peterson and Seligman's 24 virtues, Sir Iain, Shane and I gathered our potential school governors, prospective parents and students, and together we plastered an office wall with sheets of paper. This was to be our attempt to define what we wanted our teaching to accomplish on behalf of our students, and how we might achieve that. Having worked for such a long time in the target-driven culture of modern education, we began with the idea that we wanted 'incredible outcomes' for our students.

According to Ajzen's *Theory of Planned Behaviour*, the way to achieve these outcomes was by developing the intentions of our students. The way to develop those intentions was by inculcating in them the mind-sets that would allow those intentions to naturally develop. What mind-sets were those and what specific intentions did we want to develop? We began by brain-storming the outcomes we wanted: for our students to be highly motivated, for them to be good and regular attenders, to have a sense of pride in their achievements, to go the extra mile, to learn from failure, to be aware of their strengths and yet never overlook the areas in which they needed to improve.

We realised a list like this could be endless and could end up meaning nothing if we did not define the ways we could steer students here, the 'attitudes' of Ajzen's Theory. We took a step back and began to concentrate on the virtues we would have to foster in our students if these behaviours were to develop. Peterson and Seligman's list was a vital starting point – but, like others before us, we also knew that a list as broad and catch all as theirs was problematic. In covering all bases, was there a chance that every one of them might be overlooked? Could we really expect our students, some of whom would be as young as 11 years' old, to hold in mind 24 distinct characteristics at once? Could an organisation's ethos ever be as broad as that, or like in my experience of the RAF and their values code of RISE, did it need condensing and conveying in as simple a manner as possible?

Observing the overlap in some of Peterson and Seligman's virtues, we began to group certain characteristics together. After much debate, the ideas of conscientiousness, determination, resilience and perseverance were collated as 'Endeavour'.

At the same time, we had committed ourselves to what we called an 'holistic view of character' meaning that, unlike some of the schools in America focusing on character education, we did not want to limit ourselves to one particular virtue set. We would not choose characteristics focused purely on performance; we would not choose characteristics focused solely on morality, on emotional and social wellbeing, nor on our civic responsibilities. Rather, we would build our ethos around principles derived from all of these different value sets.

If 'Endeavour' was our way of capturing all of Peterson and Seligman's performance-related virtues, we would include 'aspiration' and 'achievement' as academic-related virtues, 'respect' as a social and civic-minded virtue, 'integrity' as an emotionally loaded virtue. At the end of this process, we had developed what would go on to become our singular ASPIRE code, our cultural glue through its seven corresponding pillars, each of them standing for a virtue we thought it necessary for our students to have as a habitual behaviour to succeed.

A: Aspiration and Achievement. Through the development of these character traits, we wanted our students to develop not only the highest of aspirations, but also the drive and determination to achieve them.

S: Self-Awareness. By becoming more self-aware, we wanted our students to gradually develop a greater understanding of themselves as a person, as well as their strengths and, perhaps more importantly, their weaknesses. Understanding how they perceive the world and how this may be different to other people's perspective – in other words our very own character lens – was to be an essential starting point.

P: Professionalism. By taking a professional approach to life at King's, we would encourage our students to develop pride in themselves, their inlook, their outlook and all that they would go onto undertake.

I: Integrity. We would help our students understand that integrity is not just about telling the truth. It is about being true to their beliefs and values and upholding them; it is about having pride in all that they do, always working to their true ability and behaving correctly to other people at all times.

R: Respect. We would help our students to understand that respect is not simply about being polite, courteous and good mannered but about respecting your own ability and working hard to achieve well, about valuing the differences in other people, their faiths and cultures, and looking after our planet and its limited resources.

E: Endeavour. We would help our students to work hard to achieve success through an industrious mind-set, to bring focus to the tasks laid before them, to tackle problems conscientiously and diligently, and to always persevere.

ASPIRE would become the primary vehicle of bringing our beliefs to life – a common identity that would be understood, spoken and reinforced by every stakeholder connected to the organisation. Not only this, but the values would also become interconnected to the many different channels of developing character. Interestingly, the acronym for our values based code *ASPIRE* also matched the acronym for the Theory of Planned Behaviour framework: *Attitude, Social Norms, Perceived Control, Intention, Results, Effects.*

The foundations of King's Leadership Academy in 2012, and everything we were trying to achieve in character education, is to be found in this common set of values. Making them central to the way we approached all aspects of school life, not only in the classroom but through famous role models, rituals, stories, mantras, even myths, would allow them to be a common, connected and sacred language the school needed if it was to rise above the throwaway mottos and creeds we had seen in so many of our former schools.

If the ethos of King's Leadership Academy was to be more than empty aphorism, then there had to be meaning in those words, meaning in the way we imparted them to our students, meaning in the way the school was structured around them. We would have to develop tangible, demonstrable ways of implanting these virtues in our students, to **EDUCATE** them in what these principles meant on a reductive, elemental level. If that were to succeed, we would have to find ways of measuring our effectiveness. This brings us neatly onto the next question fundamental to any attempt at teaching character: how do we know if we succeed?

Making the invisible, visible

The question of how to measure character is one that has vexed school leaders across the ages. We have already seen how relentless metrication transformed the role of school leaders and turned them into creative statisticians. Perhaps that points to a greater truth: whenever and wherever measurements have to be made, where scales of success and failure are deployed, there exists the potential for the system to be gamed. If students know they're going to be tested on character, aren't we encouraging them to prepare for that test? The usefulness of exams in academic practise has long been contested. Aren't we just testing a student's ability to keep information in their short-term memories, rather than how successfully they have internalised and invested in their education for the long term? Cramming for an exam has become an accepted part of the academic process.

Yet, if character education is about arming ourselves with the attitudes and abilities we need to have rich, successful lives long after our education is finished, wouldn't cramming be counter-productive? If character is just another discipline to be revised, is there not a chance we're falling into the same traps of old, measuring our students not on the actual character traits they have developed but on their ability to successfully navigate the test? Wouldn't that defeat the purpose of character education altogether?

The Jubilee Centre of Birmingham University aimed to tackle this very question at a conference held in Oxford in 2014. The Jubilee Centre of Character and Virtue is commonly accepted as the UK's leading authority on research into character education and how the most modern thinking can be used to better our public life. In contrast to many American thinkers – watch out for them, because we'll be looking more closely at their work later – the Jubilee Centre eschews the 'phronesis' based notion of character and, instead of focusing solely on traits that might see us strive to achieve bigger and better things, takes a more holistic view of what constitutes 'good' character, with an eye on all the many colours of Peterson and Seligman's spectrum and Aristotle's notion of practical wisdom. Founded in 2012 by Professor James Arthur, the centre has enjoyed unprecedented levels of success, directly influencing government policy on virtuous practice in fields as diverse as law, healthcare, the military and education, in particular in the field of professional ethics. Their research papers are commonly cited by central government as deciding factors in how policy decisions are being made.

The conference of 2014 was the centre's second annual gathering and brought together the best researchers in the field to ask the question: can we ever derive a credible measure of virtue? Is it reasonable to expect that virtue could ever be assessed and, perhaps most importantly, if a universal system of measuring virtue was ever to be adopted, how could we stop the system from being gamed or manipulated to a particular individual's advantage? The speakers were many and varied, touching on subjects as far afield as how soldiers recover from war and how that recovery might be plotted to the possibility of using ancient Indian scripture to measure virtue. Of specific interest were the speakers talking about the methods we might use to track character improvement, and the gamification of this data.

Jennifer Cole's paper *Can Virtue Be Measured?* was one of those addressing the problem straight on but it came with a caveat. Its sub-title: *Sure, But It Ain't Gonna Be Easy!* Cole's paper was devoted to, first arguing that there was no scientific basis why virtue could not be measured in principle, and second to defining a possible way of measuring our advancement in the application of a certain virtue. To do this, she posited grading a number of steps: first, our sensitivity to the presence of virtue-relevant stimuli, or our capacity to recognise when one of our virtues is being tested. Secondly, how we generate a virtue-specific response to that stimuli, or how we react when one of our virtues is being challenged or called upon. Thirdly, how consistent our responses are in situations with the same dynamic, or how deeply these responses have become the 'habits' we so often speak about at King's.

Measuring each of these steps could be undertaken privately, by the person in the situation, or by a third party observer. How do we tell when a person has a particular virtue, rather than just displaying its traits in a certain situation? At what point does acting on a virtue become a habit? Can the consistent display of virtue-relevant behaviour ever be metricated?

Cole's paper was a fascinating study-in-progress, a kind of first draft approach to how virtues might be measured and the most striking thing about it was its complexity. Virtues, Cole was saying, are not singular things. Her attempt at providing a framework in which we might record and grade our virtue responses is broad simply because it needs to be. Can all virtues be tracked and measured in the same way? Can we use the same criteria to measure perseverance as we would kindness? Can we measure aspiration using the same algorithm as we would to measure respect? Cole's paper attempts to do this by giving us a theoretical framework in which our designated virtues might sit, but it's far from clear how a scale of this complexity could best be applied in the context of a schooling system.

The Charter Schools of the USA were faced with the same thorny question. If we accept that character education is an admirable thing – and all of the data suggests that it should be adopted on a universal basis – the next step is finding some way to measure how successful we are at doing it. For the KIPP group of schools, the logical step was compiling a 'character report card' which, by mirroring the traditional academic report card of the American schooling system, would delineate how far each student had come in developing their specific character traits.

At the KIPP schools – according to Paul Tough in his book *How Children Succeed* – the report cards are something of a logistical nightmare, with each teacher having to grade each student on each of their 24 proscribed indicators of good character. The cards rely on the outside observation of teachers which brings problems associated with self-awareness and perceptions through their own 'character lens', the ability to evenly and fairly award a grade point for each virtue being recorded and, for their critics, leave the door open to the system being gamed. If we record virtue like this, can't students manipulate their behaviour to satisfy grade requirements?

It has long been known that people's behaviour can be negatively influenced. In his paper *Instilling Virtue,* Jonathan Webber called to mind the famous electroshock experiments by Stanley Milgram. Milgram's experiments on obedience, conducted during the 1960s when he was a professor at Yale University, put half his subjects in charge of a button that would administer electric shocks to the other half of the subjects in his study. Unknown to those in charge of the buzzer, the subjects hooked up to the shock apparatus were actually actors, asked to respond in certain ways according to the extremity of the 'shock' they had been delivered.

Milgram's experiment was startling: he showed, categorically, how most people will subject others to the most horrifying pain, if they have been told to do so by a person in a position of authority. Some of Milgram's subjects were able and willing to provide a shock big enough to kill the subject wired up to their apparatus. In his paper at the Jubilee Centre, Webber used the Milgram experiment as a kind of mirror, to impress upon us the idea that, if negative behaviours can be encouraged, so too must positive ones. Webber's paper might have been one of that day's most complex but what it came back to was unerringly simple, and wisdom that has been accessible to man for millennia.

Aristotle's original vision that we are what we do, that excellence is a habit; that habituation is key to building character and that, therefore, we as educators must seek out ways to habituate good virtue-relevant practise in our students. It's the King's 3E model by any other name: EDUCATE our students in our values; EQUIP them, through strong modelling and codified practices, with the rituals and basic social norms that allow them to express and act on those values; and, finally, EMPOWER them to make those values habits in their everyday lives.

The Jubilee Centre's 2014 conference attacked the issue of measuring and quantifying character by heavy data and academics but an earlier study, this time by the University of Chicago, had approached the same question in a different way. The Chicago study looked at the role of non-academic – or, in the parlance of the paper, 'non-cognitive' – factors in how students performed in school. Created in conjunction with the Lumina and Raikes Foundations, the study was prompted by the sense that, across the preceding 20 years of education in the USA, too much emphasis on academic pedigree and academic results had been counter productive, leading not to an upsurge in the abilities and ambitions of students leaving education, but a negative impact on their suitability for the worlds of college and work.

The principal finding of the study was that, in the American system, the standardized test score commonly used as entrance criteria for college was a poorer predictor of success – defined as college graduation, and future earnings – than the individual grades achieved at the earlier, middle school levels of education. According to the study, the grading system at earlier levels of schooling better represented the often intangible qualities a student needs to succeed; the study calls these 'academic behaviours' and outlines how they directly influence our academic performance. So, if we regularly attend school and go to class, if we consistently complete our homework, if we're active and engaged in lessons, if we're organised in collating our study materials, and if we have the social skills to interact with our classmates – and, in that way, advance our immersion and understanding of a subject – we are therefore more likely to achieve.

If measuring character by metrics, or creating report cards to track character development, reduces the process and opens it up to the possibility of being manipulated, perhaps the key to measuring success in character education lies in exactly this: if virtue cannot be directly measured or quantified in the same way that academic achievement can be, we can still use proxies to measure how well we are doing in inculcating these traits in our students.

This is the system we use at King's Leadership Academy. By relying on data that can be accurately measured, we aim to hold a mirror up against the values in which our students are being steeped in. Grades are an important part of this – according to the Chicago study's logic, the achievement of a good grade can often be a proxy for the perseverance and application of our students – but so are other, clearly definable behaviours: attendance, behaviour in class, engagement with extra-curricular activities. Importantly, we take into account the satisfaction of our students with their schooling experience, and their parents with the behaviour of their children both inside and outside the school gates.

Evidence captured so far shows that, despite the longer school day – teaching at King's finishes as late as 4pm – attendance is 3% above the national average, at 98%. Since opening in 2012 we have had no fixed term or permanent exclusions and, on average, less than five pupils (1%) are on daily report for minor infractions. Our annual pupil satisfaction survey indicates that the overwhelming majority of pupils have strong positive feelings regarding our educational programmes, feel safe in school and are making good progress. Meanwhile, 85% of our pupils regularly take part in extra-curricular activities until 5pm and 25% of each year group join the Combined Cadet Force from Year 8.

In terms of accreditation, 100% of our Year 7 and Year 8 students have either completed or are on target to complete their awards in fencing, ju-jitsu, first aid, life-saving and sports leadership. All Year 9 students are on target to complete their Duke of Edinburgh Bronze Award by the end of this school year, with Year 10s having completed their Bronze Awards already and being on target to complete their Silver award by end of Year 11. Our Ofsted report stated that "the school has been founded upon firm values and principles, resulting in outstanding behaviour. Integrity, respect and endeavour have become learned behaviours, leading to a strong and intrinsic motivation to succeed."

Academically, we are expecting three times as many of our students to achieve the government's premier performance measure, the English Baccalaureate, as state school's achieve, on average, nationally. At King's, this data is viewed as part of our success story: if our students are attending, behaving in congruence with our values and are engaged enough with our value set that it is bleeding over into their non-school lives, we are confident that our values-driven programme is being shown to be a success.

Taking the long view

We have already explored the reasons, cultural and perhaps even biological, why we're pre-programmed to go for the easiest option, the 'quick fix' that satisfies our immediate desires. How, then, do we account for those people who go the extra mile, those people who buck the biological trend and do think about the long term? Why are some people able to make hard decisions and think ahead, while others think only of the moment without any regard for future consequences? What causes some people to work relentlessly towards a distant, often invisible goal?

Researchers have already begun to interrogate this very question: if success in life does not correlate directly with our intellectual capabilities, what then is its presiding factor? Of the researchers dedicated to resolving this question, one stands out among the rest. Her name is Angela Duckworth and her seminal work, which dovetails with researcher Carol Dweck's study on the difference between a fixed and growth mind-set, concerns a quality that Duckworth termed 'grit' and which we, at King's, think of as 'endeavour'. There will be more on this later.

Duckworth had spent most of her twenties working as a management consultant before she left the world of business behind to take up roles as a mathematics teacher at public schools, first in San Francisco on America's west coast and, latterly, in Philadelphia and New York in the east. Five years of teaching exposed her to the critical similarities between the performance-driven world of business and the world of schooling where academic success is all. There was another similarity that drew Duckworth's attention. It did not take long for her to begin to see that her most academically talented students were not always the ones who did well in class, that the set of students who were consistently succeeding did not directly correlate with the set of students who claimed the highest IQs in standardized tests. Driven by the desire to understand why some children succeeded and others failed, Duckworth set about investigating what this specific quality was, what was the best predictor of success and this quest led her to leaving school and studying for her doctorate at the University of Pennsylvania.

At King's, what we call 'Endeavour', Duckworth would call 'Grit'. Grit, as Duckworth defined it in her TED talk of 2013, is the "passion and perseverance for very long-term goals. Grit is having stamina. Grit is sticking with your future, day in, day out, not just for the week, not just for the month, but for years, and working really hard to make that future a reality. Grit is living life like it's a marathon, not a sprint." Duckworth's research took in West Point military cadets, salespeople, rookie teachers in tough urban neighbourhoods, as well as students in the Chicago public school system. Along the way, her data showed that academic intelligence, or IQ, did not reliably predict who would graduate high school, or who would build a successful military career, or who would survive in a tough public service job, or which salesperson would make the most money for his or her company in any given year. The most reliable predictor for all of these things was her nascent idea of 'grit'.

Duckworth's research took her across the Americas and across the social spectrum. One of the earliest tests of her thesis was the study she carried out at the West Point Military Academy, the training programme that provides a full quarter of the officers in the US Army. The admissions process for West Point is rigorous, and reminds me of the same process I undertook to begin my training with the RAF. Along the way, SAT scores – the American measure of academic achievement at school – demonstrated leadership abilities and physical aptitude are all tested, with only the highest combined scores making it through to the academy.

As these entrance criteria are heavily weighted to academic achievement, Duckworth had a prime arena in which to road test her grit hypothesis. Statistically, 5% of cadets chosen for entrance to the academy would drop out by the end of the first gruelling summer, a three-month period in which they were rigorously drilled and tested. Duckworth began her study by having each cadet fill out a very short 'grit questionnaire' designed to measure how resilient, determined, and all-round 'gritty' they were. Duckworth still uses variations of this design to measure a base-line of grittiness now; her scale asks candidates to react to statements including "I have overcome setbacks to conquer an important challenge", or "I often set a goal but later choose to pursue a different one", and measure themselves against it. After collating the responses from the cadets, Duckworth took a back seat, returning at the end of the summer to co-ordinate the data from those questionnaires with the reality of who had stayed in the programme and who had dropped out.

The result? Duckworth's grittiness questionnaire was the only reliable predictor of who would remain and who would leave. The Whole Candidate Score – the collation of the SATs, the West Point tests and psychological assessments – might have predicted a candidate's later grades and physical performance, but only Duckworth's grit scale had predicted, with any accuracy, which candidates would make it through that first gruelling summer. Grit – not academic intelligence, or emotional intelligence, nor physical or any other mental aptitude – was the only thing that determined who stayed and who went.

Duckworth would go on to conduct similar studies in hugely different environments but, every time, her results came back the same. Whether she was testing children in a National Spelling Bee, teachers in challenging schools, salespeople in private business – or young entrepreneurs just starting to establish themselves in the world – her grit scale predicted success more reliably than any other metric designed to measure 'talent'. In fact, or so the West Point data – among other studies – showed, grit and talent were not directly related at all. Sometimes, Duckworth found, they even repelled each other, with those people thought of traditionally as the most talented showing the lowest levels of grit. For Duckworth, this represents a kind of confirmation bias.

Rational thought dictates that, if a person shows a talent for a particular skill, they would invest more time in it and in that way get exponentially better but, in reality, this is rarely the case. In schools, children with natural academic aptitude find it easier to coast. For them, achieving a top grade might be the matter of a few minutes work, whereas for a less able child, it's the matter of hours, days and weeks. Children with natural academic abilities, Duckworth contends, aren't always conditioned to persevere; if you have natural proficiency, what use is there for grit?

In an interview for the Educational Learning journal in 2013, Duckworth drew an analogy with a study conducted among New York City cab drivers in 1997, its results published in the *Quarterly Journal of Economics*. The study looked at the habits of taxi drivers on rainy days. On rainy days, more people use taxis; it's boom time for a city's cab drivers. Yet the study showed that, on rainy days, taxi drivers tend to work the fewest hours. Rather than capitalising on a rush of trade, they reach the goal they have set for their income that year and, having achieved it, simply take the rest of the day off. For Duckworth, this correlates with how talent and grit work: a talented person may work less hard to achieve the same goal as a less naturally talented person, whereas a less talented person must develop the grit and resilience to achieve the same things. Talent, then, can actually encourage us to work less hard, whereas a dearth of talent encourages us to develop grit to fill the vacuum.

Duckworth's statistics show that there's a strong corollary between abundance of academic talent and dearth of grit – that there's a tendency for one to be the inverse of the other – but she doesn't preclude those individuals who have both talent and grit in abundance. It's these individuals, she says, who go the distance, which stand out from the crowd and have the aptitude to achieve amazing things in life. The relationship she's pointing out does have important bearing to us as teachers; there can't be a teacher of many years service in the world who hasn't noticed the propensity for gifted students to struggle with failure.

Too often in teaching, students who excel are protected from failure and have no capacity to do anything other than succeed, which can leave a fragility at their core. How does a student, who has coasted through life and whose good grades have constantly been reinforced through praise by teachers and parents, cope when the inevitable moment of failure happens? How do they cope when they do not succeed in a university application or, later in life, a job interview? How do they cope with setbacks in their personal and family lives? Without having had the need to develop resilience – Duckworth's steeliness, her 'grit' – in their education, what strategies do they naturally have for bouncing back, or overcoming the odds, when life does not play out the way they wanted it to? Students like this do not know struggle, they have no practice with it. "Being gifted is no guarantee of being hard-working or passionate," Duckworth has said. What, then, can we as educators do to help develop these strategies – not just for the classroom, but also for life itself?

Duckworth's theories on grit resonated with me when I first read them; they bore direct correlation with experiences I had when I first joined the RAF. On arriving at Cranwell to report for officer training, I had barely stepped through the gates before we had been marched off to the gymnasium to complete the RAF fitness test. The RAF bleep test is infamous, not only as an assessor of aerobic fitness and predictor of all round general health, but also for the way in which it, slowly but steadily, pits mind against body and, in that way, it can be said to measure 'grit'. The bleep test involves running between two lines spaced 20 metres apart, and having to hit each line and turn in time with a 'bleep'. Very few people have completed the 21 levels of the test since its development in the late 1970s at the University of Loughborough. Interestingly, whilst I was studying at Loughborough, Lord Seb Coe is rumoured to be one of the few to have done so, during his time there as a sports science student. The bleep test, then, is not just testing our aerobic capacity – it tests our mental staying power too.

Scientists say that the body will tell us to give in and stop exerting itself when it still has up to a fifth of its reserves available. It's a survival tactic programmed into us from our earliest evolution – the body forces us to give in while it still has life, so that it has a chance to recuperate. In the bleep test – just as in so many Special Forces selection tests and training exercises – we are being tested in how willing and how capable we are of pushing ourselves beyond our normal 'give up' threshold, when the demands on the body become punishingly tough.

To pass through to the next stage of officer training, we would have to meet the RAF fitness test standard for our age group. Perhaps it was naivety, or conscientiousness, or a mixture of the two – but I approached this as a 'fail to reach this standard and I am back home tonight' scenario and, as such, I gave it 100%. So did many of the recruits around me, many of them being sick on retiring from the test because there was nothing left in the tank. Something happened which, to this day, I still cannot quite believe. A recruit – who had also navigated his way through the Air Cadets and so had been privy to what truly happens when you are on training – knew that, if he failed to reach a suitable standard, he would not really be ejected from the programme at all. Rather, he knew that recruits who failed to reach the standard would join a 'medical flight', three months of training in the RAF gymnasiums at Her Majesty's expense, and all so they could be re-tested, pass and join the next training squadron.

When this recruit – barely breaking a sweat – began to slow down and, eventually, gave up at an early Level 6 of the test, the rest of us were amazed. Only later would we learn he was 'gaming' the system. One thing was apparent to us, even then; this recruit did not have the right attitude to be able to compete, or complete the programme. If he was gaming the system then, he did not have the resilience to get through its later stages when he could not rely on trickery to get through. Eventually, he would drop out when he failed to pass the Field Leadership Camp stage of the process at the end of the 12th week.

Several other recruits dropped out within the first few days of enrolment – not to game the system and gain an advantage for further down the line but simply because they didn't deem themselves able to continue. Why, I wondered, would you go through the application phase, the three day selection phase, turn up for officer training and then throw the towel in without giving it a proper shot? The first month of the programme is hard – mentally, physically, socially and professionally – and I remember it as if it was yesterday: the 5am get ups, cleaning our rooms and blocks for inspection, morning parade by 8am, ten hours of lessons and activities, evening clean up, bed by midnight to one in the morning. This routine repeated itself for four weeks, with no weekend or evening down time and no direct contact with family and friends. It's designed to be tough, uncompromising and, specifically, to test how resilient a recruit is to being thrown in at the deep-end.

Gaining entry into the RAF College is on a par with most academic universities if not harder. As an officer, most trades require degree level education not just A level education. Why would a promising cadet routinely quit when their training had literally just begun? Was it because it was the first time that many had experienced a culture which was asking them to do things that they couldn't do, that routinely had expectations that put us all out of our 'comfort zone' and into our 'stretch zone', occasionally into our 'panic zone'? Could the ones who stayed, who faced setbacks and got back up from failure, be the ones who were the most determined, and resilient? Could it also be that they saw purpose in what they were doing, they wanted this more than anything else?

It was clear that the recruit who intentionally undertook the fitness test knowing that he was going to fail, did not have that 'hard work' and 'never give up' attitude, nor did those who dropped out on the first few days. The ones who succeeded were the ones prepared to finish what they had started, no matter what the cost. This, I would later realise, was Duckworth's definition of 'grit' in action.

Grit seems an attractive concept. At its base, it is a thesis simple enough to captivate all of us. Duckworth's work tells us that our innate intelligence, or IQ, will not dictate our future but rather that our capacity for hard work will. It is easier for us to naturally believe that we can all work harder than for us to believe we can all become more intelligent. Buying into the idea that 'grit' – or King's 'endeavour' – is the primary metric by which we can measure how far we'll go in life is wonderful for all those students who, for whatever reason, feel as if they are never going to succeed academically. Duckworth tells us: that doesn't matter, as long as you can persevere.

Duckworth is evangelical in her support of 'grit' but others are not so. James Arthur, of Birmingham's Jubilee Centre, is only one of a number of people who question the validity of grit – at least when looked at in isolation. In his paper, *Is Grit the Magic Elixir of Good Character?*, Arthur calls to mind the psychologists Grant and Schwarz who, in their own 2011 paper – *Too Much Of A Good Thing* – describe a kind of U-shaped curve of character traits. At the bell of the curve, a character trait is robust and developed and at its most useful but, at either end of the curve, the character trait – either under-developed or pushed to an extreme – is more of a hindrance than a benefit. Sceptical of Duckworth's research methods, Arthur worries that focus on grit can lead to a kind of 'romanticisation of hardship' – with the logic going that, if grit is acquired by battling through hardship then should we keep students in hardship so that they acquire this trait? He further worries about the health implications of forcing somebody to see a task through to its end, even when it becomes apparent that the task is not suited to them or their natural character.

Arthur contends that if sticking to a task and seeing it through no matter what exemplifies grit, what does that mean for students who pick a subject that they discover themselves temperamentally not suited to? Do we consider it a weakness of character for them to recognise this and change tack? Or should we consider it admirable when students doggedly see a task to its end, no matter how much they have realised the subject is not for them? Are students – and people more generally – to be thought of as weak if they simply change their minds, or if pursuing a particular task reveals something to them they had not understood before? Where does the line between admirable 'grit' and pig-headedness lie?

Arthur's critique of the thesis is compelling but not as vociferous as certain other voices, rallying against Duckworth since the publication of her 2016 work. Some detractors have gone so far as to say that Duckworth's work is built upon a kind of 'everyday racism' with its antecedents in the eugenics movements of the 20th century. In proselytising the idea that students must simply work harder, be more resilient, develop better determination, to do better, she is ignoring the social constructs that hold some students back. By focusing on grit, her detractors say, she is not accounting for the students from low income backgrounds, with unfixed or poor familial support – statistically, in Duckworth's native United States, urban or semi-urban black and Hispanic students – who might struggle more than their better-off (and more often ethnically white) counterparts in recovering from a setback. Her critics accuse her of ignoring social conditions, of belittling poorer – and, in these terms, non-white – students by telling them they must simply work harder if they're to meet the same standards as their wealthier peers, who have access to private tutors, families often more engaged with the processes of education, and generally all-round better schooling.

More strident detractors accuse Duckworth of being an apologist for bad schooling: championing grit to an extreme, they say, excuses schools for failings of teaching, of infrastructure and of good practice. For Duckworth, these critics say, a poor schooling environment is irrelevant because the onus is on the student to have the depth of character and resilience to succeed against these odds. It is easier, they say, to demonstrate 'grit' with the safety net of money, familial support, and empathetic teaching staff who are ready and willing to help students bounce back from whatever setbacks they face.

Pamela Moran, the superintendent of Albemarle County, Virginia's public schools, summed up the stance perfectly at the EduCon conference of 2015 in Philadelphia. In arguing that children from difficult backgrounds often showed 'grit' in their lives that would not be formally recognised by tutors, she said, "Sure, I want kids who are resilient, but I also want children who feel safe in school, who feel their teachers are looking out for them, and who believe schools are providing them with flexibility and opportunity versus telling them to pull themselves out of poverty by their bootstraps." For Moran, and others like her, grit is too problematic a scale; it might have benefits looked at academically, but in real world settings it falls considerably short.

Duckworth refutes these claims wholeheartedly – in fact, her 2016 book *Grit* does point out the problems of social conditions, and that her work on grit is only just the beginning of what should be a long process of building grit and resilience in our students. In fact, nothing in her work, current or historic, precludes the notion that societal influences have huge bearing on the character and abilities of our students, or their measurements of success. Nevertheless, she is inspiring spirited debate.

Grit versus EQ

Daniel Goleman, the proponent of Emotional Intelligence – or EQ – as a measure of how successful a person might be in life, is similarly unswayed – though without resorting to claims of bigotry and negligence. For Goleman, focusing on grit as a primary metric is hugely problematic. Goleman believes that what Duckworth popularised as the quality of 'grit' has long been known to researchers in the field as 'cognitive control', the quality that allows us to manage short term emotion, grapple with ourselves, and forge a path onward to longer term success.

Cognitive control, in its traditional sense, is the strength that lets us focus on a single task, to ignore distractions and to manage any emotions that might disrupt us from achieving what we set out to achieve. For Goleman, this is grit by any other name and past studies in cognitive control seem to support what Duckworth says about grit, that it's our best way of predicting the long term success of our students.

One important study conducted in New Zealand, and cited by Goleman in his review of Duckworth's work, *The Trouble With Grit* is directly comparable. In this study, one thousand students from New Zealand were rated on their 'cognitive control' when at high school, then tracked down in their 30s so that their life stories could be measured against their rating in that particular test. The test showed that those with the highest levels of cognitive control – or grit – were most financially successful; this measurement was a better predictor of financial success than IQ, and even better than the wealth of the family in which the student had grown up.

Despite all this, Goleman sees problems: prizing grit as the singular attribute driving success, he says, ignores the advantages of developing a well-rounded character with rich emotional intelligence. Grit might take a self-employed entrepreneur to great places, but there's a reason 'grit' is not high on the agenda when companies are hiring talented staff to their management boards, or other important roles. There is a reason singletons do not list 'grit' as a desired attribute when they are looking for a potential partner, lover, or parent for their future children. "People who are driven toward high achievement can be fantastic individual contributors in an organization," Goleman says, "but if that's their only strength, they will be miserable team members and atrocious leaders."

Goleman points to research from the Hay Group management consultancy, which revealed that the attributes most important in leadership were interpersonal skills, self-awareness, and emotional qualities – attributes strongly correlated to what the study refers to as coaching and affiliative leadership styles. As far as Goleman, and the research, is concerned, 'grit' or 'cognitive control' is a quality that can drive individuals onward – but, at its worst, can be damaging in circumstances where some level of co-operation and teamwork is necessary. In the modern world, that's most circumstances. Too much unchecked grit, Goleman says, can lead to failure in most modern contexts.

This is a view that other researchers into emotional intelligence have backed up. The JCA group, a careers guidance and analysis firm, who advise various FTSE 100 companies on how to get the most out of their employees by investigating and applying theories of emotional intelligence, conducted a 2012 study that showed exactly this. According to JCA, high levels of cognitive control give self-employed people a distinct advantage; when it comes to CEOs or middle managers in medium to big sized companies, cognitive control does not best predict success. Rather, these people require high scores in other emotional qualities: the ability to know what others want, to motivate others, to build trusting relationships and manage confrontation constructively. These skills – what JCA term 'interpersonal skills' – are, according to thinkers like JCA and Goleman – the ones that employees prize most highly.

Taught or caught?

It's clear, then, that 'grit' is not as simple a conceit as it first appears. Paul Tough revealed himself in his bestselling 2014 book, *How Children Succeed*, as one of Duckworth's earliest activists. That early work put grit and resilience at the heart of character education, observing that it was the development of this trait that allowed all others to flourish. Back then, Tough considered it the keystone block of character education but, by 2016, his thoughts had moved on.

In his subsequent book, *Helping Children Succeed*, Tough sought to outline the specific steps by which practitioners could begin to inculcate values and traits into school life. Perhaps his most important conclusion was that directly teaching grit is impossible. For Tough, character traits like grit could not be passed on through any method that we would recognise as 'teaching'. Rather, Tough said, grit had to be nurtured, that children had to be put in a position by which they developed the skill Duckworth terms 'grit' organically. It was the responsibility of teaching staff and other school leaders to provide the correct environment for this skill to flourish.

The nuances of Tough's change of stance hold important implications for educators of every level; Tough is effectively saying that character is not something that can be drilled into a student by rote, like the capital cities of the world or the lineage of the English Kings and Queens. Rather, he is placing the emphasis on the culture of our schools – and this key lesson is reflected in everything we are trying to do at King's.

Instructing our students in 'endeavour', like any one of our ASPIRE values, presents challenges to the traditional method of teaching. Endeavour, respect and aspiration cannot be taught and tested in the same way that our more tangible traditional subjects can be. By weaving these lessons into the fabric of our school, we aim to provide the opportunity for our ethos to be 'caught' and for students to turn our values into habits that characterise their lives. The values are also directly taught and modelled to all students for two to three hours per week by intentionally posing a series of discussions to test the ethical and moral judgement of students. Firstly, our bespoke ASPIRE curriculum helps our students become thoughtful decision makers through weekly lessons on a range of personal, social, health and economic related topics, each weaved to one of our ASPIRE values for a seven-week period.

Each year group studies the same value and topic at the same time, but topics are sequenced in age-related experiences, whilst the philosophical depth is also increased by year group to support greater levels of critical thinking and class discussion. Secondly, our Public Speaking, Philosophy & Ethics (PPE) programme aims to enhance both moral awareness and reasoning, enabling our students to debate their opinions and take the perspective of others through a series of spiritual, cultural and ethical dilemmas that focus student's thinking on more moral aspects of character. Thirdly, all students study a weekly curriculum in leadership, accredited by the Chartered Management Institute, enabling every student to earn a raft of professional qualifications. For each set of lessons, every teacher follows a four-staged approach:

- KNOWLEDGE: they deliver the knowledge of the particular topic by also reinforcing the ASPIRE value underpinning the discussion/dilemma.

- REASON: they discuss the implications of the 'Golden Mean' rule and the implications of what too much or too little of the value may lead to in reality.

- PRACTICE: they discuss scenarios from real life events or, in the case of leadership, set up practical experiences that enable students to put theory into practice and how lessons can be transferred into their day-to-day lives when 'no one is watching'.

- REFLECTION: this enables students to reflect on their reactions to scenarios and/or real life events and determine how they could improve their actions when next repeated. In PPE for example, students plan a speech and deliver it publically in front of their peers summarising their learning over the previous seven weeks and how this can be related back to the ASPIRE code.

More specifically by value, we also look to encourage ASPIRATION by naming our classrooms after universities our students visit annually and might one day attend. Our 'flight paths' are dedicated and individualised academic and career based plans designed to help each student fulfil their own personal ambition; and by inviting 'world of work' speakers to the school each month, we aim to broaden our students' horizons and bring their 'flight path' to life.

We look to foster an environment in which it is 'cool to ACHIEVE'. We break our teaching down into five-week bursts and constantly reinforce the sense of achievement students feel by progressing one more step along the ladder to mastery of a subject. We enrol each student on the Duke of Edinburgh Award scheme that, along with dedicated teaching time each week for 'leadership skills' through our bespoke and accredited curriculum, helps to build a sense of pride in a specific and highly prized qualification. Every student also benefits from regular one to one mentoring and coaching from their academic tutor who monitors their performance daily.

We encourage SELF-AWARENESS through the 'King's Experience', a series of annual pledges, trips and excursions designed to raise our students' cultural awareness and make them aware of their place in the world and not just the world inside King's Leadership Academy itself.

We look to encourage PROFESSIONALISM through our personal mentoring scheme, with each new Year 7 student buddying up with a student in the year above, who is then expected to act as their mentor and friend throughout their first year's study. Lessons in public speaking, our Academy Parliament – selected by the students from the student body, and designed to represent the needs and wants of the students to the Academy staff – and the nomination each day of a student 'Greeter', whose job it is to be the leader of their class for the day, are all methods by which we hope to develop professional habits in our students.

INTEGRITY and RESPECT are highly prized as well through our weekly lessons of thoughtful moral reflection to help reinforce and practice these values. We also look to develop these values in our students by constant reference back to the ASPIRE code they each sign upon entering King's Leadership Academy and by personal reflection sessions at the end of each learning cycle. We also invite a range of ethnic and religious speakers into school to address our students and expose them to peoples and cultures they might not yet have come in contact with.

Meanwhile, our student court, a respected subcommittee of the Academy Parliament, works alongside staff to ensure high standards of respect and behaviour. Students accused of infractions against the ASPIRE code can be brought before the court and, if found wanting by their peers, be assigned extra duties, or asked to make a public apology to the student body as a sign of atonement.

Importantly, when students misbehave and we as teachers – or the student court – must intervene, we couch it in specific terms. When we must impose a sanction on a student, we are doing so because they have behaved in a way not in keeping with the values to which they subscribed when joining the Academy and, as such, each violation becomes an opportunity for a student to self-reflect and grow morally. In this way, we argue, they are not letting us down; they are letting themselves down, by not holding themselves to the same standards as their peers around them.

In essence, by not enforcing rules or consequences as per traditional ethical frameworks and instead by reinforcing what Aristotle had always championed, practical wisdom or phronesis, this enables our students to do the right thing in the right way through strong social norms and a culture of collective responsibility. Why is this so important to our schools?

In a famous study, titled *Fifteen Thousand Hours*, researcher Michael Rutter concluded that this is exactly the kind of culture that reduces the chances of student drop out to less than 10%, compared to an almost 50% chance of drop out and delinquency if a child attends a school where poor behaviour and discipline is the cultural norm. This finding is reinforced by the fact that in five years we have yet to do a single fixed term or permanent exclusion!

ENDEAVOUR permeates all of these things, and this ability to set long term goals, to persevere and develop resilience, is the oil through which all the other values in our ASPIRE code can be transformed into habits. It's here that James Arthur of the Jubilee Centre makes perhaps his most important point in his interrogation of Duckworth's notion of grit. Grit – and, by extension, all of the character virtues we have identified – can, according to Arthur, only truly be inculcated in a student when the conditions are right.

Importantly, that doesn't just mean the school environment, nor the policies and attitudes of our teachers but rather, it points to something fundamental about our students themselves – for, as Arthur emphasises, a student can only ever be ready to absorb the lessons of their environment if their own mind-sets allow it, if they themselves are open to progression and change. With this in mind, we must turn to the next stage in the process we put our students through at King's: now that we have educated them in the values we expect them to acquire, we must equip them with the day-to-day norms and routines that will allow them to access those values and use them.

Nowhere is this more important than in the field of the mind and a crucial understanding of the way we ourselves think.

EQUIP
"Be careful of your deeds, for your deeds become your habits"

Learned optimism

We have spoken a lot about the culture of schools. Educating our students in the value set we had defined was an important first step, but perhaps of even greater importance is equipping them with the social norms and rituals that allow them to act on those virtues and establish themselves in school, work, and later life. This next section of *The Power of Character* will examine what equipping our students means on a pragmatic, tangible level and we won't stop there. There is a fundamental mind-set central to everything we do at King's, one without which the rest of the school could never successfully run, and one in which every person involved in the organisation needs to invest if the school is to enjoy continued success.

Let's all think back to a time when we were at school and starting out on a new skill, be it in a mathematics lesson, on the playing fields or in the music department. There were moments, or subject areas, where skills may have seemed to come to us almost naturally and there were other times where we found it particularly difficult to get beyond the most basic of tasks. Looking around the room, there may have been others who appeared to pick things up very quickly as if they were born with an innate aptitude for that particular skill or subject; some were just natural athletes, artists, musicians or mathematicians after all, our inner voice no doubt said to all of us at one stage.

How many of us maintained that sense of rejection throughout life for a particular subject or skill because things did not come to us as easily as we perceived it did for others? Did we even pass down this same mind-set for a particular skill to our children in order to preserve our ego? What the research shows is that whilst a higher IQ or particular body shape may give us a slight advantage when beginning to learn a new activity, our mind set to want to keep at it, to persevere and accept we can improve and gain mastery in a particular skill explains why some people flourish at things whilst others flounder.

Much of this work over why people choose to pursue or not pursue their time to learning certain skills or subjects is part of broader branch of positive psychology known as 'Achievement Goal Theory'. How we typically conceptualise goals either to satisfy our 'ego' (where we try to surpass the performance of someone else) or the 'task' at hand (where we try to surpass our own past performance) can have a remarkable effect on how long we persevere for, our levels of satisfaction versus self-imposed anxiety and, ultimately, how successfully we execute such goals. A sub theory of this is drawn from the work of Professor Carol Dweck, formerly of Harvard University and, at the time of writing, Stanford University, and it concerns whether we have 'fixed' or 'growth' mind-sets.

Mindset

Like all of the best theories, Dweck's work, first popularised in her defining *Mindset: The New Psychology of Success* published in 2006, can be boiled down to a very basic principle – and it mirrors one of the inferences of Peterson and Seligman's own defining work. Is the mind a fixed entity, unchanged by our experiences and attitudes, or is it much more malleable, capable of radical change across the breadth of our lives? Is our level of intelligence something we are born with, or is it something we acquire through hard work and dedication? It's a question that brings us back to Aristotle and his proclamations on character: do we do the right thing because we have virtue, or do we have virtue because we do the right thing? Dweck characterises her theory as being the difference between a 'growth' or a 'fixed' mind-set: do we believe our intelligence and character are immutable, or do we think they can grow and change? And how does our mind-set influence the ways we learn and teach?

Dweck began her career at Barnard College in 1967, and went on to be awarded her PhD from Yale in 1972. From a very early point, her principal research interests concerned personality and development – and, like my own, the science of motivation. Her earliest research focused on the response patterns of schoolchildren, and how some persist in the face of failure while others retreat as soon as the going gets tough. These early interests developed into a body of work across the 1980s in which she aimed to identify and define the 'theories of self' that drove these behaviours. It was this that led to her most ground breaking work on intelligence and how we perceive it in ourselves and others.

Dweck is a fascinating scholar with some of her simplest, most clearly realised ideas running counter to the assumptions of the day – in particular the idea that praising children can be dangerous. She went as going so far as to say they could have a negative effect on their well-being and sense of self, or how strategies we think might motivate others can actually impact negatively on their thirst and desire. Dweck was fiercely critical of what she saw as the deficiencies in how educators of the 1980s and early 1990s were attempting to cultivate a strong sense of self-esteem in their students, arguing that "if praise is not handled properly, it can become... a kind of drug that, rather than strengthening students, makes them passive and dependent on the opinion of others." It was Dweck's contention that giving our students straightforward tasks simply so they could be more easily accomplished, and then lavishing them with praise for it, was completely counter-intuitive. Rather than rewarding success and giving our children a sense that they could achieve great things, what Dweck said was that this belittles the student. Rather than making them confident of their intelligence because they have succeeded in their assigned task, the more natural assumption is that they think themselves stupid, not fit for higher tasks, perhaps even being patronised by their teachers. According to Dweck, the principle was correct – if students feel good, they will achieve – but the way it was accomplished was all wrong.

This simple argument was reflected in everything I'd seen of classroom life since embarking on my teaching career. The grade inflation we'd seen across the previous two decades, with examinations made easier and softer subjects grafted onto the curriculum to satisfy the quotas of Ofsted inspectors. The way teachers – myself included – had bustled classrooms of under-achievers off for residential weekends and returned them to school on a Monday morning with their exam grades already guaranteed? GCSEs in fish husbandry, diplomas in hospitality achieved in only a few days of study and yet equivalent to GCSEs that should have taken two years, our practise of constantly re-entering students into their GCSE mathematics and English examinations until they scored highly enough to be rated successful?

All of this had been intended to satisfy school inspectors and performance tables but, according to Dweck's thinking, its by-product had been to diminish our students faith in their own abilities, their own intelligence, and in doing so to limit their aspirations. At first glance it sounds oxymoronic but by helping our students get 'targeted' grades more easily, we were actually making them feel less able than they naturally were.

Martin Seligman has a term for this kind of trap: it's called 'learned helplessness'. When a person endures repeated negative situations, they often fail to learn how to avoid these situations and, eventually, they give up trying, submitting to the situation instead. Seligman conducted experiments with dogs that proved how helplessness could be acquired. In the experiment, three sets of dogs were given random electric shocks – but two of those sets were also given the means of stopping them by way of a lever built into their enclosure. When those dogs discovered the lever, they could stop the shocks at will; but the third set, whose lever did not function, was genuinely helpless for the purposes of the experiment. After this pattern had been established, all three sets of dogs were moved to different enclosures where, although they would still be shocked, they could easily escape by vaulting over a low wall. Tellingly, the sets of dogs who had been able to control their shocks in the previous enclosure quickly vaulted the wall to freedom. The last set, who had been unable to control their shocks, didn't even try; they had learned to submit to the shocks, learned how to be helpless.

A possibly apocryphal experiment involving monkeys points to the same conclusion. In this experiment, a psychologist put five monkeys into a large cage, along with a simple stepladder crowned with a bunch of ripe bananas. Naturally, the monkeys spotted the bananas straight away but, when the first monkey began to climb the ladder to reach them, the experimenter doused him with water from a hose. Importantly, he then went on to spray each of the other monkeys as well, even though none of them had gone for the ladder. Soon afterwards, once the monkeys had dried off, one bold monkey attempted to reach the bananas again only to be doused in cold water again, and for his compatriots, again, to suffer the same fate. After a little while, when a third monkey made his play for the bananas, the rest of the troop cottoned on; fearing being doused in cold water again, they leapt upon their friend, pulled him down from the ladder, and began to beat him.

The experiment becomes even more interesting next – for, at this point, the experimenter began to remove these monkeys out of the cage and replace them, one by one, with monkeys who had not been doused with any water. Quickly sighting the untouched bananas, the first new monkey raced for the ladder – only for the other monkeys to pull him down and beat him. Soon after, a second new monkey was introduced and, predictably, went for the bananas himself. Again, the other monkeys pulled him off and punished him for his infraction.

The most interesting thing was that this time, even the monkey who had never been doused in water joined in the punishing. Eventually, all of the monkeys who had been doused in water had been rotated out of the cage. Yet, the monkeys in the cage, none of them ever having felt the cold of the hose, continued to leave the bananas untouched and to punish any newcomer who tried to reach them. The lessons of these experiments are clear: learned helplessness is real, and learned helplessness spreads.

Fortunately, though, what Seligman and Dweck are telling us doesn't stop here. If helplessness can be learnt, it follows then that so can more positive mental attributes. Seligman even wrote a book about it; his *Learned Optimism* of 1991 is the founding text of the positive psychology movement. Its central thesis is that positive patterns of behaviour can be learnt just as easily as the negative. Optimism, Seligman declares, is a learnable trait just like arithmetic or ice-skating.

He proved that the cycle of learned helplessness could be broken. In an uplifting coda to his shocked dog experiments, Seligman taught the helpless dogs to escape their electric shocks. Cajoling or encouraging them did no good. The only way of doing so was to actually manhandle the dogs, moving their legs as if to replicate walking, and showing them how to jump up and out of the electrified enclosure. This brings us neatly on to one of the most important ramifications of Dweck and Seligman's complimenting works: once the dogs were forced, physically, to escape, they suddenly reacquired the ability to escape of their own accord. For we, as educators, the messages are clear: somehow, we must break the cycles of low aspiration and learned helplessness that we have ourselves been promoting. It can be done but, to do so, we must go back to the mind-sets through which we teach.

There is broader evidence to show that our actions – be they deliberate or instinctive – have a direct bearing on the way we think and feel. It might sound backward, but the scientists agree and the nuance is important: we do not always take action because of the way we feel. Rather, we can feel a certain way because of the things we do. Our actions and emotions tug and pull against each other in the most extraordinary ways.

In his popular book *59 Seconds*, the psychologist, and literary trickster, Richard Wiseman has a simple and stunning example, one which you can easily replicate as you're reading this book. Wiseman instructs that his readers take a pencil and clench it between their teeth. Upon doing this, most people's natural tendency is for the corners of their lips to tweak upwards, imitating the position of an instinctive smile. And, guess what? Those people imitating a smile report feeling genuinely happier. Rather than our bodies reacting to the processes of our minds, our minds can react to the processes of our bodies. Wiseman's trick feeds on the work of 19th century philosopher William James, who together with the Danish physician Carl Lange originated the 'James-Lange Theory of Emotion'.

The theory is simple to sum up but has untold ramifications for the way we think about ourselves. To explain, it might be most useful to use James' own example. In an article of 1884, published in the philosophy journal *Mind*, James posited the question: what happens when we see a bear? Is it that we see a bear, become frightened, and consequently run? Or is it, rather, that we see a bear, start running and are consequently frightened? What is the stimulus and what is the reaction?

Deconstructing what might be thought of as the natural order of thoughts and action has important consequences for how we approach teaching at King's. James and Dweck are both defining the same thing – that we are what we do – and Wiseman's pencil trick is the perfect example.

Sweat the small stuff

In 2004 I was invited along with a number of colleagues to attend a private briefing from Sir Clive Woodward, the head coach for the England Rugby Union side that triumphed in the World Cup of 2003. Sir

Clive had been a Leicester teammate with our head of branch within the RAF and had kindly agreed to speak to us about the core elements of his book, *Winning*. What fascinated me most was not so much the strategic thinking that took place off the field and in preparation for the field of play; rather, it was what he termed the 'critical non-essentials', a series of rituals and routines that, though non-essential on paper, Sir Clive viewed as critical to the winning mind-set of the team and what would lead to their World Cup victory.

The half-time change into a fresh shirt, the change of fabric from the traditional thick jersey to the new skin-tight material we see across many sports today, the eye coaches who developed greater spatial awareness of the players, the GPS tracking of every player on the field to monitor movement, the motivational posters plastered across the players' tunnel and dressing space, and the team chef that prepared all meals for the team home and away.

All of these and countless other examples could, Sir Clive passionately believed, make the marginal difference between winning and losing. His argument was not that a new shirt physically transformed a player; it was that these small things could create a new mind-set, a new professionalism in a game that has only just been afforded professional status. In this new world, culture and ethos trumped all: if the mind-set were looked after, the rest would follow. Sir Clive Woodward is not the only sportsman to have come to the same conclusion. Andy Flower, the Zimbabwean cricketer who, as coach, helped the England cricket team reach the top of the world rankings, had a similar approach – one that even led to the team jettisoning their most empirically talented player, Kevin Pietersen, when he was deemed to upset the team spirit in too dramatic a manner. For a team to succeed, Flower knew, culture and mind-set had to take precedence above all other things.

Taking on board the lessons learnt from Sir Clive, in 2005, I then had the privilege of being part of a small working group of fellow officers on what would become our strategic focus for the years ahead – 'Winning Spirit', facilitated by former fast jet pilot John Peters, who along with his co-pilot John Nicol, were shot down and tortured by their captors during the First Gulf War.

In addition to talking about his own experiences as a fast jet pilot and as a prisoner of war, he also spoke about the winning mindset of colleagues in the Red Arrows. You would be hard pressed to find another team in the world which better encapsulates the ethic of excellence to that of the RAF's Aerobatic Display Team. Made up of a team of nine aircraft, these are professionals who epitomise the habituation of advanced flying skills to such an extent that they are world leaders at getting the basics right and perfecting every controllable detail.

Their skills have become so ingrained through a highly tuned level of automation; it frees capacity in their working memory to focus more on superior aerial display skills that would be incomprehensible to any other fast jet pilot. It is this level of supreme competency, flying 100 feet above the ground at speeds over 400mph whilst withstanding forces of gravity up to seven times the norm, which enables them to do death defying aerial displays in front of millions of people each year with the same level of precision display after display. Further, when anything other than the norm occurs, in times of poor weather or visibility for example, pilots have such a wealth of information stored in their long-term memory that they can easily adapt to the situation at hand.

Yet, it was not until we saw first-hand how the team de-briefed one another post-training or display, that it became clear how 'what they do' surpassed anything which an untrained eye could spot – each pilot literally took their formation alignment via a single bolt on their opposite wing man's air frame, less than six feet away – to them anything less than perfect was not good enough and millimetres out created a fresh opportunity for repeated, purposeful practice and refinement.

Just like on the parade square during initial military training where new recruits practice and refine marching sequences over and over again until perfection is reached, the principle for the red arrows was just the same. This is the concept that you drill the critical knowledge and skills in a highly focused manner, adapting the goals that continually stretch people out of their comfort zone, all of the time providing immediate feedback. Decades of research provide clear evidence of what Aristotle had said all along – "you are what you repeatedly do". When we continually repeat and refine positive actions it will not only become an automated habit for life, it frees up space for new learning to take place to pursue the path to excellence. Scientists call this phenomenon 'chunking' and is the basis of how our caveman brains were able to turn all familiar routines into automatic habits in order to save time and preserve energy. The critical factor in all of this is to know or become self-aware of when a particular habit results in positive change (and you do more of it) or when the opposite is true (and you need to change it).

More recently, Sir Dave Brailsford, Director for Team Sky Cycling, has termed a strategy that led to his team's unequivocal success and one able to pinpoint, practice and refine positive habits as 'aggregated marginal gains'. Brailsford, who keeps the heart of his thinking close to his chest – given the success it's helped him achieve – has a very simple philosophy, but it's the attention to detail that makes it so fierce.

According to Brailsford's philosophy, it's easy to neglect the one per cents, too easy to shrug something off because it's minor, or incidental, or you think it doesn't matter. Brailsford's principle is that these little things add up, that pounds are made out of pennies. To put it in a way that dovetails perfectly with what we're trying to do at King's: almost every habit, good or bad, a person has is the result of the many small decisions they make over time.

In other words, if you take care of the detail and do all of the basics right, the larger things will take care of themselves. Too often we convince ourselves that change is only meaningful if there is some large, visible outcome associated with it. Most people talk about success and life, in general, as an event. We talk about losing fifty pounds or building a successful business, or winning the Tour de France as if they are singular, one off events. The truth is that most of the significant things we achieve in life do not stand alone in this way; they're the culmination of the countless moments when we choose to do things one per cent better or one per cent worse.

Brailsford discovered that aggregating these marginal gains could make a huge difference to the success of Team Sky, even down to the finest of details into how team members were trained to wash their hands to avoid infection. At King's, we make the active decision that the one per cents matter and that if we take care of the one per cents then the whole will take care of itself.

At King's, this thinking manifests itself in certain practises intrinsic to the way we run the school. We emphasise how crucial aspirations are to us through quotations, images and symbols plastered across the walls of all our learning spaces. Just like some of Woodward's critical non-essentials, displays depicting our students by year group with their graduation year and year of university entrance, are placed prominently in areas where students congregate. This constant reminder of the futures we expect for our students only underlines the aspirational qualities we are hoping to instil in them. The door of every classroom is inscribed with the name of the leading university for that subject. On the adjacent sign is the favourite book and flight path of the subject teacher.

Our intent in immersing our students in this environment is to make clear the opportunities available to each and every one of them. This constant celebration of mission and values is seen as a constant expression of what is most important in the school: values as the bedrock of our culture, traditions and history as a means of shaping contemporary objectives.

Just like what Aristotle had preached during the third century BC and as what the Red Arrows and Team Sky currently do, we practice, repeat, and refine a core set of rituals and routines with rigorous formality so that they too become an automatic and habitualised cornerstone of our student's long term memory.

At the start of each lesson, each student, upon entering the classroom, is expected to shake the hand of their teacher who welcomes them into their lesson. The importance of a good handshake is the first lesson our students receive on beginning their career at King's. On the first day of their first term, we stress the importance of making a good first impression and – as always at King's – we teach our students why; in this case how, whether consciously or not, we all make judgements within the first seconds of meeting somebody new and how we can turn this to our advantage.

Through explanation and modelling, we show how to shake hands: how to approach a person with confidence, how to keep eye contact as you hold out your hand, how to have a firm grip without having to prove yourself, how to maintain the grip as you say hello – and, finally, how to release the grip yet maintain eye contact at all times. Once our students are educated in the process of shaking hands, have practiced it in a low threat environment and are provided with feedback, we help to turn this into a habitual action by the shaking of hands at the beginning of each lesson. In effect, our students shake hands with their tutors seven times each day and then, to take students out of their comfort zones, we expect them to greet visitors to the school in exactly the same way. When visitors arrive at our classrooms, we ask first that they knock on the door, rather than waltzing straight in.

As part of our routines and rituals, each class has a designated 'greeter', a student leader of the day, and it is the greeter's responsibility to open the door, welcome the guest, firmly shake their hand and talk about their aspirations for the future. We are educating our students in why we shake hands, equipping them with the skills to do so, and empowering them to do it of their own volition. It's clear our focus on the rituals have lasting effect: parents have routinely informed us about how their child's confidence has risen outside of school. One particular story that sticks in mind is of an 11 year old visiting his dentist for a routine inspection and automatically shaking the dentist's hand on entering the room.

At the end of each morning break and lunchtime, the entire student body of King's lines up. We first began this ritual because we know from experience that these were the moments in our former schools when fights tended to break out among the student body. It also affords us the opportunity to reinforce our values, and to give our students vital experience of leading others. The line-ups begin as simple games during induction week, ordering from shortest to tallest, but slowly we work towards harder tasks, forbidding our students from communicating and encouraging the line-ups to be taken seriously. The line-ups are entirely student-led by the 'leader of the day'. This serves as a chance for any student, of any age, to take charge of the entire student body, to speak publically and take responsibility for the way the line-ups are conducted, reinforcing the three S's – Straight, Serious and Silent.

Similarly, we nominate eight 'duty leaders' per day. It is the responsibility of these students to spend their morning breaks and lunchtimes on duty. This can take the form of yard duty – collecting litter, or otherwise tending to our school ground – and checking the standards of the students around them; it might take the form of helping the caretakers keep the dining halls clean and tidy. Whatever the duty, the principle is the same: service of the students who surround us, and deep-seated and meaningful respect for the school institution itself. To emphasise the importance of this we return to the story of the New Zealand All Blacks – a team whose most senior players must 'sweep the sheds', or their changing rooms, themselves, rather than leave it to professional cleaners to clean up after them. The English cricket team, under head coach Andy Flower, were told they would no longer have attendants to carry the team's kit and that they would each be responsible from this moment on.

All of this, stiff formalities aside, is to encourage the very same thing that Wiseman encourages in his pencil trick, that James and Lange were grappling after with their philosophical enquiry into bears and the reason we fear them: by asking our students to observe the specific rituals of courtesy and respect, we're not only drilling them in how to behave in situations they'll find themselves in beyond the school gates; we're letting that sense of respect, courtesy and acknowledgement of others filter back into their minds.

We are drilling their bodies in how to shake hands, track someone with their eyes, hold correct posture and more, but at the same time we're drilling their minds in the precepts behind those actions. We're saying that these are not just arbitrary codes of conduct that exist because they have always existed, that students have to subscribe to simply because the school leaders demand it; these are manifestations of the fundamental building blocks of good character: common courtesy, mutual respect, valuing others and the simple ability to empathise with our fellows by acknowledging them as human beings just as worthy of our attention as we are of theirs.

We are following Wiseman's dictum but, in doing so, it takes us right back to Aristotle and his ancient observations: by making these actions habits, we elevate the character. It's exactly the same principle by which raw military recruits are transformed: the packing of a Bergen exactly to specification; the scrubbing of the bathroom floors to a shine; the dismantling and reassembling of a rifle so many times that a recruit can then do it blindfolded or any of the other hundred rules which had to be obeyed during training.

As Brigadier John Thompson states, everything that comes out of the military colleges, be it Sandhurst, Cranwell or Dartmouth, have to be 'inch perfect'. It's easy to argue that these tasks are a waste of time because once they're accomplished to an instructor's satisfaction they're never done again yet the real purpose is to ingrain an automatic response and cultivate dedication to community and peers. The actions are not only the actions; they're a way of cultivating character. By training yourself to be disciplined in the small detail – sweating the small stuff – you make it a habit to remain disciplined in the larger, more important areas of your work and life that can have greater consequences, especially when life or death split-second (usually moral) decisions are often required within all the confusion and panic found on the battlefield.

High expectations, no excuses

It's clear that there are ways in which the values we have identified can be developed through action. None of this is possible without making sure our students are fully invested in the idea that their characters and intelligence can change. What's more, Dweck has another observation to add to the mix, one that might even eclipse everything else because her research has shown that, whether or not the evidence proves that intelligence is malleable, those students who believe it to be malleable perform much better in academic tests than those who believe their talents are fixed and innate. Her data has shown that first measuring whether they have a fixed or growth mind-set can reliably model a students' academic performance.

As far as this thinking goes, whether or not intelligence and character are truly malleable barely matters, what matters is if a student believes they are or not, and it's this attitude, more reliably even than academic prowess, that can predict success. Think of it as a Pygmalion effect, or self-fulfilling prophecy.

The Pygmalion effect, taking its name from Greek mythology, is the phenomenon in which higher expectations lead to an increase in performance. Robert Rosenthal and Lenore Jacobson first coined it in their study of classroom activities, which clearly demonstrated that teachers who have a higher expectation of their students get higher results. Its corollary, the Golem Effect – the sense that, when little is expected of us, we achieve little in return – is named after the creature of Jewish mythology and is another kind of self-fulfilling prophecy. Often, as Dweck would agree, we are pre-programmed to fulfil what is expected of us, for better and worse.

This is remarkable stuff. Dweck's work gives absolute validation to the idea that, by nurturing a growth mind-set in our students – which by extension means ensuring we have a growth mind-set among our staff as well – we can place our students in a better position to both perform well academically, and perform well in the world beyond the school gates. How do we achieve this at King's? How can anything so intangible as a mind-set be nurtured or taught? Well, as luck would have it, Dweck's research goes on here as well, and we have drawn on it considerably in how we cultivate these attitudes at King's.

Dweck's idea that a growth mind-set opens the door to greater ambition and achievement might have come in useful earlier in my own life and that's part of the reason we became so determined to ensure our students at King's could be nurtured in it from the offset.

As a child, my aspiration was always to become a professional squash player, having taken up the game from the age of eight. I loved the game and played it every day. My weekends would be taken up with junior squash training camps or tournaments and I was very lucky to have parents who were always willing to give up their free time and ferry me all over the country to play. When I was 14, my dad became a partner, later sole director, in a squash and fitness club and there we were lucky enough to be the training hub for a local professional player, the first pro squash player for the county of Cumbria. It was during this phase of my life that I learnt an important lesson about your 'stretch zone'.

Training with a professional, my fitness and skill repertoire were always put under immense pressure as I struggled to keep up. However, this gave me immense advantages as my physiological development improved several fold times quicker than it had in previous years of training with people at the same or lesser standard. I soon learnt that, in order to improve, it was not just a case of endless practice. Practice had to become purposeful and at a rate that pushed you to a limit not too hard nor too easy, but just above where your skills level and experience level intersect. In psychological terms, this state can be described as 'flow', a theory on peak performance developed by Mihaly Csikszentmihalyi, the University of Chicago psychologist. The 'flow' experience is a unique one because it is intrinsically rewarding. In our flow zones, we become utterly absorbed in what we are doing, paying undivided attention to the task.

I often share a story with students about when we know one's character has been 'shaped'. We tend to remember actions which bring us incredible joy, or equally incredible pain or embarrassment, as it is these moments which intentionally shape who we are. I tell our students that, over the course of their education at King's, they will each sit in the main hall several thousand times. Yet, in later life, they will remember all but a few of those occasions. The occasions they remember – receiving an award, presenting an assembly, being told off for not listening – become engraved into one's mind, because it has shaped our character.

Well, aged 14, I had a moment that shaped my character. Unfortunately for me, it was not a pleasant experience nor one which I had been prepared in advance for on the psychology of mind-set and the importance of a growth mind-set. Reaching the semi-final of a national junior squash tournament, I was drawn to face the number one seed that was a player from the county of Yorkshire. All other counties feared them for their strength in depth and having the top players in the country at most, if not all, junior age groups.

This player was also the number one player in the country at the time, and as we were warming up, his 'England' T-shirt played as much mind games with me as I can imagine the Haka of the All Blacks does to opposing teams. What I had not predicted however, before we played, was being beaten 9-0, 9-0, 9-0 and not gaining a single point. Aged 14, in front of players my own age, I took this embarrassment as a personal failure and knew from then on in that I would never be able to make up the gap between where I was and becoming a professional player.

I had become convinced that the 'talent' of that player was innate or that, perhaps, the system in Yorkshire was so superior to mine that I could never compete. They must have been putting something into the Yorkshire water as some might say, some kind of magic. What I had completely failed to realise or appreciate was the incredible effort he had put in to 'become' so good. At King's, we teach a principle of leadership grounded in self and social awareness called 'Self Deception' ran by the Arbinger Institute. The main premise of Self Deception is to think 'out of the box'. Are you in the box? Well the statement that often helps, is 'the problem is, you don't realise you are actually the problem.'

At the time, the only obstacle to me progressing in my chosen field was me. Rather than appreciate all of the hours of training this player had undertaken to become so great, it was much easier for me to deceive myself and accept that this player was simply born with incredible talent to play squash. I accepted the mystery and magical side of his performance rather than the mundane hours and hours of practice every evening and every weekend. In doing this, I was taking all accountability away from my own shortcomings. In other words, I was letting myself off the hook by making excuses.

If I had continued in the same mind-set, I would not be where I am today. It was towards the end of my officer training that I finally learned the principles of optimism and having a growth mind-set. Two weeks prior to graduation, when the end of the programme was so nearly in sight, I fell at the very final hurdle. The major exercise of the 24-week programme was about to begin: a ten-day simulation of a conflict loosely based on the war in the Balkans, known as 'Exercise Peace Keeper'. This exercise took place on a military site away from Cranwell, where all the trainee officers lived and operated in the field, working either 12-hour day shifts or 12-hour night shifts. In the middle of the exercise, I found myself struggling to cope with the demands of two, ten-hour shifts as leader.

I was verging on complete panic, in real anxiety of the situation. Sure enough, when we were taken back to Cranwell for our de-briefing, I received the news I had been dreading. Along with ten others, I would not be graduating from the programme, instead I would be sent into remedial training for a further six weeks and then asked to retake the exercise. It was one last chance. The news meant joining a new squadron, it meant not graduating with the people I had started out with (to add salt to the wound, it was going to be a member of the Royal family as a special graduation reviewing officer). It meant going back to the drawing board and beginning again, this time with the knowledge that I had already failed once at the process. If we failed a second time, we would be ejected from the RAF.

It might have broken me, but by the end of the six weeks of remedial training, we were more prepared for the final exercise, both professionally and personally, than ever before. Having had the additional training and preparation, I scored full marks on both my leads – a total transformation from what I had achieved on the last attempt. It remains one of my proudest achievements, and perhaps it is no coincidence that this was one of the first moments when I understood the gift of a setback, the power of optimism and the importance of having a 'growth mind-set.'

Behavioural change is one of the most important challenges facing not only King's Leadership Academy, but also every progressive school in the nation. The principle behind it, as Dweck and Seligman showed in their contrasting ways, is simple. If we naturally become the things that we do, it follows that we must make the right choices about our behaviour and allow that to feed back into our mind-sets. If forcing a smile really does stimulate the chemical signals that evoke happiness, then we must force a smile. If a dog can only be taught to escape its persistent electric shocks by having its keeper force its legs into an imitation of walking, then to teach growth mind-set we must adopt its mannerisms.

We must go through its motions, teach our students the ways to approach their studies, and lives outside the classroom, with actions that typify those of people with growth rather than fixed mind-sets. We must get the culture correct; open our students up to the idea that their intelligence and character are not immutable things. We must release them from the fear of failure that comes with growing up, show them how to embrace challenges they might once have thought of as too difficult with a fresh and open attitude, one that sees the possibilities rather than the limitations in failure.

We must remind them that we all started out in life like my daughters: tiny human beings with no knowledge, no experience, nor any fear of trying new things and failing, a thirst to learn by trial and error. We must teach them that being the best is not the goal of education, that the process of learning is itself the end goal. This runs counter to the traditions of education across the past several decades, but – while accepting that the system of instruction and examination is not likely to change in the immediate or near future – we must shift the focus to the learning and not the result.

Dweck's *Mindset* chronicles the many and varied ways she has approached the teaching of mind-set. Her workshops stress a very simple maxim: nobody thinks of a baby as dumb because it can't speak, nor a toddler dumb because he or she can't do simple arithmetic. Yet, somewhere along the way, we begin to close ourselves off, we think of ourselves as less than intelligent if we do not automatically succeed at a given task; we begin with the capacity to grow, but somewhere along the way we become fixed. Meanwhile, the patented 'Brainology' system is a set of learning materials and workshop events that illustrate, to young children, exactly how the brain works and how it can be trained like any other muscle in the body to become stronger.

It helps educators to instil these beliefs in their classes through activities designed for exactly this purpose, activities that foster resilience, impart vital strategies for coping with failure and tackle the perennial problem of how to keep students motivated in the face of persistent setbacks. Above all of these things, though, one thing is fundamental and that is making sure the transition from a fixed to a growth mind-set is genuinely achieved. Too many schools and other organisations have taken a token interest in Dweck's work and, by sending their staff members away on mind-set training courses, believe they have successfully crossed from one mind-set to another.

In reality, this is analogous to the quick fix culture and the way teachers package off students for residential weekends, crash-coursing them in qualifications that they have not, by any rational standard, earned; grade inflation by any other name. Dweck argues that the first step to transitioning from one mind-set to another is a full and thorough understanding of what those mind-sets are and how they're dictating the decisions we make. This is not a grade that can be achieved and quickly forgotten, a certificate to put on the wall and be proud of. Going on a mind-set training course might be a good first step in adopting a new growth mind-set but teachers who've done so just to tick the correct box are, at King's, very quickly found out.

Changing mind-set is as much a life choice as it is a career one; it demands a rearranging of our attitudes and priorities across the varied aspects of our lives. We can only impart it successfully to our students, and expect them to carry those lessons on into future life, if we are completely invested. Education 2.0, then, is about much more than using a fancy trick of the mind to bolster our student chances of getting the best grades and, by that, access to a higher level of education. It's about the subtle, but most important, change we'll ever make in our outlooks, one that, by definition, will touch every corner of our lives.

Why, though, is developing the growth mind-set so important? Why do we put such onus on it at King's Leadership Academy? According to Dweck, the benefits of the growth mind-set far surpass the advancements it might offer in academic or scholarly performance. Its real world ramifications are huge. How far can somebody go in their work life if, when confronted with new challenges, they shy away because they think their talents are immutable, that the possibility of learning new things and expanding the mind ended the moment they graduated from school or university? How successful will a person be in their personal relationships if, having reached a difficult juncture with their loved one, they find themselves locked into old patterns of behaviour, unable to adapt or evolve the traits of their characters causing the clash? The growth mind-set, Dweck argues, is a vital tool for navigating a path through all of these things, the ability to develop and grow being relevant to every aspect of life.

This section of *The Power of Character* is concerned with how we build on the values that we have already educated our students; to equip them with the habits of action that will give them the best chances of success in later life. In part one we looked at the way the rate of technological progress has outpaced the changes in our social institutions. Perhaps, we contended, education just is not keeping up with the times. How can our schools best prepare our next generation for the adult world when, with such rapid and destabilising change, we can no longer accurately predict what the adult world will look like, or what the demands of its workplaces will be? Well, if the one of the drivers of Education 2.0 is to teach our students how to learn, as tautological as that might sound, the growth mind-set is key.

Failure is the route to success

Recalibrating to a growth mind-set is a long-term decision. Students with a fixed mind-set might see the end of their school days as the end of their education, or have the sense that they are now fully equipped for whatever travails life will throw at them. In a world of constant change, where a person might be expected to change careers multiple times across their working lives, this is clearly flawed thinking. According to a Future Workplace survey of 2012, 91% of millennials (those born between 1977 and 1997) expect to stay in a job for less than three years. As a rough estimate, this would mean undertaking between 15 and 20 jobs across their careers. The average worker of today is similarly skewed: as of 2015, workers in the United Kingdom stay at each of their jobs for just less than four and a half years.

For people transitioning from job to job, and especially those crossing sectors or reinventing themselves with each fresh transition, the fixed mind-set can curtail careers, constantly putting roadblocks in the way to future advancement. People with a fixed mind-set see the advertisement for a new job and think "I'd love to do that", only for it to be swiftly followed with, "if only I had the skills!" People with a fixed mind-set might go into a job interview and, confronted with a question for which they have no answer, clam up and beat a retreat, deciding that the job simply wasn't right for them after all. Ask a person with a fixed mind-set how they feel when they have to work hard to accomplish something, and they'll say, "If I have to work that hard, it means I can't have been smart enough in the first place". For people with a growth mind-set, effort is a positive thing – because it means progress, learning, and an active engagement with a process.

The same mentality is true for the students at our schools. Faced with a task they feel they will find insurmountable, students with a fixed mind-set freeze, declare the task too difficult and see effort as a waste of time that will inevitably lead to failure. Students with a growth mind-set might still recognise the difficulty of the challenge, might still expect to fail, but they will see the effort put in as part of a process towards becoming better. They will think of the effort put in, even if the challenge ends in failure, as part of a journey toward mastering the subject. At King's, we emphasise the normality of failure by our regular 'Failure Weeks' which we call 'Gap Weeks'.

At the end of each seven week block of teaching and immediately following a formal assessment, we turn our attention not to the aspects of study our students are doing well, but to those gaps that remain in their knowledge, the areas where they have stumbled or found their studies most vexing. We even dedicate a whole week to it every two months. Our message is a simple one, though at first it seems backward: we do not want to examine the things our students are doing right, we want to turn our attention to the things they're doing wrong. Organisations with a fixed mind-set want to chalk up the successes and turn a blind eye to the failures along the way.

Where a growth mind-set permeates the culture, failure is seen as a natural part of the process and, only by embracing it, does it become a step in the journey towards mastery rather than a dead-end. In his interrogation of the airline industry, 'Black Box Thinking', Matthew Syed makes exactly this point: the reason the airline industry is the safest in the world (in 2014 the chances of being involved in a plane accident were over four million to one) is because they celebrate failure. They forensically pore over every accident or near miss. In the airline industry there is no stigma attached to reporting mistakes; it's actively encouraged. If this model works for some, why should it not work for others? Can you imagine a world where your chances of being failed by your education system were less than one in a million as opposed to almost one in two in this country?

Gap Weeks are crucial, we aim to celebrate failure – or to make it a part of an everyday schooling experience – at whatever junctures we can. At King's, we want to create an environment in which each lesson is a journey from failure to success and to keep our students' curiosity building across each hour long period. To do this, each of our lessons begins with a hypothesis, a statement that our students have to either reject or confirm and, in either case, to provide evidence why. These hypotheses or statements are directly inspired by the kinds of questions students interviewing for a place at our highest ranked universities might be asked. So, for instance, at the start of a science lesson, we might begin with the assertion, 'Ladybirds are red. So are strawberries. Why?' The disarming simplicity of the question might lull our first year students into thinking the answer is straightforward but, if they were to try and answer the question straight away, most would probably fail. If you just teach children knowledge through lots of equations and how to use them, students may become just as good as the teacher in solving quadratic equations.

At King's, we want them to be able to do something with this knowledge outside of its direct context and begin to see interconnected patterns between subjects or concepts. By gradually building up knowledge and skills across the week, we look to shepherd our students to a place where they will be equipped with the intellectual architecture to provide a successful response to the hypothesis at the week's end and from which knowledge about similar concepts become easier to grapple with. We are actively showing them that the move from failure to success is an achievable process, that lack of knowledge is nothing to be ashamed of. Failure is all a part of the process known as education.

Gap Week has a practical purpose as it helps us to pinpoint those areas of academic study where students have fallen behind, and to individually tailor our responses. Its real purpose is much broader than that: Gap Week is the single most strident way we have of engendering a growth mind-set in our students. It is emblematic of the mind-set itself. By making failure central, we diminish its threat. By making it part of the process, we ensure that students know, from a very early point, that failure is a natural part of education.

By giving our students the opportunity to embrace failure, what we're really saying is that you can get better; intelligence is not a binary thing, nor is it fixed in place. By refusing to shy away from our failures, not just celebrating the things we can already do well; we're giving our students carte blanche to try. Dweck's work was very clear on this: people with a fixed mind-set, even those who believe wholeheartedly in their own innate intelligence, often trap themselves by not trying. Faced with an unfamiliar situation, a person with a fixed mind-set might either feel themselves too ill-equipped to try, or, in the event they consider themselves intelligent, too afraid to attempt a new challenge for the fear they might be found out, their immutable beliefs about themselves shaken to the core.

Those with a growth mind-set are used to failure, they consider it natural as they have retained, or perhaps even regained, that love of the learning process we all had as young children. New experiences for them are not threats. They are not challenges that have to be conquered at all costs. They are just that: new experiences, to be explored, enjoyed, or not, as the case may be. By allowing failure to exist, we take away its power. I remember with admiration (although with some fear at the time) the words of our recruit drill Sergeant at Cranwell: "Squad, today will be your worst day. But, tomorrow, after giving 100% today, will be your best day yet." In other words, we can and must always strive to become better versions of ourselves – the pursuit of excellence must become a habit regardless of what life throws at us.

Top Gun teachers

At King's, Gap Week is not the sole preserve of our students. Our staff is subjected to the same processes and it's our fervent belief that holding our teachers up to the same measures as their students is key to making sure a growth mind-set permeates all levels of the organisation. Staff are observed five times each year (with new staff also being observed weekly for the first term) and all of our staff training is personalised around their specific areas of weakness, in a direct reflection of the way Gap Weeks work for our students.

The supposition is simple: since we are asking our students to invest in the idea that they do not enter our school as either 'intelligent' or 'not intelligent', of 'poor character' or 'good character' and leave it the same way, we should not expect our staff to have similarly rigid beliefs about their talents as educators. In fact, at King's we are less interested in the particulars of a teacher's skills when interviewing for new posts than we are in the character of those candidates and, indeed, we recruit new staff entirely on the basis of their values, and how confident we are that they will invest wholeheartedly in the value system of the organisation. The staffing crisis in modern schooling is very real and, for King's, identifying the right staff is of the utmost importance. Firstly, candidates do not come armed with a trialled and tested pre-prepared 'outstanding' lesson or presentation – they have an hour to prepare one on the day of interview itself when we set a particular lesson topic or presentation question. Second, our interviews do not include the questions our candidates might expect.

There are no regulation questions about strengths and weaknesses, the ability to work as part of a team or to think on one's feet. Rather, we're interrogating the values of our candidates. "Who is the best candidate among those of you interviewing for the job?" we might ask, hoping to see both a confidence in the candidate's own ability and also a reluctance to immediately denigrate the qualities of their competitors. We might ask: "Are you the teacher you thought you'd be when you entered the profession?" hoping to identify whether that particular candidate has a fixed mind-set, convinced of their own competence, or a mind-set that will help them constantly reinvent and grow.

It's a process we all have to invest in if King's is truly to be a growth mind-set organisation. Nobody can be exempt, and even the school leaders, myself among them, must consider themselves on a journey of development. I can clearly chart the ways I have grown as a teacher across the lifetime of King's Leadership Academy: my increased ability to personalise lessons to different levels of ability; my improved style of questioning, not closing off avenues but phrasing my addresses in such a way that they better encourage fuller responses, higher orders of thought. I can clearly chart my weaknesses too, and be unashamed of proclaiming them. For me, my development has come about most prominently in the way in which we mark and feedback to our students' about their work.

When I was at school, our books were marked once a month and, looking back, this feels incredible. By the time our work was being marked, we had already moved on to new topics and debates. Further, there was also a sense of learned helplessness when we received our books back. By marking, highlighting and correcting our mistakes, our teachers actually trained us to be helpless, and not be held accountable for our own actions and shortcomings. As such, we were never trained to re-read, check, correct, improve or reflect on our submitted notes against any form of exemplary work. A week is also a long time to a student; a month longer still. Without real-time feedback, as soon as is reasonably possible after a piece of work is undertaken, how can students benefit from interaction with their teacher?

When I began my teaching career, marking was a chore that we, as teachers, had to endure. The dreaded weekend mornings that had to be devoted to it before any form of relaxation could begin or the constant reminder every time you opened the car boot and saw a pile of books waiting to be marked. Like many other teachers, my motivation in marking was that if I didn't do it, my head of department would find out and I would be disciplined for it. Teachers in this mind-set, as I was, are being externally motivated, and coerced into marking their students' work. Some teachers might only mark students' work regularly to assuage a feeling of guilt that might well up if they do not. This is just as much of an external motivator as the fear of being disciplined for not meeting a target. Similarly, lack-lustre marking – simply flicking through a students' work, offering a perfunctory comment and a tick – is evidence of the 'me first' quick fix culture we were trying to avoid in founding King's. This is a style of marking that prioritises saving a teacher's time and effort over genuinely cultivating good practise and learning in our students. In the end, it is a lose-lose scenario.

Providing timely and constructive feedback to students is one of the most important tasks we can undertake as teachers, equally it has to be carefully managed to ensure a work life balance for our staff. We are only too aware of the numbers of great teachers leaving the profession in their droves because of the insurmountable pressures of book marking, lesson planning, and observations, to name just a few. Feedback is critical to putting our students – and, in parallel circumstances, our staff – at being in our state of flow. This is the point at which we are pushed just out of our comfort zone, into what Csikzentmihalyi calls our 'stretch zone' or that zone where we are constantly being challenged so that new learning is constantly taking place. Ever tried to teach yourself a musical instrument? Those who teach themselves to play an instrument often report a sense of 'plateau', a time when their natural learning ability peters out and, without the guidance of a tutor, they fall into a pattern of playing the same old pieces over and again, enjoying the ritual but never getting any better. Without the feedback and guidance of someone further down the road, their talents are never stretched. They move out of the 'growth' mind-set, which would encourage them to constantly grow and get better, and slip into a 'fixed' mind-set, one which reinforces the false belief that this is who they are, what they are, and that they will never take the next step.

For people in their mid 30s to 40s, the film *Top Gun* can often score in their top ten films of all time (or is that just me). Whilst not everyone knows that *Top Gun* actually exists (as the U.S. Navy's Strike Fighter Tactics Instructor programme) fewer still may make the link between the principles of training detailed in the film and Csikzentmihalyi's theory of Flow. *Top Gun* was formed during the latter stages of the Vietnam War when ariel combat during the mid-1960s saw more American fighter jets being out manoeuvred and shot down than their MiG flying opponents. *Top Gun's* mission was to train an elite group of fast jet pilots into their state of flow by pushing them to their aerial and physical capabilities by an even more elitist cadre of 'friendly' trainers, playing the role of enemy MiG pilots and flying their aircraft. Every day, having been pushed to their limit to see what was capable, using different tactics for different scenarios and all the time gaining high quality feedback to improve, it pushed them into a constant state of development.

The results of *Top Gun* were dramatic. Between 1970-1973 over 12 times as many North Vietnamese fighter jets were being shot down compared to American planes, even though the number of planes in the skies stayed similar to pre-1969 levels.

Taking inspiration from this model of training, at King's we see constant feedback as a way of keeping our students – and through constant appraisal, our staff – in a state of flow. For this to work, feedback on performance has to be immediate or real time, developmental and accurate. Since the foundation of King's, and through constant staff training and on-going debate, I have seen my own mind-set regarding marking (or live feedback as we call it) change dramatically. Where marking was once a chore to be endured, now I see reviewing books and making notes on a cribsheet as a reflection of my teaching and as a way of interrogating what my students were getting right but, more importantly, what they were getting wrong each lesson. Now I was ready to adapt the content, seating plan or types of questioning for the next. I have come to see the immediacy of feedback as a vital tool in how I plan and feed forward the most effective forms of delivery into my next lesson, recognising that there is no point in moving on from one topic to the next when students are still making common mistakes.

In effect, I have moved from a mind-set in which the motivation to mark my students' work was driven more by external factors, by words such as 'ought to' and 'have to', instead changing it to a 'want to' mind-set driven by more internal motivators. This includes the desire to be better in my chosen career, to be proactive, to develop my own talents and hold students personally accountable for their submitted work and get them to improve. When I had bought into the real purpose of checking students' work – and how that reflected on not just my students' performance, but my own as well – I could take the first steps to developing a mastery of my subject, and marking became less an extrinsic-led activity ('I do it because I have to') to being a self-directed, intrinsic led activity ('I do it because I want to do it – this is important to me'). This subtle shift allowed me to invest so much more of myself in the activity and to unlock a deeper sense of motivation.

At King's, recognising weaknesses and failure is a vital developmental tool for staff as well as students. Staff are given feedback on a weekly, often daily basis through our coaching programme. They are given deeper feedback every seven weeks via a more formal and in depth observation model. In effect, we treat our staff in precisely the same way as we do our students during their formal Gap, or Failure, Weeks. The principle is that we keep both staff and students in a state of constant learning, or persistent 'flow'. We do not mark them down for the things they have done poorly, or incorrectly, but identify the focus areas for them to develop over the next learning cycle. We break the skill down into weekly chunks and provide real time feedback at each stage. We all observe each other weekly in dedicated 'walk though' slots as part of our timetable, with classroom routes discussed, plotted in weekly coaching meetings and written into our personal action plans to identify the best teacher to observe for a particular focus. New staff at King's are allocated a personal coach from a senior team of practitioners who are there to constantly challenge their thinking and daily practice. They are even timetabled to do their weekly planning at the back of more experienced teachers so they can pick up the routines, expectations and teaching techniques from those who have done it for longer.

The goal in all of this is just like the Top Gun pilots – to gather quick and candid feedback to improve and help internalise and refine new practices and increase the speed we act to our constantly changing conditions. In other words, to make our OODA loop more refined and effective. The analogy we use at King's is that it would be pointless to drive a car by constantly looking in the rear view mirror; we must drive by looking forward through the windscreen. Acknowledging past mistakes, or poor performance, is important but brooding on it, or being overly critical of oneself, is not. We configure our feedback to encourage development, rather than to criticise. By embedding an interrogation and celebration of failure in the way our school works, by placing an emphasis of firmly 'doing it' at the heart of the organisation, we put the growth mind-set at the heart of everything we do.

As the school continues to grow year on year and as we welcome a new set of staff to the academy, the need to bring these staff closer to the level of the best performers becomes ever more important. As such trainees from the previous year become the trainers for the next all aligned in the purpose of sharping our skills and the drive for continuous improvement.

Shining lights

King's is not the only school challenging long held conceptions about what constitutes good teaching and how best we can instil good patterns of behaviour in our students. Other progressive schools are also charting new territory in their efforts to equip students with the tools – be they practical, psychological or emotional – that they will need to succeed in later life. In London, the Floreat Education Academies Trust (founded by Lord O'Shaughnessy, Conservative peer and Baron of Maidenhead) is dedicated to building programmes of character education in its primary schools. Floreat's mission, which expands as they add new schools to its 'family', has important mirrors with King's. By harnessing the power of character and virtue development at an earlier age, it seeks to harness the power of character education when children are at their most impressionable.

The Floreat 4C system is a neat parallel with King's 3Es: by focusing on CURIOSITY, CHARACTER VIRTUES, CORE SKILLS, and CULTURAL KNOWLEDGE, their stated aim is to "enable children to flourish by developing both their minds and their morals." This is a holistic approach, rooted in the belief that a society has a responsibility to cultivate good values in its children, that cultural knowledge should be widely shared, and that schools are society's best tool for developing the kind of world in which people are curious, hard-working, are good and do good for others.

The organisation styles its type of study as one that is 'taught and caught', with classroom lessons first addressing the types of virtuous behaviour they seek to instil, their especially-tailored Virtue Literacy programme using children's stories to explore ideas of character and virtue in class, and finally their 'Service Learning' initiative giving students the opportunity to practise these virtuous behaviours, first inside the school and then out in the wider community itself. The approach is analogous to King's EDUCATE, EQUIP and EMPOWER but, at Floreat, the range of virtues they look to develop is broader, and further broken down. At Floreat, bravery, humility, forgiveness, gratitude, empathy and perspective are all traits with specific 'character' lessons and specific practises attached, yet are virtues also reinforced throughout the academic curriculum by the people studied in history, the stories taught in English, the depth of problem solving in mathematics, all of which can have ethical dilemmas and famous role models attached.

Another London establishment known as School 21, in East London, approaches character education in a subtly different way. Its founder and principal, Peter Hyman, a former speechwriter for Tony Blair – places a heavy emphasis on oral skills and student well being. School 21, which caters for students aged anywhere between four and 18, was founded out of the belief that too many young people were leaving school without the qualifications needed to realise their dreams. Importantly, even those students who had achieved good grades at GCSE and A level, were under-prepared for a working environment that demanded different things: creativity, the skill to adapt and continue learning, forthrightness and good interpersonal skills.

For the founders of School 21, the traditional schooling system had made even high-achieving students unimaginative, too focused on exam preparation and exams, too quiet and unforthcoming. To remedy this, School 21 focuses on developing another set of values analogous to King's: expertise, professionalism, eloquence, grit, spark, and craftsmanship. More importantly, it places the responsibility for developing these attributes into the hands of their students themselves.

Students are encouraged to reflect on their learning; on the way they have approached projects, not only in academic ways but also on their successes and failures in resolving problems, or in demonstrating the school's designated character traits. Each student keeps a permanent and self-reflective portfolio, evaluating their approach to each of the school's characteristics and, rather than have lessons dedicated to these traits, they are expected to knowingly demonstrate them across each of their academic subjects. As history teacher Joe Pardoe put it: "At School 21, it's not that we don't have a character curriculum; it's that our curriculum is designed to build character." Much of this is inspired by the work of educational researcher Ron Berger – an American public school teacher, author of *An Ethic of Excellence* and founder of the Expeditionary Learning organisation – whose central tenet is that modern schooling is more about quantity than it is quality.

By redressing that balance – focusing on the quality of the time we devote to our students, not the number of qualifications to which we can guide them – we can begin to get more value out of the everyday schooling experience. This conscience of craft, what School 21 terms 'Beautiful Work', helps to develop a working environment underpinned by Berger's ethic of excellence that inspires responsible attitudes to school, homework, and performance on the part of the student taking personal responsibility of their output. As a result of students developing mastery in a particular area, high-perceived control becomes part of their self-image, which makes them more likely to be self-efficacious in other areas too.

These are just two of the many schools now investigating the benefits of good character education – and many of them under the auspices of the Jubilee Centre, and its national listing of schools of good character. King's Leadership Academy is just part of the sea change in how we are re-evaluating the purpose and processes of education. These schools might vary in how we all approach the same challenges – defining our value systems differently, focusing on different traits and methods of habituation – but our differing visions of Education 2.0 still have one vital process in common: the need to first educate in a virtue, then to equip our students in the tangible practises and mind-sets necessary to act on those virtues; and, finally, as we will now see, the need to empower our students with the confidence and wherewithal to carry those virtues onward into later life, to turn them into habits that characterise their behaviour outside the school gates and into whatever field of work or study they enter next.

EMPOWER
"Be careful of your habits, for your habits become your character"

The Nelson touch

Educating our students in our proscribed value set, then equipping them with the habits and mind-sets necessary to generate success, means nothing unless our students are empowered to act on the values that they're now steeped in. Having the confidence that they will make good decisions across the rest of their lives is the next vital step to Education 2.0, and in this section, we will turn our attention to the future: what motivates us and keeps on motivating us, how can a student take control of their own lives and their continuing education, and how can the most modern theories on autonomy and the perception of self, impact on our work in education?

In part one of *The Power of Character*, we touched on the principle of Mission Command, which is the sense that soldiers in the field must be empowered to make split second decisions, or else risk dramatic losses of life. Countless lives were squandered, in conflicts of the past, when soldiers were treated as the mere tools of their generals, safely hidden in garrisons and command tents behind the front-line. They were confronted with unexpected circumstance, relaying orders from above before responding. The fierce resistance on the Normandy beaches of June 1944 is only one of a great number of stories plucked from the annals of history in which soldiers, unable or unwilling to make decisions of their own, paid the ultimate price for their hesitation.

In modern, urban, 'asymmetric' warfare, there are no longer any certainties. Insurgents have stopped playing by the so-called predictable 'rules of war', suddenly the bigger and less manoeuvrable forces have become the most vulnerable. The military cannot afford for commanders in the field to make bad decisions that may result in the loss of civilian lives, nor can the countless lessons on the 'rules of engagement' be muddled or confused during the fog of war that risks the welfare and survival of themselves and those whom they command. The question is how do they prepare people to make good split-second decisions in such a fast-changing environment?

Brigadier Thompson uses the analogy of moving between oil and water to describe this change of fluidity in tactics: "as moving from the complicated to the complex. We must now train people and empower people to be able to react and morph quickly to the complex environment." As such, soldiers are tutored in the ability to make good decisions for themselves and quickly; rigorously drilled in the beliefs of their value-driven organisations through simulated practices and scenarios made as realistic to the battlefield as possible, so they can then be entrusted with the duty of making those decisions in the field. In essence, a person trained on good character is more likely to approximate the right decision in the heat of the battle during even the most high pressure and chaotic of moments.

I can still clearly remember the briefing that was to be my introduction to the principle of Mission Command, led by a senior Air Officer in early 2004. Over the Middle East, the skies were being patrolled not just by fighter aircraft, flown by experienced pilots of an officer rank, but also by unmanned air vehicles or UAVs. The difference was that, even though they had the same fire power as other aircraft, these UAVs were not being controlled in situ by an experienced pilot who had navigated his or her way through many years of formal education, university education, officer training, and several phases of flight training. Instead, they were being flown by an operative several thousand miles away at an air force base in Nevada, USA, sitting in front of one of the most advanced computer terminals available and holding a joystick. What made the Air Officer's account even more dramatic was that the person at the control was a young Senior Aircraftsman, one of the most junior ranks in the military. Yet, they had been delegated with sufficient autonomy to make a split-second decision and make a strike.

This was a paradigm shift: the rigidity and rigour with which decisions were made by rank had eased, and those closest to the information now took control.

Such is the strength of the value system in which all soldiers are educated that military psychologists can reliably predict the decisions they will make in situations of high stress. Research has shown that, to an incredible level of accuracy, those decisions are more often than not the same. The implication is extraordinary: there is a high enough level of correlation between the values in which a person is instructed and the decisions he will make in instinctual situations to reasonably assume that one has direct bearing on the other.

In his book *Team of Teams*, General Stanley McChrystal describes at length his use of Mission Command principles with groups of Special Force operatives under his command. Rather than waiting hours or days for a decision to be made once senior officials had assessed all the information held by troops on the ground, and then get it 90%-100% right, mission command was now able to empower the same troops to make split second decisions in the hope that they would get it right 70% of the time. In other words, their thinking was: better to get it right 70% of the time now than wait and for the moment to have passed.

What good, they argued, was a 100% approved and accurate decision if it was too late to be of any use? As it turned out they were actually getting it right 90-100% of the time straight away, this was because the troops were aligned to the intent of the commander and to the values underpinning the organisation.

The principle of Mission Command has historic antecedents that it is important to recognise. What we think of as the standard doctrine of Mission Command – that a commander gives orders in such a way that his juniors understand the mission's intentions, their own roles in it, and that they are then entrusted, within certain bounds, to do the job without being managed in detail from above. This was being employed in the German and Prussian armies as early as the 19th century.

It is likely that our own Admiral Nelson inspired these processes when he brought elements of Mission Command to the British Navy in the early years of that same century. As far as we can tell, Nelson realised that the key to successful naval operations rested in a form of shared consciousness after he survived the battle of Cape St Vincent in 1779. This particular battle, the opening salvo of the Anglo-Spanish war, was led by Sir John Jervis, an admiral who relied on signals to direct the ships in his armada as if they were the pieces on a chess board. Jervis being the only one making any real decisions, treated his vessels and their crews as extensions of his own.

As a result, the battle was becoming a long and drawn out chase until Nelson broke formation and sailed out of line to head off one of the Spanish vessels. Nelson had read the situation perfectly and used his initiative but no other ship did; instead, they waited until the Admiral understood Nelson's motives and instructed them to follow. It was a lesson that radicalised Nelson's attitudes toward leadership. A year later, when he set out to destroy the French fleet sailing out of Toulon, he did just that, by giving the individual commanders of the ships under his command a level of autonomy and decision-making powers previously unheralded.

This was a revelatory moment for Nelson and he would go on to develop it in bold and interesting ways. At the very core of his plan for the Battle of Trafalgar in October 1805 was what would later be termed as 'the Nelson Touch'. This is the idea that individual commanders should act on their own initiative as required. This was reiterated in his final piece of advice on 9th October 1805: "No Captain can do very wrong if he places his ship alongside that of the enemy." The strategy employed by Nelson and his fleet on 21st October was just the tip of the iceberg: the hard work had taken place over the many preceding months and years, through which he had trained his captains to think and act just like him; he nurtured a team where every captain would make exactly the same decision as Nelson would have done, had he been on that ship himself. If Nelson could succeed in implanting such a simple but clear framework of intentions in the minds of his captains and could then debate their own reactions, then it would follow that their minds would be prepared. Simply put, Nelson's intentions would become the same intentions as their own.

Of course, the supreme test of this kind of thinking comes when the commander is killed or removed from the arena. This was exactly what happened at Trafalgar. Less than an hour after the HMS Victory opened fire, Nelson was carried below deck injured. The battle would last for another three hours and twenty minutes and Nelson's fleet would ultimately be victorious, even though he was not there to direct its every move. What Nelson had done before the battle was of far greater importance than what he did during it. The lesson for today might be that Mission Command simply enables you to achieve more with whatever you have got. Its overall effect is probably best summed up in the words of army doctrine: "Commanders who are in each other's minds and who share a common approach to the conduct of operations are more likely to act in concert."

What does this have to do with Education 2.0 and our endeavours at King's? Well, the principles of Mission Command might have originated in the armed services, but only by accident or as a by-product of the times. Nowadays, the principles of Mission Command are in fact being employed by big business, government institutions, leading sports teams and all kinds of other organisations – from the big to the small. Companies from as diverse fields as Walmart, the retail giant of North America, The Ritz Carlton Hotel Group that is famous for its service and quality, and Valve, the computer game developer and distributor, are employing its tenets to maximise the potential of their staff. In 2014, Walmart's senior vice-president of talent development, Celia Swanson, reported that the inspiration for their adoption of Mission Command tactics came from observing the veterans employed in their stores, and how they carried the cultural values of their past military lives onward into civilian life. Gabe Newell, Valve's CEO, made headlines when he went one step further, declaring that there were absolutely no managers at his company, and that only by entrusting each individual to make their own decisions, free from any chain of command, could the perfect working environment be achieved.

When we give the people at the frontline more authority, good things happen. When we force them to push information up, it just creates more bureaucracy. The CEO of the Ritz-Carlton famously said, "My lowest paid employees have all the contact with my customers." In other words, if you want to know what's going on on a daily basis, it's the people at the frontlines who hold the key. The company is famous for the freedom it grants its employees and its Institute and Leadership Centre has welcomed tens of thousands of executives from other companies so that they too can learn from their practices. In the sporting arena, one of the most successful teams on the planet, the New Zealand All Blacks also use it as part of their cultural blueprint.

In his book 'Legacy', chronicling the history of that team, author James Kerr charts the development of Mission Command under Graham Henry's reign leading up to their World Cup triumph in 2011. There appears to be no coincidence why the team is so successful – they have a select group of generals on the field who take control of a situation that endless team training scenarios and managers prep talks could never begin to predict. The managers and coaches sit well away from the action on the field in the stands or in private boxes; their work is done long before the game is played. This stands in stark contrast to the many sports that appear to rely on constant orders being shouted from the sidelines from their manager.

All across the business world, leaders are waking up to the benefits of Mission Command and reaping its benefits in terms of share price, staff loyalty, and morale. In a sense, it's alarming that it's taken so long for the business world to wake up to the benefits of a system that, by investing in high levels of trust between senior and junior employees, can allow their organisations to become more flexible, to react more swiftly to the day to day realities of a constantly shifting marketplace, and promote strong cultural bonds.

Schools are no different. One of the clearest lessons I learnt in my first schools was how the lack of autonomy given to staff could diminish their engagement with the job, even in schools where strong leaders had worked wonders to impose a rigid culture and to turn a failing institution around. One of the central tenets of Education 2.0 is the lifeblood of a school is its teachers. To take the military analogy to its fullest, the teaching staff are a school's soldiers sent out into the field. If this is the case, then we must take the lessons that the military learnt as our own, empowering our teachers to take ownership of their classrooms, to make decisions for themselves – all within the confines of our shared values and culture. At King's, we seek to do just this: the school our teachers work in is theirs as much as it's ours, and in this sense of shared ownership we hope to find a very modern form of motivation. This also creates a win-win scenario, as when teachers feel empowered and respected, they are more likely to empower their own students and treat them with the same level of respect.

Motivation 1.0

What makes workers work is a debate that has been raging as long as there has been employment and the answers as to why continue to change. Think back to the middle of the 19th century, the explosion of factories, railways, and mills that came with the advent of the steam engine and the Industrial Revolution, and the answer seems straightforward. Workers worked because not to work was to fall into poverty and die, and a factory overseer quite clearly made decisions over the lives and deaths of his workers. For those workers, motivation was all about the traditional reward and punishment matrix, the 'carrot and stick': the carrot of their wages at the end of each week, the stick of the overseer's implacable gaze.

At the beginning of the 21st century, the question is not quite so simple especially in the UK, with its universal healthcare service, system of benefits, and other structures of support. Most of us have jobs, but what makes us perform in them, what makes us invest, care, and work to our fullest if not the threat of unemployment hanging over us? By extension, what motivates a student – by nature captive in a classroom – to learn? It's this question of motivation that has intrigued and commanded the attention of researchers like Daniel Pink, whose seminal work *Drive* charts the changing attitudes to motivation – and how we're on the cusp of a new age of understanding exactly what propels us.

Motivation was my own area of research, when I studied for my doctorate under the auspices of the Royal Air Force. Three years into my military service, tasked with researching how the military might create fitter, more robust soldiers, I began to spend half my time at the University of Birmingham. I would undertake an examination of the psychological determinants of exercise in order to better understand the motivational dynamics at play. Why do some people exercise regularly and others choose not to? Why do all service men and women spend the first years of their career exercising regularly (partly because they have to and partly because of the 'carrot' of meeting an end of course fitness level), then stop as soon as the 'stick' is taken away? Why do some people stop exercising, start again, then stop?

These are questions which have bewildered yet intrigued health and exercise psychologists for decades, and later I would find that they directly paralleled what is happening in our classrooms. Why do we all start off as curious beings with an incredible thirst for learning as babies and toddlers, then for this to shut down for many of us during childhood and adolescence? Why do so many children stop learning after compulsory education age? If the greatest resource educators can tap into is students' natural tendency to be curious and want to discover new things, why is education also a domain in which external controls are strictly imposed?

My early research revealed that, when formal fitness training ceases, new military recruits tend to retreat from continuing the practice. Rather than inculcating a way of life, or introducing that new recruit to new long-term habits, the end of fitness training was often the end of fitness itself. As it transpires, the recruits rarely bought into the vision of their commander – the 'intent', the 'why', the 'vision' for why they were undertaking fitness training in the first place – and, hence, they rarely undertook the behaviour of their own volition. This, I would later understand, is exactly the same top-down coercive approach seen in our schools. Learning is seen as a means to an end, the generation of good exam results, rather than a practice to be undertaken for its own reward. The question was: why was this happening, and what could be done to subvert it?

A common belief in the military is that physical training sessions are to be used as an aversive 'character building' experience: by putting recruits through increasingly arduous tasks, the military helps them develop strength of character and perseverance. At the same time, there was also an expectation that the participants should enjoy the process enough that they should voluntarily repeat the activity throughout their career – that these same arduous sessions would encourage the participant to volitionally come back for more. Holding both these things together in mind is a difficult task. Put together, they hold a somewhat contradictory message.

The effects of this are damaging in a variety of ways. Holding both counter-view points in head at once creates a kind of self-fulfilling prophecy, one I can also see across other 'educational' or 'training' environments. When the student (or in our case recruit) is no longer interested in what is being taught, the teacher (or in our case instructor) must resort to external controls to make learning occur. Rather than being engaging on a fundamental level, students have to be coerced into learning and that begets a vicious cycle: control only leads to more control. As my research showed, when new recruits stopped their training, a large proportion were never seen in the gymnasium again – even though those facilities were free, designed to be welcoming, and all recruits were given long lunch breaks with the idea that they would use them for exercise.

Something had to change. When the Second Gulf War erupted in 2003, the conditions – in extremes of climate and altitude – started to place immense physiological demands on all service personnel. The days of 'I don't need to be fit to do my job because I am a 45-year-old desk officer' were gone. If you were a service employee, you could be out on the front line at a moment's notice, regardless of age, rank or gender, and be in a working environment of 50-degree heat, living and operating in austere conditions. An unfit serviceman or women within a military unit could now not only have compromised the effectiveness of operations but also could ultimately have jeopardized the safety of themselves and others around them.

Equally, the physical demands of a particular role became dictated by extrinsic factors that could not be altered to account for a reduction in physical capability over time i.e. as one ages or puts weight on. Imagine a scenario on operations where a 50-year-old serviceman proudly stated: "I am not allowed to lift that because of my age or medical restrictions". The expeditionary warfare rule became that, if you were fit to be deployed, whether as a twenty-year-old man or fifty-year-old woman, you were fit to be asked to do the same thing. There could be no excuses.

This put the military's physical training regime into the deepest scrutiny. What were we doing that was not effective at developing long-term health and fitness in our recruits? What if basic training had established the correct motivational climate from the outset? Would it have made the exercise experience a more positive one for the participant, thus encouraging a life-long love of activity? Was it possible to motivate our recruits – and, by extension, our students – to motivate themselves?

Though my research led me to looking closely at patterns of physical exercise, more specifically it led me to interrogate our attitudes towards it. How could we motivate new recruits to better levels of physical fitness? What factors shape motivation? What drove some soldiers to higher levels of performance than others, what made some maintain that level of performance on a long-term basis?

All of these were questions that my research sought to answer but whatever the varied results of my investigation, one discovery underpinned it all. This was the idea that, for a soldier to be motivated to advanced physical fitness, outside motivating factors, our traditional 'carrots and sticks', were obsolete. The real route to creating fitter, more resilient soldiers lay in making exercise and health a 'habit' in their everyday lives – and this brings us straight back to Icek Ajzen's *Theory of Planned Behaviour*, and the idea that the development of the appropriate culture could positively influence the decisions a person made. The reason why some soldiers were successful in habitually exercising was just that – they had redesigned their lives after compulsory training had ended that enabled them to continue with this behaviour – the habit of exercising and associated motives were greater and more important than the reasons for not exercising.

I spent seven years earning my doctorate in the sciences of motivation and habit formation, collating and interrogating data from a broad range of subjects, but the principles of modern theories on motivation, especially as they pertain to the business world, are hiding in plain sight. All you really have to do to understand the new science of engagement and motivation is open any national newspaper and look at the preponderance of stories, rapidly growing since the economic crisis of 2008 and the policies of austerity that followed. Stories chronicling the abuses of low-paid workers, workers on zero hour contracts, or those working for the big multinational corporations whose power and influence has grown exponentially since the dawn of the 21st century.

Consider Amazon, the online retailer and distribution company. A worker in an Amazon warehouse, employed to fulfil orders taken over the company's vast website, is given a handset that instructs him precisely where to go in the sprawling warehouse, which packages to collect and where to take them. The handset allots him a specific length of time, measured in seconds, to find each product; as he moves across the warehouse, it tracks him, the seconds counting down, and sounds an alarm if he has moved off track or made a mistake.

A BBC investigation of 2015 found that such close monitoring and control had critical impact on the mental health of those employees. One remarked, "We don't think for ourselves. Maybe they don't trust us to think for ourselves as human beings." That the system is ruthlessly efficient and that the end result, the service to customers, has been rated as second to none by independent surveys, has never been in doubt. Neither is the fact that the company has the second highest staff turnover rate of all Fortune 500 companies with new staff staying, on average, for less than ten months.

It's not hard to draw the conclusion that the two facts are directly related: a motivated staff is a happy staff, but when every aspect of what makes us an individual is taken away, when we are not trusted with making even the smallest decisions, when our every move – in this case, even the pattern and timing of our footsteps – is scrutinised and controlled, our motivation evaporates. Anyone who has worked in a call centre, reading from a script without any opportunity for elaboration or improvisation, will recognise the feeling: when our actions are not our own, when we are playing puppet to somebody else's controls, what joy do we take out of our lives? Without joy, can we ever prosper and flourish?

Motivation 2.0

There is strong evidence to suggest that our happiness as human beings is directly related to how in control we feel of the journeys we are each on. Aristotle once described the good society as one which enables its people to flourish and be personally fulfilled – to have purpose and meaning, to master new skills and reach new heights and be able to connect with people in their social milieu – and one of the most prescient thinkers in this field for our time is a man named Edward L. Deci. Deci and Richard Ryan, his colleague, are the authors of *Self-Determination Theory,* or 'SDT'. This is a body of research that seeks to explain the very things that make us tick, one that has been instrumental in our Aristotelian approach to create 'the good society' at King's Leadership Academy.

I first came across Deci and the SDT in my military research, in the same moment that I investigated Icek Ajzen and his *Theory of Planned Behaviour*. Whereas Ajzen's theory investigates the antecedents to our behaviour and determinants over our decisions, Deci and Ryan's theory delves into why we are impelled to act (or in some cases not to act). Brought together, their theories describe a condition of living that might be called 'the pursuit of personal worth and freedom.'

Born in 1942, Deci is a Professor of Psychology at the University of Rochester in New York City, one of the United States' premier private universities. It is here that he directs the University's unique 'Human Motivation Programme.' His seminal work of 1995, *Why We Do What We Do*, seeks to distil all of the complexities of a lifetime devoted to the study of human motivation. Like all the best thinkers, Deci's principle might seem simple but it revolutionises the way we interrogate the way we act. The traditional view of motivation, Deci argues, is as an external driver – the sport's coach's pep talk to his team, or the motivational speaker's inspiration speech – but what Deci, along with his colleague Ryan, worked to prove was that lasting motivation comes from inside. Fraudulent motivation might come from the traditional carrots and sticks of reward and punishment, but according to these theorists the only genuine motivation comes from the authentic self that drives each one of us. "External pressure," Deci wrote, "can sometimes bring about compliance", but not motivation in its truest sense.

In fact, much of Deci's work has gone toward showing the difference between motivation and compliance, when we're compelled to do something by punishment or reward. It's in this grey area between the two extreme poles of motivation that Deci locates some of his most interesting thinking: an investigation into whether behaviour is autonomous or controlled, and what effects each have on us. Now, if I take you back to how my mind-set changed with regards to the daily task (some may say chore) for teachers of marking student's work, you will see how one's motivation can move up or down the continuum from at times being highly controlling to other times when it is more volitionally endorsed; or as Deci states '…the degree to which the regulation of a non-intrinsically motivated behavior has been internalised'.

A key principle of SDT is the more self-determined our behaviour, all of which are driven by three underlying and intrinsic human needs (more on mastery, autonomy and relatedness later), the greater the level of our intrinsic motivation and the longer we will repeat the behaviour and reap greater benefits. A further advantage of this theory is that it also explains how we can be extrinsically motivated for a specific behaviour; yet still demonstrate an element of self-determination in our behavioural regulation as this diagram shows:

	Continuum of Self-Determination				
	Low				High
Amotivation	Extrinsic motivation				Intrinsic Motivation
Belief related to Learned Helplessness	External Regulation	Introjected Regulation	Identified Regulation	Integrated Regulation	Intrinsic Motivation
'I mark my students book, but I am not sure why'.	'I mark my students books because I am told to'.	'I feel guilty if I don't mark my students books'.	'I want to mark my students books to learn new things'.	'I mark my students books because it's important to me'.	'I mark my students books because I enjoy it'.

It is Deci's contention that controlled behaviours run contrary to what makes us human – that the hidden goal we all share is the urge to express ourselves according to the dictates of our intrinsic selves, and to hold complete mastery over our purpose and direction in life. Deci argued that when we act autonomously, it infers that we are acting according to our authentic selves that also aligns to the upper stages of the continuum – identified and integrated regulation and intrinsic motivation.

This is similar to what Aristotle termed eudaimonia, the inherent sense of joy and personal fulfilment on completing an activity which is central to who we are and what we stand for. Yet, when we are being controlled through introjection and external forms of regulation, we are acting "without a sense of personal endorsement", and this makes our actions groundless (even hopeless in the form of amotivation); we're puppets rather than puppet masters. And just like when I was marking my books because I felt compelled to do so out of guilt or worried about getting into trouble from my superiors, actions pursued for these extrinsic reasons have been empirically shown to lead to ineffective, negative, and short-term behaviours.

Deci writes about the wide and negative effects of mindless compliance to controlling bodies – whether they be parents, lawmakers, educators or employers – with a sense of real vitriol. He calls it nothing more than 'profound alienation', and it's easy to recognise it in many aspects of our everyday lives.

Think back to a time when you've been compelled to do something. Then compare it to a time you've chosen to do something, and consider the difference of feeling and emotion between the two acts. Now consider the same act. When we choose to take the bins out on an evening to improve our living environments, doesn't it feel different to being coerced into taking the bins out by a family member or loved one – even though the two acts are identical? When we choose to visit an ailing acquaintance, doesn't that feel different to the times we would rather be doing something else but find ourselves bullied into it, or perhaps bully ourselves into it to assuage our guilt?

According to Deci, society has since time immemorial been built upon a reward and punishment basis. When we behave well, we're generally rewarded: a gold star at school, a bonus at the end of each year for a banker who's performed admirably for his company. This is the type of motivation we grow up with and which we implicitly understand. Is it the natural one?

Across the length of *The Power of Character* we have harked back to the joy toddlers and tiny children take in learning for learning's sake – that sense that an activity can be its own reward, and instinctively is, until we develop enough to start assimilating the way the world traditionally works. Might this not be the 'authentic self' on that so much of Deci's theory is predicated? As fortune would have it, others have carried out experiments with exactly this theory in mind.

The pioneering psychologist Harry Harlow's experiments with rhesus monkeys demonstrated that an activity could itself be the reward, with the monkeys consistently engaging with the puzzle apparatus Harlow gave them, despite there being no reward for the completion of any puzzle. Deci's own experiments went on to show that engagement in an activity previously found stimulating – a mathematical puzzle, a linguistic teaser – can actually decrease if a monetary reward is attached. It's for this reason, counter-intuitive as it sounds, that programmes designed to reward students for schoolwork by paying them to complete assignments have tended to fail wherever they have been introduced.

Traditional methods of motivation suggest that people are simply algorithms: we might respond to external stimuli, but not in a complex or nuanced way. If this was the case, why do children shirk at school? Why do we coast and become passive in jobs we once longed for? Might it not be that a simple reward system is not actually motivating to our authentic selves? Certainly this is Deci's thesis: that rewarding a person is, on some level, always interpreted as a method of control, and that, since human beings long to be the agents of their own destinies above all other things, rewards run counter to our instinctive goals. It might even be that we can see evidence of this in the events that led up to the economic crash of 2008.

Why was the reward – or bonus – system not enough for our bankers? Why do we repeatedly see bankers making riskier and riskier trades, taking greater and greater gambles – to the extent, in 2008, that it precipitated a global crisis? Might it be that the rewards of big pay run counter to the desires of the instinctive self? Might, in Deci's own words, "people's intrinsic motivation [be] undermined by extrinsic rewards"?

We have already seen how, when people are solely oriented toward rewards, they usually resort to the route that takes least effort in order to receive them. That's our 'quick fix culture' by any other means. As early as 1968, psychologist Richard DeCharms was espousing his belief that people have a fundamental need to feel masters of their own destiny even on a micro level, to know that they and they alone determined the choices that they make.

If we accept this logic then it follows, as Deci states, that both threats and rewards that 'coerce' in a kinder way provoke deep-seated feelings of negativity. Author and researcher Daniel Pink goes further. For Pink, the traditional carrot-and-stick matrix is flawed in seven deadly ways: it extinguishes intrinsic motivation; it diminishes performance; it crushes creativity; it encourages shortcuts and unethical behaviour; it becomes addictive; and, it fosters short-term thinking. Pink's example is particularly apposite for our structure at King's: "if students get a prize for reading three books," he says, "many won't pick up a fourth." Rewards do not set targets to aspire to; too often they set limits to our aspirations.

When companies are not meeting their targets, their instinctive response errs toward either reward or punishment: we either reward staff for increasing productivity, or punish them for not accomplishing enough. In schools the system is strikingly similar: children not trying hard enough will often find themselves in trouble, and those who do are often rewarded – either with intangible rewards, gold stars or certificates of merit designed to lift their self-esteem, or sometimes even tangible rewards. Various programmes have been trialled, offering cash incentives to encourage students to work hard and achieve good grades – but the debate about what best motivates students to success is fiercely fought.

There's a very clear argument that goes: if a student is not equipped with the necessary skills to achieve success in their examinations, how does offering a monetary reward realistically help them to do any better?

Very quickly we come back to the circuitous thinking of old, and Carol Dweck's findings on how the by-products of our well-intentioned endeavours can have negative impacts on our perceptions of self: by offering a monetary reward for success, what we are really saying to students is that they are being lazy, that they need to be cajoled, that they can do it if only they changed their attitude.

We are making the assumption that students do not want to learn, or that workers do not want to work – and that's a form of patronisation that builds barriers and fosters antagonism between teachers and students, between workers and employers; it is the engendering of an 'us vs. them' mentality to the detriment of us all. Rather than looking at the root cause of a problem that students might be under-prepared for their examinations, we are sidestepping the real issues. It's the quick fix culture of old. Even for students able to fulfil their exams, who do respond to cash incentives – and the evidence shows that, in some instances, this can be successful – our message is unclear. Rather than rewarding success, we are actually turning it into a transaction and that is the very thing that undermines the purpose of education in the first place. What's more, we're exonerating ourselves as educators; we're neglecting to interrogate ourselves and whether we're doing the best by our students, and instead laying the blame for poor performance on issues of attitude and effort.

Here's where Deci's *Self-Determination Theory* is vitally important. If we accept that one of the fundamental goals of human life is to achieve a kind of mastery, required to have self-direction, over our own destinies, then tactics of punishment and reward are necessarily obsolete. If the route to true motivation is in belying these traditional methods and moving beyond, then Education 2.0 can only locate the true spirit of motivation in empowering our students, putting them in the place where striving for excellence and achievement is a 'habit' in their everyday lives, making them masters of their own destiny.

Any attempt to do this, especially within the confines of a necessarily rigid schooling system, brings us back to questions of culture, educating our students in the right values, equipping them with the right mind-set to build on these virtues, and making certain the culture in which they work is so steeped in these virtues and mind-sets that they are empowered to act on them.

Start at the end

At King's Leadership Academy, Deci's *Self-Determination Theory* might be thought of as the engine room: the driving force that propels everything we do. Despite the time and energy we invest in establishing, inducting and educating on our values, despite the lessons we structure to equip our students with the social norms and rituals we perceive as a necessary part of success beyond the school gates, nothing we do inside the academy itself will have lasting effect unless we can empower our students to act according to those values.

Throughout their education, our students are encouraged to express themselves, to enter discussion and debate passionately without the fear of failure. They are shown, in tangible ways, that success in school and in life is not about innate talent but about applied effort, and that envisaging a bright future – the aspiration central to our ethos – is the first step to achieving it. Posters around school display possible futures: 'YOU TOO CAN BE A DOCTOR' announces one; 'YOU TOO CAN BE AN ARCHITECT' announces a second; 'YOU TOO CAN BE A TEACHER, A LAWYER A PILOT, AN ENGINEER!'

In a tactic inherited from the American Charter School system, classrooms are named after prominent universities so as to raise awareness of possible next steps in education and raise aspiration. Together with our learning cycles – targeting the things our students can do better rather than simply rewarding what they have already achieved – our Gap Weeks and our 'character passports', which track our students' skills from EDUCATE to EMPOWER and allow them to gain formal qualifications in coaching and as leaders of programmes, we are giving our students the mental tools to make their own life choices, to be able to envisage a future for themselves and then, through structured planning, make that future happen. Beneath it all, we're looking to access what Deci calls the 'true motivation' of the self: the motivation that comes to do better, to engage on a higher level, when an individual feels in control of their own lives.

In a rigid environment like a school, where a pupil's time necessarily has to be timetabled and where many aspects of life – what they wear, what structure their days have, what behaviours they are and are not allowed to commit – are proscribed from above, encouraging a sense of autonomy presents a significant challenge. Students have to attend school – so how to make them feel empowered, rather than coerced, by the experience? This close supervision in the classroom might sound like a child's worst nightmare, but in an atmosphere where students thrive, they come to appreciate the orderly environment as it makes learning easier – structure and stricture literally liberate learning.

Further, both inside and outside the classroom, social norms trump rules. Rules are a form of top down control whereas norms are self-enforcing. Rules are there to be broken, you cannot break norms; if you do, you only break your integrity and professionalism whilst losing the respect of your peers. Encouraging the individuality of our students, through self-expression – and a particular focus on the creative aspects of education, with Daniel Pink observing that people can express themselves more fully in creative areas than rigid academic ones because "routine work can be automated; artistic, empathic work cannot" – is important, but our focus on aspiration is key.

At King's, we try to fulfil our students' creative thirsts by dedicating every afternoon to the creative arts in the first two years of school, and a full afternoon of weekly creative enrichment for students in every other year group. If a student knows that their school life is building towards an ambition they personally hold, one true to their most fundamental selves, then their engagement in the learning process takes on a different pallor. School, for students with a specific ambition, is a stepping-stone to leading the lives they envisage, rather than a succession of hurdles put in the way to vex and frustrate.

It is for this reason that, at an early point of their King's education, each of our students builds a personalised 'Flight Path'. This plan, which they will keep with them, adapting with the turning of each academic year, is a document that has its headline as that student's ultimate goal – whether that is to become a doctor, a laboratory scientist, an architect, a teacher, or whatever other profession they choose. Beneath that, there is a breakdown of the steps the student will need to take in order to achieve it. So, if a student wants to become a veterinarian, the 'flight path' would show them what university degree they would need to attain and at what level; this would then dictate what A levels that student needed to undertake, this would dictate what choices the student should make at GCSE.

Young people's ambitions naturally morph as they grow and change and, at King's, 'Flight Paths' are never set in stone. If they were, they would run the risk of becoming coercive measures to be resented by the very students they're put in place to support but it is a vital tool in our lexicon. Through them we hand agency back to our students. The very existence of a 'Flight Path' is asking our students, "So, what do you want to be?" and telling them that we're here to help them achieve it. In these circumstances, learning is positioned as being for the students, rather than a problem they have to overcome simply to satisfy the school system. Our roles are transformed: we are not the cruel taskmasters in our student's lives; in a very real way, we're the servants, there to facilitate them in achieving whatever they desire. The mentoring we offer our students is therefore personalised, attuned to a specific 'flight path' and, ultimately, directed by the student. This might involve the setting of specific academic or character targets, tailored visits to universities or other important places outside the school, or the invitation of specific visitors to the school, designed to advise and inspire.

'Flight paths' are there to be ambitious, realistic, and unleash personal responsibility for every child whatever their aspirations may be. We accept no excuses for starting point or any pre-conceived labels they may have been allocated by their previous school – reaching one's goal is a consequence of setting the right path, working hard and making the right choices day in, day out.

For a student to know what they want is critical: it's the first vital step toward self-awareness and taking control of their own paths in life. In his bestselling book articulating *The Seven Habits of Highly Effective People*, author Stephen Covey emphasises the need to be "proactive" and to "start with the end in mind", both strategies we teach our students in the first year, as a way of making it clear that our ambitions are within our grasp, if only we know the right steps that will take us there.

We have all known people with big ambitions who, vexed by circumstance or lack of confidence, have failed to fulfil it and lived with regrets ever after. Seligman and others would call this a kind of learned helplessness. This is the trap that exists when 'I will' becomes 'I wish', when we lose our conviction that achieving what we most desire is possible and begin to look for excuses; or, instead of finding ways to make our dreams happen, fall back on the safety net of 'I could have been an X, if only I was more...' confident or intelligent, or whatever the most comfortable emotional crutch is for the individual in question. It's for this reason that we must empower our students to believe in their own abilities, that innate talent is just a myth and that anything can be achieved with the right focus and work ethic.

We have already seen how fundamental Carol Dweck's 'growth mind-set' is to life at King's – and how, only in ensuring our students believe that hard work and application can reposition themselves in life, how intelligence and character are flexible and how nothing is innate, can we unlock our fullest potential. How do you instil self-confidence and not fall into the traps that Carol Dweck has chronicled, those moments when, in seeking to do good, by bolstering our students' self-esteem, we in fact do bad, by undermining our expectations of them? How do you raise confidence and self-esteem without falling into the praise trap, or making our students dependent on the 'sugar rush' of satisfaction short-term praise can give?

At King's, we build confidence into our curriculum with lessons devoted each week to the skills of public speaking and the challenges of leadership. To enable students to become more 'mastery oriented' and to develop the growth mind-set vital to long-term learning, we praise students not for their abilities but for their attitudes and effort. Our rituals and expected social norms, too, go some way to building self-confidence. Remember Richard Wiseman's pencil trick, and how the body can itself relay a message of happiness back to the mind? Consider the way King's students are taught to hold eye contact, to track a speaker as they speak; consider the message these actions are sending back to the brain. These are the building blocks of self-confidence, the ability to hold one's own in conversation with, and presentations to, others – and underlying all of these factors is the importance of culture. For it is in culture that Ajzen's *Theory of Planned Behaviour* and Deci and Ryan's *Self-Determination Theory* intersect.

MAP: a new paradigm

Ajzen's work dictates that a prerequisite to developing good intentions is the confidence and self-efficacy that comes from knowing how our peer group might react in any given situation, and Deci's *Self-Determination Theory* suggests that to be properly empowered we must feel in control of our own decisions in life. This follows that only by putting our students in the most influential surroundings, only by exposing them daily to the values by which we believe they should live their lives, only by ensuring they absorb these lessons even when they are not actively learning, can we ever help them develop lasting character traits.

Understanding *Self Determination Theory* is a critical step in shepherding out students to brighter futures, but it docs not stop there. At King's, where staff's value sets are ranked equally with their academic credentials, empowering our staff is also a critical part of school culture. We firmly believe that it is not just what we teach, but how we teach it, or as the saying goes, character is both 'taught and caught'. Teachers who therefore espouse the human need for relatedness and whose positive, trusting relationships are founded on kindness and caring for others, will make a significant difference in children's lives. Without relatedness, a teacher's influence is greatly diminished, but with it, students are more likely to feel respected, secure and are more open to failure and strive to be more successful. Nowhere is the power of relatedness more evident than by psychologist and psychotherapist Haim Ginott:

> "I've come to a frightening conclusion that I am the decisive element in the classroom. It's my personal approach that creates the climate. It's my daily mood that makes the weather. As a teacher, I possess a tremendous power to make a child's life miserable or joyous. I can be a tool of torture or an instrument of inspiration. I can humiliate or heal. In all situations, it is my response that decides whether a crisis will be escalated or de-escalated and a child humanized or dehumanized."

The moral of this verse is that, as teachers, parents or leaders, we all possess a staggering level of influence to make a lasting impact, positive or negative, on a person's life. It is for this reason, that hung in every classroom at King's is the poem taken from an ancient Chinese proverb to remind our staff of their primary role as a craftsman of character:

> "Be careful of your thoughts, for your thoughts become your words. Be careful of your words, for your words become your deeds. Be careful of your deeds, for your deeds become your habits. Be careful of your habits, for your habits become your character. Be careful of your character, for your character becomes your destiny".

Our outward facing image, which manifests itself daily through our thoughts, words and actions, will also become our habits of character if continually repeated. Our words do not just impact how we feel about ourselves, they also impact how others think and feel. Even if we make hundreds of positive comments and actions every day, a single flippant negative remark, even if made from a good intention, could create its own legacy and ultimately change someone's destiny. Indeed, a 2016 global survey on what makes a great teacher had this very disposition voted in as number one by a range of educational stakeholders (including students themselves) across 23 countries; and, as such, we only recruit staff that can demonstrate the passion, enthusiasm and imagination to succeed in our environment. It doesn't stop here; hiring great staff is one thing, but ensuring they make the greatest contribution to the school is another.

It was Steve Jobs, former CEO of the technology giant Apple, who said, "It doesn't make sense to hire smart people and tell them what to do; we hire smart people so that they can tell us what to do". The sentiment can be applied equally to schools as it can business. Why seek to hire the best and then not trust them to be the best possible versions of themselves they can be? Why seek to hire talented individuals, only to micro-manage and direct every aspect of their careers, to the point at which they have been robbed of the intrinsic motivations that once drove them?

At King's, achieving the right balance of support and challenge for our staff is a seismic part of achieving the right aspirational culture. Creating this culture of constant aspiration is one of our primary aims, and here the writings of Daniel Pink are particularly instructive. In his study of motivation *Drive,* Pink describes a 'Goldilocks' situation for students and workers alike, one in which we are set tasks that are not too easy and not too hard. Tasks that challenge our current capabilities and allow us to develop a tangible sense of progression, but also ones that are not so difficult that they stymie us from the start, ones that encourage us to develop and grow without ever patronising us by making us feel we have been set tasks below our natural levels of ability.

It is here that the engendering of the growth mind-set and our sense of flow can truly be found. As with our students, we look to ensure a 'Goldilocks' zone for our staff by the employment of one important principle: leadership roles in the school, heads of department and other managerial roles, are constantly available and to be challenged for. An English teacher promoted to Head of English is secure in that role for only a year before others can apply – alongside the Head in situ – for the role for the upcoming academic year. If the middle leader currently in post has done a good job and hit their self-directed targets, they will be in pole position to retain the role for the following year should they wish to re-apply. Equally, if they have done a great job, they may have the confidence to apply for an even more senior post in this new round of middle and senior leadership roles.

All candidates are expected to write their own job descriptions based on the long term objectives of the academy, prompted by a single sentence 'vision statement' provided by the school leadership and describing what we expect of the year ahead. According to principles of Mission Command, we are not delineating how we expect this to be achieved, only what we expect to be achieved. The rest is up to each candidate to proffer. Through this we hope to develop a culture of constant aspiration, in which all our staff – ourselves included – are constantly aspiring to be better versions of themselves.

In the schools I first worked in, coasting staff were a curse; in residency, I had seen the most senior and experienced staff coasting in easy classrooms while the most inexperienced staff were left to tackle the most problematic. This is one of the most toxic situations for a school, when heads of department or other school leaders who achieved a particular role many years before no longer deserve to still be in the post – yet, because of labyrinthine bureaucratic process, are unable to be removed.

At King's, with a culture of constant aspiration and responsibility built on a shared value set, we have never seen coasting of this kind and if we do, it will be short lived because of our systems. The key to engendering this passion and drive in our staff is unlocking the potential for true motivation, as proscribed by Deci, Ryan and Pink. If the key to developing fitter, more robust soldiers in my own doctoral research was in determining what kind of value and culture they had to inhabit in order that health and fitness became an accepted 'habit' of everyday life, what kind of culture, and what specific steps, are key to making a teacher feel valued and committed to the schools in which they work, and the students whom they serve?

Across the business world, staff with a sense of ownership over their roles – if not their places of employment – report higher levels of commitment, motivation and productivity. Technology giants like Google go to great lengths to ensure the happiness of their workers: dishing out free ice creams; free lifts to work; free dry cleaning; and, perhaps most intriguingly, the opportunity to spend 20% of their time on projects that they can initiate and are entirely responsible for seeing through, with the absence of external pressures and scrutiny from higher up the chain of command.

The computer software giant Valve goes to similar extremes, having renounced all managers and allowing all staff the opportunity to create and direct projects of their own imaginings – all with the result that staff feel empowered, take ownership of the company's direction and, therefore, its successes. Research undertaken by Professor Alex Edmans of the London Business School suggests that there is direct correlation between the happiness of a company's workers and the returns of its shareholders – a fact that Edmans directly credits to how invested a company is in making its staff members happy.

Levels of autonomy come in many different forms. At Google and Valve it might be the opportunity to spend part – or the entirety – of the working day on a project you yourself have instigated. At smaller companies, it has been shown that something as simple as moving your desk, deciding where you work and who you work alongside, can have a disproportionate effect on how we think of our work and our levels of productivity.

In 2004, Deci and Ryan proved this themselves when, on studying the workers at an American investment bank along with Paul Baard of Fordham University, they recorded greater levels of job satisfaction in those employees whose bosses encouraged their own sense of autonomy. At King's, we seek to replicate this effect through our annual MAP projects. MAP – or Mastery, Autonomy, Purpose – projects are inspired by the work of author Daniel Pink, who himself uncovered the idea and branded it as 'MAP' by looking at the basic human needs identified in the *Self Determination Theory*. For Deci and Ryan, these are the three elements of true motivation that allow us all to move up the continuum from external sources of motivation and onto more autonomous forms to guide our behaviour. These are our natural drivers for self-efficacy and to **master** a particular subject or skill (what Deci & Ryan termed Competence); our **autonomy** in deciding what we will do and when and how we will do it, as expressions of our intrinsic selves; and our **purpose** and social capital (what Deci and Ryan termed Relatedness). Pink argues that the key to unlocking the highest levels of motivation is in dedicating ourselves to a purpose greater than us.

SODD off!

At King's, MAP projects reflect the business strategies employed by the various tech giants we have considered – Google, Valve and many others, who allot a certain percentage of their employees' time to employee-led and employee-driven projects, workers empowered to build and invest in projects of their own devising to enhance the company as a whole.

At King's, each staff member – school leaders included – is given a free period each week in which to work on a project of their own devising, without guidance or direction. These projects could be any manner of things and in the past they have included our Monarch System for rewarding students; our Wednesday Enrichment scheme, which makes every Wednesday afternoon dedicated to over fifty different extra-curricular activities; our Leadership Institute that allows our students to gain formal coaching and leadership qualifications and themselves help younger students progress. The one thing they have in common is that they are designed to better the school culture and experience, and they're being driven not by us, as school leaders, but by teachers and our staff on the ground who have direct experience of the aspects of school life that could be better, forgotten corners of the school experience that need their champions.

Through MAP, every single member of our staff – from new recruits to seasoned hands and school leaders – can embody our 'SODD' OFF principles, each one a derivative from Boyd's OODA loop: when they SEE a problem, they ORIENTATE a plan and resources toward it in order to solve the problem; they DECIDE to DO something about it and act in order to help improve the system. In this way, our MAP system is analogous with the Japanese philosophy of Kaizan, a common feature in Japanese industry.

According to the principles of Kaizan, everything that is done can always be fine-tuned and improved. What works well for the notable car giant Toyota can work well for us too. By focusing on an area of interest, MAP projects can be an excellent mechanism for staff to become experts in a particular field, and can be a superb catalyst for promotion too. To top it off, by completing a MAP project, staff start their journey in gaining Level 8 (or MPhil equivalent) 'Chartered' status as a leader and manager, through our partnership with the Chartered Management Institute ran in conjunction with our very own Institute of Character and Leadership (which originally came about as a teacher's MAP project!).

As I write this now, one MAP project stands out from the rest. MAP projects are more than a gimmick; they are the outward manifestation of one of King's core principles. Earned autonomy by seeking continuous improvement, the refusal to defer responsibility, and aspiration are all bound up in MAP. There is a saying that punishment and sanctions stop the rot, but only praise and rewards truly change behaviour from within. This theory is embodied in the Monarch System, one of King's Leadership Academy's most transformative MAP projects. Tom had been teaching at King's for less than half a term when he realised that the school reward system had become lethargic and lacking in enthusiasm. What he saw was a system that had been fit for purpose in a small school, but had not adapted to the needs and aspirations of students as they grew older.

For the past two years, good behaviour had been rewarded with raffle tickets in class; at the end of each week, these raffle tickets were placed into a pot and the winner selected for various academic prizes at the start of the whole school assembly. Tom had recognised that, because there were only ever two winners each session, the raffle tickets were being devalued. The chances of winning had become so slight that investment in the raffle by the student body was at an all time low. Stricture and structure had always been high on the agenda at King's, but now it was time to develop a system to celebrate success.

Tom's goal was to find a way of investing the senior year group at the time – those in Year 9 – to reinvest in the reward system. His first step was to look for inspiration from other organisations and through his

Teach First connections, he heard about a successful reward auction system being used at REACH Academy, a school for pupils aged 4 to 18 in Feltham, London.

At REACH, the end of each term was marked by an auction where students could bid for items with the 'praise points' they had been allocated across the term. Points were worth prizes and the more points a student had gained, the better the prize they could bid for and hopefully buy. Education companies such as Vivo have been selling a similar system into schools for some time – asking the school to pay an exorbitant annual subscription to the service and using their set point system for prizes that can be 'cashed in' at any time. The underlying problem with importing this kind of set-up into King's, however, was that it lacked any link to the values and ethos of the school – it is a bought in system made by somebody external to the organisation.

What if, Tom began to wonder, a school could produce its own system internally and for free, but make the points system competitive through an online and live auction whilst being aligned to our value system? In this way an element of competition might be added to the system, with students encouraged to outbid each other, or even group together to ensure they could not be outbid, thus generating a sense of real team spirit.

Tom's system rewarded students with credits – or, in the new language of the system, 'monarchs' – for high performance, attendance, random acts of kindness (where a student goes the extra mile, contributing to a wider community project, picking up a piece of litter or unexpectedly going out of their way to help a fellow student), participation in after schools clubs and sports' team. Monarchs are also rewarded for healthy eating at lunchtimes – and, conversely, they're taken away for poor performance, ill attendance and behaviour. Data for each student is tracked online, with every student receiving a weekly 'King's Bank Statement' detailing their total number of monarchs. Here's where things get unique – because Tom's system also allows for monarchs to be retained term to term, gathering interest for being in a 'savings account' – and thus teaching our students valuable lessons in how to defer gratification, a skill we feel is vital in the face of today's 'I want it now' society.

Delaying gratification is an interesting science and a valuable experiment that was first conducted by Walter Mischel in 1960, when he was a resident professor in psychology at Stanford University. Mischel's experiment was striking in its simplicity. Children, on average aged four-and-a-half, were led into a room and asked to sit at a table, on which sat a single marshmallow. Mischel told each child that they were free to eat the marshmallow at any point but, if the marshmallow was still there when Mischel returned to the room after a five minute absence, they would be given two marshmallows and allowed to eat both.

The point was to test how strong-willed each child was, how much they could delay their gratification for a greater reward further down the line. Some children gave in and ate the marshmallow straight away. Some were seen to struggle with the decision before giving in. Others managed to hold out for the reward. Mischel's experiment is only really interesting when the follow up data is studied. Mischel's follow ups showed that those children who were able to delay their gratification and resist the marshmallow had stronger SAT scores in the long term and, importantly, were more successful in their chosen careers.

The Monarch system, then, not only revitalised the academy's flagging reward system; it also tapped into one of the sciences predicting a student's success. It became another small piece of the King's puzzle, contributing to developing the right mind-sets to condition our students for success in the long term, outside the school gates.

MAP projects like this are entirely personal, but they're more than that; they're our way of saying to our staff that we value their input, that they have ownership of the organisation and its successes, that they're not just extensions of us as school leaders but the most valuable resource we have – and that they can make a tangible difference to the way the school operates. Not only this, MAP projects can often lead to a personal journey of self-discovery and also rapid promotion. Some of the school's major projects have been highlighted and led by our potential 'stars', which have required considerable strategic leadership on a par with experienced middle and senior leadership roles. It means that whether you have been teaching one year or ten years, there is no limit to what you can achieve.

In Tom's case, the MAP project provided him with a 'voice', an opportunity to at one and the same time transform the school and to prove to the school leadership that he was worthy of promotion to a senior role – which he was duly given. At King's, staff are not bound by hierarchal structures and a system of 'seniority'; ours is a true 'meritocracy'. We want every one of our staff to be on course to developing mastery of their chosen profession. Every week, each member of staff will complete a strategic walk-through of other teacher's classes: the teachers they have been asked to observe are ones we have identified as having particular strengths that the observing teacher might develop, and in organising these walk-throughs we're looking to promote a sense of shared responsibility, all of our teachers invested in the development of their peers. On top of this, every member of staff is assigned their very own coach; each week, coaches lead a reflection on the week's walk-throughs and discuss what might be gleaned from the lessons that have been observed.

We look to empower our staff in other ways too, and here those principles of Mission Command come back into play. When problems arise in school life, as they inevitably do – perhaps there are problems between students, class engagement, or students in absentia – the instinct of a teacher in another organisation might be to seek clarification or help from higher up the 'chain of command', but at King's we belie that.

Too often, in our past schools, teachers would claim a problem as 'not their responsibility' if it didn't fall within their classroom hours, or explain that they have seen a student from another form group throwing litter on the playground – passing the problem over to another member of staff. At King's, we consider this 'below the line' thinking, passing the proverbial 'hot potato'. Instead of allowing the buck to be passed, we seek 'above the line' accountability.

In practise this means that our staff do not have rigid areas of responsibility; if something happens and requires action it is everyone's responsibility, starting with the person closest to the information.

Imagine the scenario on the cricket field when the ball goes high in the air but the fielder stops on the edge of his or her 'area of responsibility' as the team all watch the ball fall to the floor three metres in front of the fielder, stood still on his line. The scenario is as comical as it is absurd yet in schools, and in most businesses, that is exactly how we operate.

At King's, if a ball is dropped – for example, if a child walks past their form tutor without them noticing they have their shirt out – we want several other people close by to dive, catch it and clear it up. Our teachers are analogous to the soldiers out in the field who must make quick, informed decisions of their own.

At King's, we call this our SODD OFF principle. As the polar opposite of SID (See a problem, Ignore it, then Deny it ever happened in the first place!), teachers must SEE a problem, ORIENTATE a course of action and resources towards that problem, and then DECIDE to take action and DO it. They must personally take charge of situations as they arise and act promptly, rather than defer action and responsibility to somebody else. We are empowering them to reach new creative heights in our MAP projects, yes, but we're also empowering them to stand up and take responsibility in more specifically challenging moments. We are asking them to take part in a school culture where we are all accountable to everybody else, and we all have responsibility for the successes and failures of the school – and, in doing so, we're granting them the autonomy to get things done, to express themselves, to gain mastery in their profession in a way that teachers micro-managed and controlled from above rarely have.

In effect, we're telling them that it's they, not us, who control the way their careers will progress and change; we are handing them the keys to their own futures and, if Deci, Ryan and the rest are right, then what we're really doing is opening the door to them for true, deep-level motivation, and satisfaction of the intrinsic self.

ENTRUST
"Be careful of your character, for your character becomes your destiny"

Excellence must become a habit

If you were to stand in the atrium of King's Leadership Academy, Warrington and allow your gaze to run from left to right along the sweep of the atrium wall, you would be flung back in time more than two thousand years. There you would see words that have echoed through the ages, words to which we keep returning to time and time again: 'You are what you repeatedly do. Excellence is not an act, but a habit.' These four words: 'Excellence is a Habit', were chosen to be the most prominent and striking feature of the academy's entrance hall. This was a deliberate act in the knowledge that words literally create the thoughts, deeds and actions of the world our students and staff inhabit daily.

Aristotle's words are as true today as they were in his own time. Perhaps he was the first one to recognise the true value of character, but it seems likely that there were others before him, stretching back into a time immemorial, which drew the same conclusions. Because Aristotle's famous quote goes to the core of what we are as human beings, it encapsulates that very human desire to do better, to be better than we were the day before, and the day before that.

Too many schools fail because they focus on the tip of the iceberg, because they opt for quick fix solutions and, unless we stand against the tide, it is only going to get worse. In an age of instant gratification, where the 'I want it now' mind-set dominates and attention spans are dwindling, how do we buck trends and inculcate in our students the drive to succeed? How do we set them on the paths to fulfilling and enriching lives?

Well, if the most modern thinking in which we have now steeped ourselves has any light to shed on this dilemma, it's that we must hark back to Aristotle himself: excellence is not an act, but a habit. The wisdom, it seems, has been here all along. Just like my military research showed, creating fitter and more robust soldiers meant making sure that exercise and good health were habits in their daily lives. In schooling it is no different: aspiration, effort and achievement must all become good habits, and it is our role as educators to ensure our children develop them.

Habits are difficult things to acquire. Do not just take that from anyone, case studies show that less than one in twelve of us actually succeed in sticking to a New Year resolution. A 2009 study was published in the *European Journal of Social Psychology*, led by Phillippa Lally and colleagues from University College London, that actually measured how long a habit takes to form. Recruiting 96 undergraduate students and asking them to adopt a new health-related behaviour linked to an established daily routine (i.e. eating a piece of fruit with their midday meal), found that the average time it took for their new behaviour to become habitualised was 66 days, although this varied greatly between participants from 18 days to as much as 254 days.

Anyone who has ever been on a diet will recognise the dilemma: you begin the week in good spirits, determined to make a change in your nutritional life; the first few days, when the passions are high, are easy and you wonder why anyone ever told you it would be so hard. As the days creep by your defences drop, you begin to tell little lies to yourself such as that you could eat just one slice of cake, or just one pastry because nobody will ever know and, after all, it's only one. Very quickly, that one becomes two and that two becomes three. In only a matter of days, the willpower you had stockpiled so ferociously is gone, and the diet you had entered with such high aspirations is just another failed experiment along the way.

The diet industry is built on exactly this model, luring its customers in with promises of rapid weight loss, sometimes even promising its permanence, and then luring them back in with another new diet when the old one has failed and been forgotten. If only a healthy, well-balanced diet could become a habit and the accepted norm in a person's life, then the chances of it failing or being forgotten would be crushed. Our habits are the things that we do without thinking.

This is exactly what the King's 6E model is seeking to do. We have already seen how Icek Ajzen's *Theory of Planned Behaviour* tells us our behaviour is shaped. Firstly, by our attitude toward the behaviour we are about to perpetrate; secondly, by the social pressures we feel to either engage or not engage with certain behaviours; and, lastly, by our sense of how much we are in control of whatever our behaviour will be. If Ajzen's theory still holds weight, habits are the end result: the culmination of our attitudes, the social norms we enact daily, and how great we perceive our control over our own destiny.

The King's model seeks to develop beneficial attitudes through our value set; it seeks to generate shared social norms – so that peer pressure is always in a favourable, rather than negative, direction; and finally, by looking to Deci's *Self Determination Theory*, it seeks to give agency back to the students, expanding and encouraging the sense that they have mastery over their own lives and a level of autonomy which we all so desperately wish to seek. If we get all these things right – in other words, if we can put our students in a place where they believe their choices will lead to favourable outcomes, where they are supported by their social milieu, and where they are confident they have full agency in the decisions they make – they will be empowered to act.

By being empowered to act, they will form habits that will, thereafter, form the basis of the decisions they make and continue to make in later life. The debate about capturing character, measuring its successes and strengths, and whether specific character traits can be directly taught, will continue to be argued for generations to come. At King's, our thinking is clear: good character is not an act, nor a succession of acts, but a set of habits that it is our responsibility to propagate in our students. Good character cannot be taught by lecture or seminar, by rote or examination; character can only be found in culture.

*

King's Leadership Academy, Warrington is only at the start of its journey; there is much cause for hope, but there are still many unknowns. Four years into our odyssey, we can point to levels of attendance, predicted exam success and engagement that statistically surpass many schools in the United Kingdom. It is really the unrecorded stories, the successes that it is impossible to metricate that mean the most and have the longest lasting effect on us as teachers. In what other profession could you gain the satisfaction of watching a child formally labelled as 'problem' and 'uneducatable' and diagnosed with attention-deficit disorder be transformed by the school culture to a calm, professional member of his peer group, a member of the combined cadet force and leading star of the major theatre production? In how many other schools would you have student's staying true to the value of 'integrity' and booking themselves in at reception for a detention later that day because they realised they had forgotten to pack their homework that morning? Or see a boy beginning his leadership field trip terrified of the water, transformed to being the leader of his group, piloting their boat across the waters of Lake Windermere after investing so deeply in the school's championing of 'endeavour'? The true outcomes of these events, along with countless other student stories, may not be truly revealed anytime soon and may lie dormant for many years to come.

This is a phenomenon known as the 'sleeper effect'. When awoken in times of crisis or free fall as children or as adults, these profound experiences will have sharpened their characters to meet the demands that life can often throw at us. Teaching is a profession like none other, for more often than not its rewards cannot be measured directly. Even so, they lodge in the memory and will remain there forever.

What successes our first students will have at GCSE and A level, what universities they attend and what successes they make out of their lives – all that is for the future. For now, the present is adventure enough. Having been recognised as the first National School of Character, King's Leadership Academy has increasingly found itself used as a model for how character education might work more broadly, particularly for those with the greatest need. As government conversation steers toward making character education a formative part of the schooling experience nationwide, King's has already taken its first steps to spreading its model.

The architect

Liverpool is a wonderful city, and not just because that is where my wife is from! My late grandfather used to recall, with great affection, the many memories he had of the Carlisle regiment with which he was posted to Liverpool with during the Second World War. The local lads there had been 'salt of the earth', who stepped out with him onto the beaches of

Normandy during the D-Day landings. Yet, Liverpool is also, relative to the other major cities of the United Kingdom, presented with significant challenges: a relatively recent history of chronic unemployment, poor wages and lack of aspiration. Common sense tells us that the family is the first and foremost incubator of character for our children, when the quality of the parent-child relationship becomes strained, even non-existent, due to a number of contextual factors, the moral fabric of a society can soon unravel. The suburb of Bootle typifies this: predominantly a white working class suburb, famous for its long history of shipping, the town's economy – once centred on the docks and their associated industries – has been waning since the closure of the docks in the 1980s. By 2006, Bootle was one of the poorest wards in the country, with unemployment two to three times higher than the national average.

In 2014, Hawthornes Free School in Bootle was put into special measures under its first Ofsted inspection. Hawthornes had only been in existence since 2012, when two high schools – St Wilfrid's High and St George of England High – had been amalgamated.

The amalgamation had, by all accounts, been a messy process. Neither school had been able to sustain their existence due to falling birth rates in the borough, as well as a surplus of places at competing schools. The more affluent and academically aspirational parents often chose to educate their children out of the borough to areas such as Southport and Formby, where more middle class schools were ready and willing to take them to combat their falling rolls. St Wilfrid's and St George's had become victims of the shifts in Bootle's demographic and the way out was to combine resources.

At around the same time that King's Leadership Academy was formed, the rebranded Hawthornes opened its doors but the process was cruel, with around 100 staff members losing their jobs. The impact this had on the newly formed school's culture was detrimental. After a spate of further problems, it looked as if Hawthornes had failed before it had barely begun. In 2014, with the school struggling to produce a new culture and ideology, it was put into special measures under its first Ofsted inspection. It was then that King's Leadership Academy became involved.

Taking on a failing school is a great risk but in 2015 Sir Iain accepted the challenge. Hawthornes became the first satellite school of the newly formed Great School's Trust. Where the new culture and rituals of King's had been relatively easy to develop because we started with the blank slate of a new school, transforming the fortunes of Hawthornes was going to be a different matter altogether. Here the challenges were not the same as they had been at King's; here Sir Iain and his newly appointed team, which included a number of high performing staff retained from the previous administration, would have greater hurdles to leap over such as staff who were already in situ and could not be recruited in the same way that we hired staff of a particular mind-set to work at King's.

The culture, social norms, and rituals that the staff were looking for were missing and so the old culture had to be dismantled and rebuilt stage by stage, with staff buy in required on every step of the journey. In taking on the challenge of Hawthornes, Sir Iain was resolute in his belief that every child had the capacity to succeed at the highest level and that no child should be left behind. In a 'turnaround' school this belief was going to be tested to the extreme.

Yet, it was also at this point that I remembered with great fondness one of Sir Iain's teachings on the Future Leaders programme and how taking on a failing school required the belief similar to that of Michelangelo and his Renaissance masterpiece of 1504. Here was a lesson in how vision, hope and huge expectations could defy all the odds. For those not familiar with the story, the very same piece of marble which was discarded as trash by a number of renowned sculptors of the day was seen as treasure in someone else's eyes. Only when Michelangelo took to the task, some 40 years after the first sculptor had rejected the challenge, did Michelangelo see his vision of David, a project that would take a further two years of his life and once finished would become one of if not the most famous sculptures this world has ever seen.

The Great School's Trust would continue to spread its message in the same year when the Academy Trust took on stewardship of its second satellite school: University Academy Liverpool, formerly called Shorefields, in the suburb of Dingle. Mention the name 'Shorefields' to the people of South Liverpool, and the name of the school is well known – but sadly for the wrong reasons. Located in the south of the city and bordered by the district of Toxteth, famous for its riots, Dingle is a suburb very different from Bootle. The centre of Liverpool's ethnic minorities, Dingle has a higher proportion of non-white British families than anywhere else in the city.

From the perspective of schooling, a low proportion of households here have English as their main language and Shorefields School celebrates over 30 different languages on a daily basis. Managing the complexities of religion and the will of the area's many Muslim families to have their daughters educated separately from the boys of the school was going to be difficult. The school had been a serious concern for Ofsted for longer than it was not a concern, having already changed its name from Dingle Vale to Toxteth Tech then to University Academy Liverpool. By November 2015, after failing four of its previous five inspections, it was the institution's last chance. No amount of extra funding and special help – a rebrand under a large national academy chain, new leadership by two separate National Leaders of Education, huge investment of time and capital – had been able to turn the school around. At a point at which only 14% of the students were reaching the government benchmark of five good GCSEs including English and mathematics, it once again fell to Sir Iain and the work of The Great School's Trust to rescue a school from closure.

Taking on and turning around a failing school requires great courage. The Liverpool newspapers might have written about Sir Iain as a 'super head' parachuted in to work his magic, the reality was far different. Failing schools are a civil rights issue; the unspoken truth is that schools fail in tandem with the societies they serve. Rescuing them is not a single, fleeting act but a commitment to long-term change, to addressing aspects of the society it is sometimes apolitical to mention. The hundreds, often thousands, of children who have been failed by the state and grown up to build a society not of aspiration, where education is valued, but of learned helplessness and handouts.

A day that I spent observing the school under the previous administration that had once been University Academy Liverpool made clear exactly how vast the challenge being presented to the incoming team was going to be. With over 40% of total staffing taken from supply agencies, the culture was unrecognisable and, at times, intimidating. The school's corridors were unruly, with scuffles commonly breaking out in-between lessons and during break times. Lessons were often unable to be taught, with a distinct lack of observable social norms, structure or routine. In one mathematics lesson I observed, the supply teacher visibly gave up halfway through the class, choosing to focus his attentions on a small corner of the room where a minority of students wanted to learn. In another class, a technology lesson had to be abandoned and a senior member of staff attempted to intervene, only for them to fail to control the situation as well.

Things did not transform immediately upon coming under the trust's stewardship when it was re-branded as King's Leadership Academy Liverpool. The first step in transforming the school culture was to recruit new, exceptional values-driven leaders; ones whose personal vision aligned to the tenets laid out in the trust's cultural blueprint, and who believed as passionately as we did about the moral imperative of character education. Miracles do not happen; changes are not made overnight. Soon after beginning work, the deputy headteacher who had been newly appointed had his car keys stolen by two students but they luckily failed to reach his car in time to take it.

Nevertheless, the students in question did not return to the school after that point. Taking over the school revealed systemic failings in what had gone before. It quickly became apparent that the older students in the school had not been taught certain core subjects including science, a task that made the new team's crusade feel even more perilous than they had thought.

In turning around a failing school, the core principles are not revolutionary; in fact, it stark simplicity was key. Sir Iain and his team identified a number of steps to lasting cultural change. Each step would take an incredible amount of will from the staff involved, and first of all this meant that they had to have the right staff. Above all, there needed to be the same culture of responsibility and accountability among the staff in our satellite schools that we had at Warrington, with teachers all responsible for their classrooms, their corridors, the lessons they delivered and the results they strove to achieve. For the staff this would have to be a lasting cultural change, but the situation also necessitated a period of unapologetic and coercive leadership.

This flew in the face of what we had achieved at King's Warrington, but in a situation in which supply staff were embedded in a system of excuses and poor standards, and in which many of those staff would need to stay in post for the remainder of the term, the new leadership team had to enforce strict rules to make a rapid transition. Only after this could the new team transition to a leadership style closer to what we had at King's Warrington, one in which the principles of Mission Command were taken to heart and in which trust and personal responsibility were key.

Eventually, they would be in a position in which all staff – new and old – stepped outside of the old culture of blame and excuses, and instead began to 'own' every aspect of the school. They introduced the SODD off principles: 'my' responsibility became 'our' responsibility. As all the teachers learned to sweat the small stuff, the school finally had a framework for lasting change.

So much for the staff, but an equal focus also had to be on the students. The first step to lasting change was to get all students regularly attending lessons as nothing could ever improve if students were not present. The second step was to get them behaving, if they are not behaving then learning cannot take place. The third step was to get them learning if they were not learning, there could never be the necessary change in culture of steps four and five – achievement through unwavering belief.

Through the holidays preceding both takeovers, great effort was put into the rebranding of the schools. Every corridor, stairwell and entrance hall was decorated with pictures of students, details of universities and top careers, motivational quotes and, most crucially of all, widespread promotion of the ASPIRE values.

By the time the students returned to school after their holidays, the only thing that remained of the old regime was the building itself; everything else was changed. The focus on behaviour began at the school gates, with uniform standards being rigorously enforced. Students who did not meet them were being sent home to return correctly dressed. Each member of staff was required to own the corridor outside their classroom space and walking on the left professionally soon became the norm. Lessons began, as at King's Warrington, with a strict line up and handshake on entrance.

Within the first few weeks, the students who refused to conform either learnt to do so, or were sanctioned. Over time, as structure, stricture, and routine became more and more embedded; the school began to achieve the consistency that it needed. Teaching focused on mastery for the first time, homework was set regularly for the first time, the school day was extended by an hour to aid catch up and remedial teaching, and a huge enrichment programme made students feel wanted and cared for.

At Warrington, we had the luxury of running a school with parents and students who actively bought into the new vision. Indeed, if it had not been for the will of the parents, the original King's Leadership Academy would never have materialised. The trust's turnaround schools did not have that luxury. Sometimes, in life, you cannot just wipe the slate clean and start again. Each of the trust's turnaround schools had unique challenges, but in transforming both, Sir Iain and his team had to overcome one big hurdle: how to align the existing staff, students and parents into a vision of their future that they were, in many cases, conditioned against. How could he ask them to accept the value system of King's Leadership Academy and get them to buy into it as a daily part of their lives? In this, there are no short cuts.

The children and wider families of the trust's turnaround schools had been repeatedly let down by 'super heads' brought in for the quick fix; ours would be a lasting change, one that reached the roots of school culture. This kind of change requires an extraordinary amount of belief and energy from all participants, starting with a vision that is clear and understandable. As luck would have it, the current principal of King's Leadership Academy Liverpool is himself a local resident of Toxteth, living just 400 metres from the schools gates and whose wife was once a student of Shorefield's as it was then.

Similarly at the Hawthones, the principal is a long-term member of the previous administration. In both schools, nowhere could the desire to make a great school for the community be better felt than those leading it. Every community deserves a great secondary school where children can turn their dreams into reality and that's exactly what both principals and their staff are doing here.

The good news is that, within two terms, Hawthornes was taken out of Ofsted's special measures category. The success was replicated at King's Liverpool but quicker, with the school being taken out of special measures for the first time in any of the staff's careers, after just one term of support by the trust. When young people attend a school where they feel valued, safe, and that their teachers have their best interests at heart, they will work harder, suffer fewer distractions, become more motivated and, ultimately, achieve more. By pursuing a character-driven approach to education, The Great School's Trust has demonstrated a new way to successfully transform even the most challenging of schools.

Looking at the schools now, you would be hard pressed to imagine them as they were. With both schools now moving through their second full year under the trust model, the changes in culture and ethos are dramatic. Lessons are purposeful, corridors are calm and disciplined, teachers can teach and experiment their craft with confidence and without fear of failure. Their passion for aspiration is everywhere from the members of staff with PhDs to backgrounds as GPs and academic researchers. Students are being exposed to high quality subject practitioners whose mere presence and background is positively intoxicating. Students all go on an annual leadership residential camps, the trust's character and leadership programme are now taught as weekly lessons.

These values are also reinforced by programmes such as the Duke of Edinburgh Award and National Citizen Service, now part of the core curriculum for students. As part of the King's Experience, students regularly visit the Russell group universities to develop their academic aspiration, take part in annual visits to museums and theatre productions to develop cultural awareness, complete accredited awards in the arts, and in 2016 we became the first trust to have a combined cadet force in each of the three academies with specialisms in the Royal Air Force and Royal Marines.

The transformation of these schools marked a new chapter in the trust's school turnarounds. The difference for the trust – and for the staff, students and communities that the schools serve – is that these takeovers are not short-term 'surgeon' or NLE headteacher projects; these schools are permanent pieces of the Great School's family.

We have already seen how we are not alone in our crusade to change the face of modern education. Across the United Kingdom a new breed of school leader – driven by different innovators with different histories – share one uniting principle: we are all looking for something new, something transformative, something that rejects the conventional ways of doing things and instead adopts a more adventurous, passionate, and heartfelt approach. Perhaps that is the one thing lacking in the standards of modern education: passion for the project at hand. For too long, schooling has been done by rote, just like the monkey story, and the 'we do it this way, because this is the way it has always been done' mind-set.

Now, at last, innovative educators are beginning not to bend to the system's inadequacies but to butt heads with it. King's, Floreat, and School 21 – all of these institutions are different, but what each of them show is an intolerance for accepted norms and a willingness to embark upon a crusade in support of our children. Progressive theories about child development and the nature of teaching are finally being embraced but this is not enough. In order for these schools to flourish, they must not be constrained by bureaucratic process and, like King's, the self-interests of the local government system.

Headteachers must be free to run the schools their way, rather than subscribing to a one-size-fits-all code; they must be freed to hire and nurture committed teachers in ways specific to the cultures and demands of their own schools. They must be supported in being individualistic, committed and passionate and they must do it free of the culture of fear that constant metrication and inspection promotes.

There are challenges ahead, but ones with which the trust is already engaging by taking over stewardship of failing schools in the local area. As of 2016, it was awarded 'fast track' status in recognition of the speed in which the turnaround of the Hawthornes and University Academy schools took place. Later in the same year, the trust announced two bids to found new free schools in the wider local area, with a second free school being established inside Warrington itself in response to the four-fold demand for school places that the original King's Leadership Academy can no longer satisfy.

Further afield, the trust was awarded permission to build an alternative provision unit, where those students at risk of dropping out and becoming NEET – or not in employment, education or training – can be provided for, with an academic curriculum entwined with character and leadership development, and run in partnership with an existing Great School's academy to draw upon for staffing and expertise.

We are facing these challenges head on, but as we grow and get exponentially bigger, new problems will arise. How can a school culture first started at King's Warrington in 2012 be replicated on a large scale and outside of the purview of its original creators? How can a school system that concentrates on aspects of character be rolled out nationwide, without then becoming victim to the scales and rankings that large-scale endeavours necessitate, and therefore without opening the door to temptations to game the system? How can a move away from data analysis to oversee a vast schooling system be affected without losing sight and control?

These are challenges currently without answer, but that does not mean we should not be confronting them, piecing together our answers bit by bit as the school years continue. To turn away now would be an example of the quick fix culture at its worst. One day, with the proper passion, commitment, and resilience to turn away from easy answers in favour of ones that actually work, we will find our way.

Beyond Aspiration:
A Field Manual

The Power of Character began as both a chronicle of the failings in modern day education and how the crusade of the Great School's Trust, initially through King's Leadership Academy Warrington from 2012, went on to define a new way of educating our children, an Education 2.0 that could provide a blueprint for the future. In actual fact, the benefits to be reaped by investment in character are not the preserve of education alone. Across the world, businesses, governments and other organisations are waking up to the fact that the accepted sciences of motivation, work ethic and why we do the things we do are increasingly out-dated and, by harnessing the hidden power of character, are transforming the way the world is run.

Education 2.0 can be stripped down and applied across so many fields of life, and in this final section of *The Power of Character*, that's exactly what we'll do: break down the code to its root elements. In that way, we will show how these fresh new approaches to education are, in fact, fresh new approaches to life at large. In this next section, we'll work through the simple mechanics of *The Power of Character* as it applied to King's Leadership Academy, breaking off at junctures to invite you to apply the same mechanics and rationale to your own life: to your business, to your charitable organisation, even to your home life and family. You too can reap the rewards of investment in the new sciences of character.

ENGRAVE: A TEN STEP GUIDE

The character code begins with a set of universal virtues (not British or any other country's for that matter), human behaviours that transcend cultures, religions, national, and political boundaries. These behaviours also meet the principle of 'reversibility', by which we mean that these are behaviours you would want somebody else to do to you. Respect, tolerance, kindness, and gratitude are only some of the behaviours we find venerated across the world, no matter what the idiosyncrasies of any specific culture. A virtue, as we think of it, is something that cannot be physically broken, a character trait that will always stand the test of time.

To start thinking about the character code as something we can apply in the real world, we must then think of it as contextual. The virtues that we have identified must become real-world properties, not merely ideas. In his book *Principle Centred Leadership*, Stephen Covey uses the analogy of your virtues as the physical terrain of a landscape; now think of your 'values' as the map that aligns to that specific landscape and your character as the internal compass which points you in the right direction at every decision juncture. Values come from the beliefs of your culture and your organisation; they are a contextual manifestation of universal virtues.

No value set can be universal as, in the real world, no person, culture or organisation is going to align perfectly with what we think of as 'universal' virtues. Values are how we, in a real world context, navigate those universal virtues. They are the way we interpret and express those universal virtues for a real world situation. The trick, as we have seen, is to develop a belief system that connects universal virtues with contextual values. That's exactly what Seligman and Peterson were trying to do in developing their definitive list.

There is no doubt that the will to believe is the first and most critical step in any change process. We at the Great Schools Trust held the unwavering belief that every child – regardless of background, post-code or starting point – could succeed academically and personally, become driven, law-abiding citizens, could go on to win a place at one of the country's leading universities, and then have the choice of pursuing a career of their dreams and becoming a leader in their chosen field.

In order to put this into a real world context, we identified a set of values based upon this belief – our ASPIRE code, through which we would provide real world context for the universal virtues underpinning everything. By identifying the behaviours we wanted to see in students – in our case, to be hard working, to be punctual, to attend school and behave well at all times, to dress smartly and never give up – we then worked backwards to identify the 'antecedent' to each behaviour. It was through this process that we identified and named each value we considered most important.

TASK ONE:
WHAT IS YOUR BELIEF AND PERSONAL VALUES?
We had a simple belief: that every child could succeed. From this, we defined a list of conscious and observable behaviours (or 'habits') we knew it was necessary for every child to exemplify if they were to reach that success. From this, we worked backwards to identify a value set that would naturally give rise to these behaviours. Through this process, we constructed our seven-pronged ASPIRE code.

Look at your own organisation: your business, your sports team, your chess club, your family. Can you follow a similar process to identify what the value set specific to your organisation might be?

1. What is the eventual outcome you want? In a business, this might be increased productivity; in a family, increased harmony. Now turn this outcome into a simple belief statement.

2. What behaviours can you identify that will lead to that favourable outcome? In a business seeking increased productivity, punctuality, hard work, and communication might be key. In a family seeking increased harmony, so might be listening more closely to one another, resolving conflicts in a calm and methodical manner. Whatever the behaviours you think are the most important to achieve each outcome; employ the SMART principle to each of

them individually which will provide focus and clarity. Are they: Specific, Measurable, Attainable, Realistic, Time based.

3. Extrapolate backwards. What values could you put at the core of your organisation to give eventual rise to those behaviours, to then lead onto the outcome you desire? Remember that this can be the thorniest of questions. What balance of values do you need? Too much determination can lead to a lack of empathy; giving too much to others can lead to a lack of self-awareness or self-respect. In a business looking to increase productivity, perseverance is key; but what of respect for those around you, curiosity, creativity, fairness and leadership? For a family, fairness and forgiveness might be key but what of courage and teamwork, of humour or (to quote Seligman and Peterson) the appreciation of beauty?

Once we had identified the specific sub-set of values that we have considered vital to developing the right behaviours and habits in our students, thus setting them on the road to our particular definition of success, the next step was to build a framework that we could use to lead students from value to behaviour to life-long habit: following the pathway we had originally created in reverse.

As we have seen, Icek Ajzen's *Theory of Planned Behaviour* posits that humans behave rationally when they are making decisions in situations with which they are familiar. In other words – we behave according to our principles in situations that have become habits for us in the past. According to Ajzen, when we 'intend' to do something, we are more likely to carry out that behaviour than if we left it to random chance. Ajzen goes on to argue that our 'intention' to act is facilitated by three things: our attitude to the behaviour, whether we find it to have a positive or negative effect; the 'social norm' attached to the behaviour – or whether or not those closest to you believe a particular course of action is the 'right' one; and our perceived 'behavioural control' – or, in layman's terms, how much we feel we are in control of our own behaviour and destiny.

The trust takes this three-step process to heart and incorporates it into everything that we do through our 'E' approach, with our principal aim being to create the right intentions in our students. Let's take, for instance, the example of 'going to university', central to our aspirational ethos. If we were to leave the thought of going to university entirely to our students and their parents, there's a chance they would reach the age of 18 before properly considering what this means.

By that point, a whole world of external influences would be pulling the student in different directions; a proportion of students would apply to university even if the school had never mentioned the word, but another proportion of students – who might otherwise have succeeded at university level – might not have that clarity. For them, university might have been a pipe dream, or something they never entertained at all. What if 'going to university' was an explicit and taught part of the school experience? What if schooling was tailored to developing the intention to apply for university and succeed there from the beginning?

It's part of our credo that we steer our students to the best possible outcome by leading them through a version of the *Theory of Planned Behaviour*: first by creating the intention to act in a certain manner; then by ensuring that their attitude to the behaviour is a positive one, and by making sure that the 'social norm' allocated to that behaviour positively reinforces the action; finally, by putting our students in a position where they have the control over whether or not to act – where they are in control of their own destinies. To put it more simply, we EDUCATE them through knowledge, then EQUIP them with the necessary skills and finally EMPOWER them through opportunities and the will to act.

TASK TWO:
CREATING NEW HABITS
Identify a long-term goal for your business, family, personal relationship or other organisation. Think of it in terms of the *Theory of Planned Behaviour*:

1. What is the 'intention' you hope to create? In a family, this might be the intention to commit to a weekly bonding activity together; in a business, the intention to adopt a new strategy or reach a new target.

2. What 'attitude' toward this new behaviour do you want to create to ensure its smooth running? In the same family situation, this might be about reinforcing family activities as a positive experience, rather than something to be endured; in the business situation, perhaps this means making sure employees are truly motivated to work rather than being coerced into it.

3. What 'social norm' might be needed to encourage family members or employees to adopt the new behaviour wholeheartedly? In a family, this might be creating an environment in which a family activity is a 'cool' thing to do, rather than a tiresome duty; in a business, this might mean creating a sense that striving to reach the target is for the benefit of all, rather than something being demanded by overseers.

4. How can you think of the 'perceived control' of those in your business and family? Does every member of your family, or employee in your business, have a sense that they control their own destiny? Do they have the skills and confidence to do what is expected?

We want all of our students to aspire to higher education, and in particular to know that it is realistic that they can attend any of the leading universities this country has to offer. To get here, first and foremost we need to develop in our students the 'intention' to act – the intention to go to university from an early age. To set them on this course, we first educate them in the value of aspiration, the benefits that come with an aspirational mind-set, with inspiring examples of this forming part of our weekly curriculum. This sets the groundwork – it gives them the 'intention to act', that is the first step on this journey.

The second step on this journey demands that we shape a child's attitude so that the intended behaviour is one that is seen as positive.

Our primary means of this takes us right back to the taught ASPIRE curriculum but it also places emphasis on aspects of culture and environment. How do we shape the culture of our academies so that university and aspiration are a positive part of the daily educational experience? This translates to classrooms being named after leading universities, talking about university through our 'greeter' speeches, school assemblies in which we explore the value of aspiration. Wherever we can, we take tangible steps to reinforce the message that attending university is a positive and attainable thing, a possibility for every one of our children.

TASK THREE:
HOW CAN YOU CHANGE YOUR CULTURE?
Consider your family, business or other organisation. Now that you have defined your target, or the outcome you'd like to see, think about the aspects of culture that might help you get there. If, in a family, your intention is to have weekly bonding activities, how can changing the culture of a family best position you to get there? Is shared time important? Are meal times solitary or communal affairs? How might interrogating the culture of your family help you reach a stated goal?

Meanwhile, in a business situation, what aspects of culture are prohibiting – or at least not contributing to – you reaching your goals? How might small changes in culture change the tone of your business, and then feed back into employees' attitudes towards it? If aspiration is key, how might reinforcing the methods of career progression at your business motivate staff? Crucially, is there a defined culture at all at your workplace, or is culture something that happens in the absence of a defined cultural policy? What effect might defining culture have on a business that is devoid of cultural direction?

The third step we take to shepherding our students along the *Theory of Planned Behaviour* is in shaping social norms so that the intended behaviour is seen as an accepted part of the educational journey. In the university example, this means shaping social norms so that attending university is the 'default setting' – the accepted next step students would take after completing their A levels.

We want an environment in which graduating from a trust academy and beginning a university career is to be expected, and where deviating from this path is out of the ordinary. This means every child investing in their personal 'flight path' – their personally tailored route to achieving their dream – from the very first day. We use the ascent of Everest as a way of framing this journey, with each milestone being seen as a 'camp' along the way to the summit: first GCSEs, then A levels, then a university degree, and finally their chosen career. By having a destination in mind from the beginning, and then through careful research, mentoring and workplace internships, students learn how to work backwards from their career and life aspiration so that they can work out what they need to achieve along the way.

During this period we use inspiring stories – including the life of Eric Weinmeyer, the first blind man to climb Everest – to give students a sense that anything is achievable, as long as you have the power to dream and the ambition to work hard every step of the way. We also bring aspirations into reality through inspirational role models. The academy, for example, has welcomed over four astronauts for them to share their personal 'flight paths' with students.

TASK FOUR:
WHAT ARE YOUR SOCIAL NORMS?

Think of social norms as they apply to your business, family or other organisation. What are the social norms as they exist now? In a family, are constant arguments and bickering the norm? Do you eat separately or in front of the TV, or do you eat communally around a dining table? Is basic mutual respect a social norm or is it, as in many cases, an oddity? What family rituals do you observe that give your family the sense that it's a coherent unit?

Do the same for the business or other organisation to which you belong. What are the social norms at your place of employment? Is there a sense of respect to managers and supervisors? What rituals are in place during the work day? Do staff members turn up late, or create divisions with others? Is there a sense of unity, or an us-versus-them mentality between employees and employers? What adjustments in the social norms of your organisation might better give a sense that the entire company is pulling in the same direction?

Once we have established the appropriate social norms at King's, our attention turns to how our students perceive the control they have over their own journeys. Everyone faces setbacks and failures at certain points across their lives yet it's a central tenet of our academy that, if a student has the inner confidence to bounce back from failure or to re-align a 'flight path' that has gone off course, they can accomplish anything. Instilling perceived control in our students is therefore paramount. To make this a reality we focus on how to manage failure, how to incorporate setbacks into part of the natural process of education and appreciate its benefits. We look to give our students control over their own journeys by showing them how setbacks are a natural part of any career, and empowering them with the appropriate tools and mind-sets to bounce back from them.

TASK FIVE:
HOW DO YOU REACT TO SETBACKS?

Think of perceived control and how we manage setbacks and failure as it applies to your family, business or other organisation. We use our regular Gap – or Failure – Weeks to incorporate setbacks into a natural part of the culture. How do you manage this in your own worlds outside the school gates? In a family situation, how do you resolve conflicts? As parents, how do you discipline your children and how do you support each other? How do you deal with negative feelings about your own capacity to parent? How does your family unit bounce back from the inevitable breaks in communication that happen from time to time?

In your personal relationships, do you see breakdowns in communication, or occasional arguments, as reasons your relationship is not working – or as opportunities to develop and grow?

In a business situation, how do you incorporate setbacks and failure into your staff routines? Are setbacks punishable, or are they seen as opportunities for an employee to gain mastery of their chosen career?

We feel that, by shaping attitudes, creating strong social norms and instilling perceived control in our students' actions, we shape an 'intention' to act. By shaping their attitudes through educating on our values they will know what the good thing is; by equipping our students with the right social norms, they can see and feel what the good thing is through repetitive practice and strong role modelling; and, by empowering them with the appropriate levels of perceived control, they can experience what the good thing is autonomously. It does not stop here. This code might shape what our students do, but just as important is the question why.

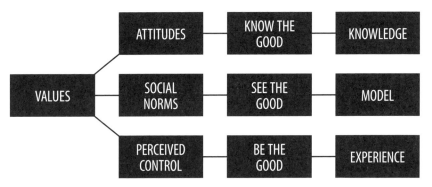

Why we do the things we do has been at the heart of *The Power of Character*. The Theory of Planned Behaviour might help us shape the what, but the why is a different, much more nuanced beast.

Many of us 'intend' to do the right thing – something that we know is positive and supported by our family and friends, a behaviour that we mostly have control over and could carry out habitually. Yet we do not always do it. Anyone who has entertained a new diet or exercise regime will recognise this in themselves: few of these ever materialise into a long-standing habit; rather they are picked up and put down, seemingly whenever the initial surge of enthusiasm for the change begins to wane.

Here, we would argue that this is because we have failed to 'internalise' the behaviour, failed to make it a part of our true selves. Rather than turning it into a habit that we perpetuate because it brings us inherent pleasure or joy, we perform the behaviour for an external or extrinsic reason. This is because we are being coerced into it, whether that is by those around us or the nagging voice in our own heads that tells us this is something we should do, whether we truly want it or not.

This is exactly what I saw within my military research on why troops failed to exercise after their compulsory training ceased. They had all exercised daily for months on end, yet when given the opportunity to stop training because the 'stick' or fear of punishment was removed, they did so. Why? They, and the service, had failed to internalise the value of exercise through more autonomous motives.

As we have seen, we confront the challenges of why we do the things we do through Deci and Ryan's *Self Determination Theory*. The key tenets of the *Theory of Planned Behaviour* help us determine what behaviours we choose, but only by understanding the underlying tenets of the SDT can we determine whether these behaviours will ever be carried out habitually or over the long term. This is important because, unless new behaviours become habits for life, we will never ENGRAVE them on our inner selves – and engraving is the final step of our 'E' programme:

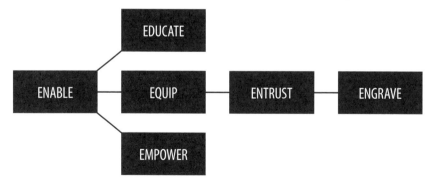

Let's go back to the example of 'going to university'. So far, through our values code, we have EDUCATED by shaping attitudes; we have EQUIPPED by creating strong social norms; and we have EMPOWERED by giving students the perceived control – or what we call self-efficacy –

over their actions. What we have yet to do is ENTRUST our students to perform the intended behaviour, because this can only come through the shaping of a culture and environment based firmly on personal leadership.

In their *Self-Determination Theory*, Deci and Ryan identified three universal human needs – the need for autonomy, or to have choice over your own journey; the need for competence and mastery in your own skill-set; and the need to have a strong purpose and direction in life. We look to help our students do the very same.

We want to give every child complete autonomy over their 'flight path'; the final destination of their journey is determined by them alone. Whether they aim to be a doctor, a lawyer, an airline pilot, a construction worker or a diplomat – that is their decision. The stages they might take to reach that goal – the 'camps' along the route to the 'summit' of Everest, to use an old analogy – are researched by each student as well. Careful mentoring by tutors only helps facilitate this process; the process belongs to the student, supported by targeted conversations to help return them to their core goals and the importance of 'aspiration'.

TASK SIX:
LEARN TO DEVISE A PERSONAL FLIGHTPATH

Consider autonomy in your own life. Do you feel as if you have complete control over the journeys you are making – whether those journeys are personal or professional?

Consider devising a 'flight path' for yourself. Where do you see yourself, personally and professionally, in five years' time? Repeat the exercise for intervals of ten, fifteen and twenty years. Life will throw curve balls at all of us in this time, but a strong flight path can help navigate the storms.

Once you have committed to an end goal, what steps can you break it down into? What camps do you need to reach in order to get to the summit? Have you set SMART goals in order to reach each camp?

Could 'flight paths' be of benefit to members of your family, your employees or colleagues?

Having a 'flight path' is a key tool on claiming that sense of individuality that, according to Deci and Ryan, we all need to assert if we are to achieve full contentment in our lives – but so too is the ability to achieve mastery of our chosen field, the self-efficacy of the SDT. Psychologist Albert Bandura defined self-efficacy as the belief we have in our own abilities, the confidence that we can accomplish a certain task or achieve a certain goal. It's nothing less than a sense that we are worthy and accomplished, and it can be the determining factor in how we approach any of the challenges life throws at us.

We all have a natural desire to master an area in which we might feel important. At the academy, this means that through careful research, planning, and reflection, every child's personal 'flight path' is linked to the GCSEs, A levels and university courses that their flight destination requires. So, for instance, if a child wants to become a sports scientist, they will be aware from an early age which universities offer them the best opportunity to pursue this career; and, working backwards, what A levels and GCSEs they will need to get them there. Along their journey they will be exposed to a plethora of role models, workplace visits and internship opportunities that will help cement belief in their own abilities and future potential.

TASK SEVEN:
WHAT'S YOUR MOTIVATION?

Think back over the last few weeks of your life. Were there moments when you felt motivated to do something solely because of external pressures or rewards? What things did you do because you had to do them – whether because of societal or peer pressure, or even the pressure you put yourself under – and what did you do because, on an internal and instinctive level, you wanted to do them?

Our human drive for self-determination and self-actualisation must come from within – from intrinsic as opposed to extrinsic motives. Now consider the three intrinsic desires common to all humans for self-determination. Firstly, our perceived level of competence or MASTERY when completing a task; secondly, our level of choice or the feeling of AUTONOMY we have over the task itself; and, finally, our feelings of relatedness to both the PURPOSE of the task and the people involved in the task – does it align with the value set of who we are and what is important to our belief system?

Are there moments you can identify in which a change in mastery, autonomy or purpose might move you from external motivation to intrinsic motivation?

The final part of Deci and Ryan's *Self-Determination Theory* points to unlocking the truest, most vital form of motivation there is: a motivation driven not by external factors, by punishment or rewards – as in so much of modern life – but by internal factors, the deep-rooted desire to do something and do it well; the true motivation that comes from the intrinsic self.

This sense of purpose is vital to developing true intrinsic motivation; it's the difference between a dieter who diets purely because of societal pressure to lose weight, and a dieter who embraces long-lasting lifestyle change because they are being driven to do so by something deep inside. At the academy, it's the difference between a student going to university because we tell them they have to, or because societal pressure coerces them into it regardless of how they feel, and students wanting to go because it satisfies them on a deep, internal level.

It is crucial that we help students unlock motivation from within. It's central to our work that, if students believe they can achieve places at universities and subsequently have great careers, if they have the right attitudes and if their peers around them believe the same things, if they have a mastery of their own destiny and are willing to work hard to get there, then the behaviours they perform are likely to be accomplished by intrinsic means.

We are not coercing our students to behave in a way we dictate; we are putting them in the correct place, developing the right mind-sets and behaviours in them, that they are driven to achieve these things of their own volition.

TASK EIGHT:
MISSION COMMAND

Identify a time in recent memory when you have been assigned a task. Were you instructed in how to accomplish that task down to the smallest detail, or did you have the freedom to plot your own path towards success, just as long as the end goal of the assignment was reached? How did it feel to be 'micro-managed'? How did that differ from a time when, left to your own devices, you have found a route to a successful outcome without defining direction?

Now identify a time when you have assigned tasks to others. Perhaps it's an employee, a business associate, a student at the school where you teach, or a child of your own. When you assigned that task, did you explicitly dictate how that task should be completed, how that summit should be reached or that goal achieved? How did dictating so closely affect the task? Was it achieved to standard and, even if it was, how did that affect the relationship between you, issuing the task, and the person completing it?

Consider morale in your home or workplace. How might this change by investing in principles of Mission Command? Might the person to whom you are assigning a task be able to complete this without being directed in their every movement? What benefit might this be to their morale and sense of purpose? Try assigning the task without monitoring it. How has this changed the result and, more importantly, how has it changed the relationship between the two of you?

The final step is more of a cautionary 'check point' to consider at every decision making juncture. Did you know that our brain computes over three billion separate bits of information each and every second, and two thirds of it comes from what we see. Our sight therefore is the dominant human sense and as such it is important to be mindful that we may see the world not necessarily as it is objectively, but as we are conditioned to see it through our very own virtual reality. This is our unique character lens that is a representation of our personal beliefs, values, attitudes, norms and self-efficacy.

This lens enables you to make a decision over something where another person might arrive at a completely different conclusion. The difference between a good or bad choice, or one which ultimately may lead to perceptions over what constitutes good or bad character, are often subjective to the lens of the person observing that particular behaviour. How do you prevent yourself from seeing things only through your view of the world? How do we see things 'eyes wide open' and arrive at a unified end goal?

Now, consider that our perceptions are framed by the many experiences taking place each and every day in our lives – our families, our schools, our work environments and our social circles. When perceptions are different, people may not like or understand what you are trying to achieve or are asking them to do and will implement it poorly or, at the worst, subvert it. If we can take into account not just our frames of reference but listen to others and be open to their perceptions (also termed perspective), we are more likely to gain a much more objective view of reality and share a common purpose towards an intended goal.

TASK NINE: BEWARE OF PERCEPTIONS!

Each time you issue a directive – whether that be to tidy a bedroom, complete a task at work, or another family chore – think about the power of perceptions and the multitude of perspectives around us. Might the person to whom you're assigning a task hold a different belief and value set to yours? If so, how might you align their view point to your intended vision?

Have you 'imposed' your vision onto them or have you 'brought' them towards it? What might talking to them about your intended end goal do to their personal motivation and buy in to the vision? How might the end goal benefit them as well as the organisation? How can their points of view be taken into account to help shape and strengthen the intended outcomes further so that they feel as much a part of it?

How has this changed the result – and, more importantly, how has it changed the relationship between the two of you?

The 6E system developed by the Great Schools Trust, through King's Leadership Academy Warrington, is a way of moving from value to habit in six steps, a process of developing – or changing – behaviour that has, until now, been rooted in the educational experience, but which can be applied to life in general. This, in essence, is the heart of everything *The Power of Character* has been trying to show: by identifying a specific value set, we can shepherd ourselves to lasting change in our lives. We are unlocking the hidden power of character: the power to take charge, the power to identify where we have been making missteps and to get back on the tracks we deserve, the power to determine the courses of our own lives.

TASK TEN:
THE 6Es IN YOUR LIFE

As a final reminder, run through the 6Es and apply them to your own work and life situations. How you apply them will clearly depend upon the nature of the situation, but they stand as pillars of character that will help point you in the right direction and inspire others:

1. ENABLE. What are the values specific to your own beliefs, the beliefs of your family, business or other organisation? How do these align to universal virtues?

2. EDUCATE. How do you shape attitudes inside your family, business or other organisation? How do people know what the good thing is in any given situation?

3. EQUIP. What social norms are needed in your specific circumstance? How do you create these social norms through close attendance to the culture of your family, business or other organisation?

4. EMPOWER. How do you give people self-efficacy and that sense of personal leadership? How do principles of Mission Command work in your organisation?

5. ENTRUST. How do you create an environment in which intentions become habits?

6. ENGRAVE. Finally, how do you create habits that people will still enact when nobody else is watching, and when peer pressure to take the opposite path is strong?

Einstein famously said that insanity was doing the same thing over and over again and expecting different results.

Just like the principles of Mission Command, *The Power of Character* is not a linear process. Rather, it is a constantly evolving cycle operating within the complicated to the complex. There is not a finish line to celebrate crossing or a final destination at which we know we have arrived. *The Power of Character* is just that – a complex code. Once you break into a new paradigm of operating, you enter a new stage of growth that, in turn, brings its own new challenges and its own unique code. You may at times need to go back to step one and start the cycle again in order to unlock a new path to continue your journey to flourishing and transform the way you live.

Those of us who excel at something are the ones who can, just like the pilots completing the OODA loop or members of staff completing the SODD principles, most rapidly repeat the cycle. Just like the best parts of life, there are no short cuts to good character – yet, the more you use the code, the faster you will progress through each cycle. It must be grown from the root up and the only way to consistently apply this model is to intentionally build our character over the course of time – to be a constant gardener – to engrave a mark on our life and those of others so deep that its leaves an enduring imprint when we are gone.

Afterword

The contents of this book had been percolating in my mind ever since I took the step back into the world of education in 2009 and my mind was suddenly opened to the myriad changes taking place in our educational landscape. I had just left the 'character factory' of the British military and, on stepping back into the world of formal schooling, what I discovered was nothing less than an 'sausage factory', a world in which, by increments, our schools had been transformed into a mechanized industry, taking in children full of potential and promise, and spewing out exam grades that were often meaningless and, even more importantly, detrimental to that child's future prospects.

When we look back at life, we often focus on the moments that have shaped us. For me, this realisation would change the direction of my life. Think of a moment in your own life that has changed you, you will often see that these are the moments that shape our very character. We remember the people who changed us, the events in our lives that were exceptionally stressful, embarrassing.

Equally so, the events that made us stand out, exceed our expectations, and think of ourselves as greater, more full of promise, than we had ever thought ourselves to be are also remembered. The Great School's Trust, initially through the creation of King's Leadership Academy Warrington, has been nothing less than an attempt to create an environment which can create moments like this in our students' lives, moments that can intentionally shape positive habits and as such shape their character forever and for the better. The journey is only just beginning, because this journey will last a lifetime.

This story of character, and how it can have such a transformative effect not only on our lives as individuals, but on our societies, our civilisation itself, is a complex but vital one. *The Power of Character*, and the chronicle of King's Warrington and its partner academies, has been my small contribution toward the subject and, in its own way, I hope has unlocked some of its mystery. Character might seem like an old-fashioned concept but it has never been more vital to understand its hidden power; philosophers might have talked about it for millennia, but contemporary policy makers are finally having their interest in character reignited.

Technologies rise, empires grow old and then fade away, societies transform and crumble and grow again, but the values we hold dear now are the very same that we held dear as primordial man, or in the civilisations of a classical or prehistoric age. These values transcend time, religion and culture, and never fade away. Being kind, tolerant, and responsible members of society is as important now as it was thousands of years ago. The love and discipline of our parents, the temptations and affirmations of our closest peers, the examples set by the role models we encounter across our lives – these things are the inputters to our character, and they have never been more needed than they are today.

My investigation into the power of character, and our attempt to implement best character practise has opened my eyes to the wealth of research, dialogue and debate being undertaken by some of the world's most learned researchers into this very field. Not everyone agrees on everything, but common to all these thinkers is a unifying thread: character matters, whether we frame it in terms of 'Emotional Intelligence', 'Grit', or any one of a dozen other different titles. All of the behavioural scientists agree that strength of character is a better indicator of a child's future success in life than the academic markers which have, until now, been our only way of gauging, measuring and, in too many cases, restricting the innate potential of our children.

The story of King's Leadership Academy has been the story of how one school could transition these theories into real life, how we could make the latest research and thinking manifest in our classrooms and how, as a trust, a blueprint for character could be placed into schools facing great difficulty and help change their fortunes around. It has been a story about our natural drive for flourishing, our desire to be good people – to be of good character. It is also a story about one school's journey to becoming the nation's first School of Character in little more than three years from its inception and the help and inspiration it has given two former failing schools. For far too long there has been a mismatch between what science is telling us and how our schools operate. The goal of this book has been to repair that breach, to show a working 'solution' and a manifesto for the next generation of education, our very own Education 2.0.

The late Stephen Covey, whose *7 Habits of Highly Effective People* has been an inspiration throughout the writing and research of this book, suggested that almost every significant breakthrough is the result of a courageous break from traditional ways of thinking. Education 2.0, then, is our own paradigm shift. If the whole purpose of a school is to develop every facet of a child, why, then, up and down the country, do the overwhelming majority of our schools continue to focus far too heavily on the metric of exam results and obsess over Ofsted inspections? What could a paradigm shift in the way we run our schools and classrooms look like and how could it be achieved? As Covey says, "To do well, you must be good. And to do good, you must first be good".

I had always thought of teaching as a branch of leadership, and leadership skills had been drilled into me during my military career. It was not until the founding of King's, and our focus on developing leadership in both our students and our staff, that I truly appreciated how critical leadership skills are to the life chances of our children. In essence, good teachers are good leaders. Yet, even now, we use terms such as 'classroom management' and 'behavioural management' in our schools. As a trust, we deliberately changed this terminology to 'classroom leadership' and 'behavioural leadership'. The distinction is incredibly important.

Reflecting on the words of the management consultant and author Peter Drucker: management is about getting by or, in our case, 'managing' the system to get the best ranking in the performance tables and stay in the good books of Ofsted. But, leadership? Well, leadership is about doing the right thing per se: not right for the league tables, not right for the system, but simply right. It is about accepting that there is a simple and unalienable definition of 'right', one that transcends everything else and this brings us right back to the value systems that underpin organisations like ours.

Doing the right thing, being values based and principle centred, has been a complete paradigm shift, of the kind Stephen Covey championed across his writing life. What this paradigm shift relies on are remarkable school leaders, remarkable teachers, parents who are willing to take a leap of faith into the unknown; and a common and shared purpose by all of these stakeholders. It requires a long-term commitment on the part of schools. If we want a fairer, more just, more productive society, we now need to focus more on what Doctor Martin Luther King called the 'content of our character'.

Despite what the science is telling us, despite revolutionary writers and thinking increasingly challenging these centuries-old norms, I have observed that there remains a systemic refusal to see the problem staring us in the face. Why should the tail, made up of government-led performance measures and inspectorates, continue to wag the main body of our educational system?

Only the other day did I receive an invitation to attend a conference on British values and the delivery of character education in our schools – its closing title 'what Ofsted is looking for'. Too often, the failure to see that a problem even exists expounds the problem itself. The solution stands right before us – ourselves and what is truly best for our children.

For some reason, we have lost sight of the true purpose of education. The Greek philosopher Heraclitus really did have it right when he said, very simply, that: "character is destiny."

As my eldest daughter embarks on her educational journey into primary school, how can I rest assured that the development of every facet of her character will enable her to flourish? In a world where exam grades and league tables are still of paramount importance, where the infrastructure and economy underpinning our educational system still prioritises grades, even when they are sometimes meaningless, above everything else, how can I be confident that she will have the best start in life and be afforded the best chances of later success?

Unless the model being pioneered by schools like King's Leadership Academy – and, as we have seen, we are not alone – finds itself rolled out into more and more schools, how can children be best shepherded on their way? Not being able to hold a conversation on trigonometry or 20th century history at a dinner party is unlikely to ever be a game changer for my daughter when she eventually leaves school or university but we know that without character, without such qualities as aspiration, respect and endeavour, she will not venture far.

I felt compelled to commit the lessons of *The Power of Character* to paper because, on looking around me at the current state of education in our country, it is clear that in spite of the progress some are making, most of us still rely on the same old methods, the same old attitudes, and as a result we are continuing to leave our children behind. In an age in which the gap between the haves and have-nots continues to widen, provoking discontent and political upheaval across the nations of the world, providing the best education for even the poorest citizens has never been of more paramount importance.

Perhaps my first lesson on leaving the military and joining the world of education was that children from poorer families are less likely to go to university and, whilst at university, are less likely to see it through. I had spent much of my life being blissfully ignorant to the incredible levels of deprivation and struggles that exists for many people until I was exposed to the families and communities served by some of our most urban and challenging schools. Can only Superman save them? I can vividly remember this question being posed by Sir Iain during our Future Leaders training, followed by the inspirational story and yet heart breaking words of Geoffrey Canada whose story of New York's Harlem Children's Zone has featured in this book:

> "When I first found out that Superman wasn't real, I was about maybe eight. And I was talking to my mother about it. And she was like, 'No, no, no. There's no Superman.' And I started crying. And she thought I was crying because it's like Santa Claus is not real and yet I was crying

because there was no one coming with enough power to save us. I really thought he was coming to rescue us. The chaos, the violence, the danger. No hero was coming". – Geoffrey Canada

For the many in poverty who fail to be served by a good school, the only hope out of a life of poverty may still rest on the existence of a mythical, magical superhuman, yet in reality what I had seen when I visited the best that the charter school movement of America had to offer were everyday superheroes devoting their lives to the most vulnerable of children and turning them into first generation university graduates.

As a child (and even occasionally now at Christmas), I must have watched the film Superman tens if not hundreds of times. I think I, like most of us, are captured by the fantasy of having power that no other possesses. Having reached the end of this book, I now begin to wonder whether we have a superhuman figure within all of us, a power that is unique only to the beholder and which, when unleashed in the right way, can be an incredible force for good. It is something that may lie dormant in many for eternity, but with the right circumstances and people around you, anything is possible.

Having written this book, I can now for the first time truly understand what Joe-El meant by his final words to his son in this very film. For over 30 years I thought he was talking about the super powers that he was passing onto Kal-El. I now know he was talking about the passing down of his character:

"You will travel far, my little Kal-El. But we will never leave you, even in the face of our death. The richness of our lives shall be yours. All that I have, all that I've learned, everything I feel, all this, and more, I bequeath you, my son. You carry me inside you, all the days of your life. You will make my strength your own, and see my life through your eyes, as your life will be seen through mine. The son becomes the father and the father becomes the son. This is all I can send you Kal-El".

You see character is real, terribly important and may be the one thing that can bring back some sanity into our classrooms, living rooms, boardrooms and communities – we all have a duty for those who we serve, those who we lead, for those who we teach, and most importantly for our children who we raise in order to educate, equip and empower them with their own super power.

For our young, it remains my fervent belief that where you live should not have to determine your destiny, and that a group of progressive and like-minded school teachers can open a remarkable school in any neighbourhood anywhere – and, more importantly, not charge nor select. The achievement gap in this country remains stubbornly hard to break and this is something that educators have long wrestled with, and with which they will no doubt continue to wrestle for generations to come.

Do we just accept the achievement gap for what it is, continue to develop the areas served with good schools and educators, forget about the rest and hope for the best? What else can, and should, we teach students that will help them get along in life? What are the habits, the skills, the strengths in life that people, especially young people, require in order to flourish? How do we get our children to connect with others in a world that seldom relies on face-to-face communication and keep their future firmly in sight when there are so many distractions, and when we are steeped in a culture of immediate gratification and success?

If *The Power of Character* can get us even a single step closer to answering these questions, then it has been a worthwhile success.

I do not believe that Homo sapiens have existed for so long on earth because of our ability to process numbers quickly or to hold rational thought without being distracted. Rather, I believe we have survived precisely because we possess the very skills that no examination can measure: qualities such as sensitivity, empathy, imagination and many more. It is by recognising the values of our emotions, our motivation and our character that we have survived and thrived; it is only by returning to these ways that we can progress.

Ultimately, we can worry about the world of character as much as we like, but the only person's character with which we must truly be concerned is our own. It is only our own character over which we have ultimate control. Few of us make the connection between our life's achievements and character in this way. When I reflect on Doctor Martin Luther King's statement, "Intelligence plus character – that is the goal of true education", I think of my closest friends and the people I most respect. We are all drawn to people by forces that go beyond intellect and success, drawn to them because of the intangible, often unspoken, merits of their character. How long before we wake up, as a species, and recognise that character is all – that everything else is a sub-set of character, that everything we do would be easier to understand, easier to process, easier to learn, if we turned to the merits of character first. How might the world look if it had more teachers, more school leaders, parents, communities and business leaders who looked to character education as a real asset, one that could holistically better the world? What if we collectively turned our backs on short-termism, on tip of the iceberg thinking, and took more time to build our young people's self-worth through a firm foundation of principle-driven values? What if we then took the time to nurture them for the long term, confronting both *what* we do and *why* we do it?

This journey toward self-discovery is not finished yet. *The Power of Character* rationalises many years of thinking and practise, but it is only the first step in what I intend to be a long life steeped in the wisdom of behavioural scientists, trying to put those theories to tangible use in a problematic and often fractious world. As the politics of our 21st century lurches further toward division, enmity and an 'us vs. them' mentality, developing good character will only become more important. Our understanding of character is far from complete, and just as the behavioural science continues to flourish and change, so will the Great Schools Trust continue to grow and adapt.

In fact, as I write these words, we have just received permission to open a second free school in the area of Padgate, only half a mile from our current school. The significance of this site will resonate with readers because it was here, in Padgate, that local man Gary Newlove was murdered in 2007. It was in Padgate that his attackers were born and raised, and from which they were taken to serve their life sentences, in 2008, for the unimaginable violence that they had meted out on this man, as they had done countless others. Character education is not an immediate salve for all of the world's ills, but the transformation from school-as-exam-factory to school-as-social-service, to seeing our schools as vital cogs in society's wheels, helping turn out children of good character, not just good grades, could have no stronger symbol than this.

The lessons of *The Power of Character* have focused on the educational community, but they do not stop there. Good character, good values, as we have seen, transcend time, cultures, religions and continents and so too, I hope, do the lessons of this book transcend the boundaries of business, communities and families. Character matters, and if this book has one simple, short message to take away, it is that it matters for us all.